"A fundamentally radical author . . . Baker is an essayist in the tradition of GK Chesterton and Max Beerbohm, writing winning fantasies upon whatever chance thoughts may come into his head."

*—Financial Times*

"Baker's new essay collection, *The Way the World Works*, is always absorbing, merging his interest in solid, tangible objects with his devotion to the life of the mind. . . . Simply dazzling."

*—Seattle Times*

"Baker splashes around happily in the English language, looking for new and amusing ways to bring his subjects to life. . . . His writing is deeply *moral*—not in a preachy sense, but in the sense that it emerges from the way he sees the world."

*—Slate*

"Baker's essays suspend you every few sentences or so, as you savor the silence he creates and enjoy the weightlessness you feel leaping from one thought to another."

*—The Daily Beast*

"Baker looks at the world around us in a way that is not only artful and entertaining but instructive."

*—Charleston Post & Courier*

"Baker, naïvely eager yet wise, employs his precise and evocative words to cherish and dissect, illuminate and interpret, gild and strip down things common and uncommon in such a manner that we appreciate what a splendid creation we inhabit."

—*The Barnes & Noble Review*

"[Baker] writes with charm and humor but also with a literate, clear-headed insightfulness. . . . Highly recommended."

—*The Portland Book Review*

"No matter how often one reads Baker, the style remains a surprise. . . . He is one of the most important writers we have."

—*The Telegraph* (UK)

"Full of the kind of cognitive sharp left turns that betray a true gift for metaphor. . . . For all his descriptive flourishes, Baker still has a way of getting to the precise heart of a matter."

—*The Independent* (UK)

"Baker offers gorgeous prose and poses important questions. . . . A delight to read."

—*Publishers Weekly* (starred review)

"A thoughtful collection . . . Baker is a champion of beauty on the verge of vanishing."

—*Kirkus Reviews*

# Praise for Nicholson Baker

"Baker is one of the most beautiful, original and ingenious prose stylists to have come along in decades."

—Charles McGrath, *The New York Times Magazine*

"His prose is so luminescent and so precise it manually recalibrates our brains."

—Lev Grossman, *Time*

"Nicholson Baker is such a swell, smart writer that he rarely—maybe never—tips his hand. . . . In Baker's view the mundane, closely enough observed, may be the skate key to the sublime."

—Carolyn See, *The Washington Post*

"Baker writes with appealing charm. He clowns and shows off, rambles and pounces hard; he says acute things, extravagant things, terribly funny things."

—*The Boston Globe*

"If only more of the literary world worked the way Baker does. . . . You cannot deny the courage of the writer. . . . Baker is singular."

—*The Buffalo News*

## ALSO BY NICHOLSON BAKER

FICTION

*House of Holes*
*The Anthologist*
*Checkpoint*
*A Box of Matches*
*The Everlasting Story of Nory*
*The Fermata*
*Vox*
*Room Temperature*
*The Mezzanine*

NONFICTION

*Human Smoke*
*Double Fold*
*The Size of Thoughts*
*U and I*

# The
# Way
## *the*
# World
# Works
## — *Essays* —

# NICHOLSON BAKER

**SIMON & SCHUSTER PAPERBACKS**
New York   London   Toronto   Sydney   New Delhi

Simon & Schuster Paperbacks
A Division of Simon & Schuster, Inc.
1230 Avenue of the Americas
New York, NY 10020

Copyright © 2012 by Nicholson Baker

First Simon & Schuster trade paperback edition August 2013

SIMON & SCHUSTER PAPERBACKS and colophon are registered
trademarks of Simon & Schuster, Inc.

For information about special discounts for bulk purchases,
please contact Simon & Schuster Special Sales at
1-866-506-1949 or business@simonandschuster.com.

The Simon & Schuster Speakers Bureau can bring authors
to your live event. For more information or to book an event,
contact the Simon & Schuster Speakers Bureau at
1-866-248-3049 or visit our website at www.simonspeakers.com.

Designed by Joy O'Meara

Manufactured in the United States of America

The Library of Congress has cataloged the hardcover edition as follows:
Baker, Nicholson.
  The way the world works : essays / Nicholson Baker.
    p. cm.
  I. Title.
  PS3552.A4325W39 2012
  814'.54—dc23
                                    2011052741

10  9  8  7  6  5  4  3  2  1

ISBN 978-1-4165-7247-3
ISBN 978-1-4165-7248-0 (pbk)
ISBN 978-1-4165-8398-1 (ebook)

# CONTENTS

# CONTENTS

## Libraries and Newspapers

## Technology

## War

## Last Essay

# FOREWORD

B ack in 1982, when I was just getting going as a writer, William Whitworth, the editor of *The Atlantic*, called to say that he was putting together a 125th-anniversary edition and he wondered if I had anything short to contribute to the front of the magazine. Flattered, I wrote something that tootled around in a ruminative way called "Changes of Mind." Other pieces followed, and I allowed myself to believe that I was helping to bring back the personal essay, which had fallen out of fashion. Some of my heroes were G. K. Chesterton, Christopher Morley, Alice Meynell, William Hazlitt, William James, and Samuel Johnson. By 1996 I had enough for a collection, *The Size of Thoughts*. Now it's 2012 and time, it seems, for a second and slightly heftier accrual. The first section of the book, LIFE, is made up of autobiographical bits arranged more or less chronologically; then come some meditations on READING and being read to. After that I tell the story of how I sued a public LIBRARY and talk about the beauties and wonders of old NEWSPAPERS; and then comes some TECHNO-journalism and writings on WAR and the people who oppose it, followed by a LAST ESSAY that I wrote for *The American Scholar* on mowing the lawn. I like mowing the lawn, and it didn't seem quite right to end the book with an impressionistic article on my unsuccessful efforts to master a series of violent video games. You'll find things in here about kite string, e-readers, earplugs, telephones, coins in fountains, paper mills, Wikipedia, commonplace books, airplane wings, gondolas, the *OED*, *Call of Duty*, Dorothy Day, John Updike, David Remnick, and Daniel Ellsberg. In a number of places I've changed a title, or restored a sentence or a passage that was cut to make something fit. I hope you run into a few items that interest you.

My thanks go to Jofie Ferrari-Adler at Simon & Schuster, and to all the careful, kind editors I've worked with on these pieces, especially Deborah Garrison, Henry Finder, Alice Quinn, and Cressida Leyshon at *The New Yorker*, Anne Fadiman and Sandra Costich at *The American Scholar*, Robert Silvers and Sasha Weiss at *The New York Review of Books*, Jennifer Scheussler and Laura Marmor at the *New York Times*, and James Marcus at *Harper's*.

# Life

# *String*

I was two years old when we moved to Rochester, New York. We lived in an apartment on a street that was only a block long, called Strathallan Park.

The shortness of the street was perfect, I thought: it had two ends and not much middle, like a stick that you pick up unconsciously to tap against a fence, or like one of those pieces of string that the people in the food department at Sibley's, the downtown department store, cut from wall-mounted spools to tie up a box holding a small cake. You could run from our end of the street, near University Avenue, all the way to East Avenue, the grander end, without having to stop to catch your breath, or almost, and when you reached the far corner and turned, panting, with your hands on your knees, you could look down the whole straight sidewalk, past the checkering of driveways and foreshortened snippets of lawn to where you had begun. Everything on my street was knowable by everyone at once.

A few of the lawns along Strathallan Park were, though small, fastidiously groomed—they were bright green and fluffy, and they were edged as well: using a blunt-bladed manual cutter at the end of a push pole, the lawn tenders had dug narrow, almost hidden troughs or gutters in the turf next to stretches of sidewalk and along walkways, outlining their territories as if they were drawing cartoons of them. The edge gutters looked neat, but they could wrench the ankle of a small-footed person who stepped wrong, and they held dangers for tricycle traffic as well: if you were going at top speed, trying to pass another tricyclist on the left, with your knees pumping like the finger-knuckles of a pianist during the final furious trill of his cadenza, you could catch your wheel in a gutter and flip or lose the race.

Some parts of the Strathallan sidewalk were made of pieces of slate that sloped up and down over the questing roots of elm trees (one elm had a mortal wound in its trunk out of which flowed, like blood, black sawdust and hundreds of curled-up larvae), and some parts of the sidewalk were made of aged concrete, with seams cut into them so that they would crack neatly whenever a growing tree required it of them. These seams made me think of the molded line running down the middle of a piece of Bazooka bubble gum, which you could buy in a tiny candy store in the basement of an apartment building near where we lived: the silent man there charged a penny for each piece of gum, machine-wrapped in waxed paper with triangular corner folds. It had a comic on an inner sheet that we read with great interest but never laughed at. Or, for the same penny, you could buy two unwrapped red candies shaped like Roman coins. These were chewy, and they let light through them when you held them up to the sun, but a red Roman coin couldn't do what a hard pink block of Bazooka gum could as it began to deform itself under the tremendous stamping and squashing force of the first chew: it couldn't make your eyes twirl juicily in their sockets; it couldn't make all your saliva fountains gush at once.

When you pulled part of a piece of well-chewed gum out of your mouth, holding the remainder in place, it would lengthen into drooping filaments that were finer and paler than thread. And I was thinking a fair amount about thread and string and twine in those Strathallan years—*twine* is a beautiful word—about spools of thread, especially after I got the hang of the sewing machine, which I drove as you would a car, listening for and prolonging the electric moan of the foot pedal just before the machine's silver-knobbed wheel began to turn, and steering the NASCAR scrap of fabric around a demanding closed course of loops and esses. When you floored the Singer's pedal, the down-darting lever in the side of the machine rose and fell so fast that it became two ghost levers, one at the top of its transit and one at the bottom, and the yanked spool on top responded by hopping and twirling on its spindle, flinging its close-spiraled life away.

Sometimes my mother let me take the spool off the sewing machine and thread the whole living room with it, starting with a small anchor knot on a drawer handle and unreeling it around end tables and doorknobs and lamp bases and rocking-chair arms until everything was interconnected. The only way to get out of the room, after I'd finished its web, was to duck below the thread layer and crawl out.

I was wary of the needle of the sewing machine—my father told me that a sewing machine needle had once gone through my grandmother's fingernail, next to the bone, and I didn't like the long shiny hypodermic needles, called "boosters," at Dr. Ratabaw's office one block over on Goodman Street. One morning, just after I took a bath, wearing only a T-shirt and underpants, I climbed down into the lightwell of a basement window in the back of our house, and in so doing disturbed some yellow jackets that had built a set of condominiums there, and I got several dozen short-needled booster shots at once, and saw my mother's arm set upon by outraged wasp abdomens that glinted in the sun as she brushed them off me. I tried to be braver at Dr. Ratabaw's office after that.

So that was my first street, Strathallan Park. Everything was right nearby, but sometimes we traveled farther afield, to Midtown Plaza, for instance, where I saw a man open a door in the Clock of Nations and climb inside its blue central pillar. There were thick tresses of multicolored wire in the Clock of Nations, each wire controlling a different papier-mâché figure, all of whom danced back then, in the days before Midtown Plaza went into a decline and the clock froze. We bought a kite and some string at Parkleigh pharmacy and took them with us to the greensward behind the Memorial Art Gallery, where there were three or four enormous trees and many boomerang-shaped seedpods that rattled like maracas. There wasn't enough wind there to hold the kite up, so we took it to a park, where it got caught in a tree and tore. My father repaired it on the spot, and even though it was now scarred, heavy with masking tape, we managed to get it aloft again briefly before it was caught by the same tree a second time. That was the beginning of my interest in kite flying.

Then, when I was six, we—that is, my sister, Rachel, my father and mother—moved to a house on Highland Avenue. It had a newel post on the front banister that was perfect for threading the front hall and living room, which I did several times, and it had a porte cochere and six bathrooms, a few of which worked, and it had an old wooden telephone in the hall closet that connected to another telephone in a room in the garage. The phone was dead, as my sister and I verified by shouting inaudible questions into either end, but there were interestingly herringboned threads woven as insulation around its cord, and because the phone had never been much used, the threads weren't frayed.

Highland Avenue was, as it turned out, also a perfect length of street, just as Strathallan had been, but in the opposite way: it went on forever. In one direction it sloped past Cobbs Hill Drive, where I always turned left when I walked to school, and then past the lawn-and-garden store, where my father bought prehistoric sedums every Sunday; and then it just kept on going. In the other direction it ran past our neighbors' houses, the Collinses, the Cooks, the Pelusios, and the Eberleins, and past a suburban-looking house on the left, and then it became quite a narrow street without sidewalks that just flowed on and on, who knew where. On Strathallan, our house number had been 30; now it was 1422, meaning that there must have been over a thousand houses on our street. In fact, it wasn't even called a street; it was an avenue. Avenues were, I gathered, more heavily trafficked, and therefore more important, than streets—Monroe Avenue, East Avenue, Lyell Avenue, Highland Avenue—they reached into surrounding counties and countries, and because the world was round, their ends all joined up on the other side. I was quite pleased to be part of something so infinite.

Soon after we moved in, my grandparents gave us a hammock made of green and white string. We hung it from two hooks on the front porch, and I lay in it looking at the fragment of Highland Avenue that I saw through the stretched fretwork of its strings. I could hear a car coming long before I could see it, and as it passed, its sound swooshed up the driveway toward me like a wave on a beach. That's when I counted it. One day I counted a thousand cars while lying on that hammock. It took about half an hour or so—a thousand wasn't as close to infinity as I'd thought it was.

And Cobbs Hill Park, half a block from where we lived, was, I discovered, one of the best kite-flying places in the city. My father was able to put a box kite in the air, which I never could; once it was up it was like a rock, unmoving, nailed to the sky. The key to kite flying, I found, was that you needed to lick your finger a lot and hold it in the air, and you always had to buy more rolls of string than you thought you needed, because the string manufacturers cheated by winding their product in open crisscrossing patterns around an empty cardboard cylinder—it looked as if you were holding a ball of string that was miles long, but in fact it was only eight hundred feet, which was nothing. One way or another, we always ran out of string.

To put myself to sleep at night, I began thinking about kites that never had to come down. I would add more string, half a dozen rolls of it, and when I knew the kite was steady, I would tie my end to a heavy ring in the ground that couldn't pull away and then I would shinny up the kite line with sticks in my pockets. I'd climb until I was a good ways up, and then I would make a loop around one foot to hold some of my weight, and begin knotting a sort of tree house out of the kite string to which I clung. The kite would be pulled down a little as I worked, but it was so far up in the sky that the loss of height didn't matter much, and I would use the sticks that I'd brought along as braces or slats around which I would weave the string, emulating our hammock's texture, until I had made a small, wind-shielding crow's nest like the basket in a hot-air balloon. I would spend the night up there, and the next morning, as people arrived in the park with their kites, they would point up at me and be impressed.

But that was just how I got to sleep; my biggest real moment of Cobbs Hill kite flying came around 1966, when I was nine. I was given a bat-shaped kite that year. It came from England via Bermuda in a long cardboard box that said "Bat Kite." The wings were made of black, slightly stretchy vinyl, with four wooden dowels as braces, a fiberglass crosspiece, and a triangle of vinyl with a metal grommet in it, where you tied the string. It was entirely black, a beautiful kite, but I wasn't able to get it up in the air for more than a few minutes because it was so heavy.

Then one weekend my old tricycle rival, Fred Streuver, and I went up to Cobbs Hill on a day when there was a hard steady wind blowing in from Pittsford Plaza, and the bat kite went up and it stayed up. We were stunned. What had we done right? We began feeding out the string. The kite seemed to want to stay up in the sky. Nothing we could do would bother it. It was hungry for string and it kept pulling, wanting to go out farther, over the path near the tennis courts. I tied on another roll, checking to be sure that I'd made a square knot—the kind that gets stronger and tighter the harder you pull on it. Our black bat was now out past the lilac bushes near Culver Road, and it was high high in the air, visible all over Rochester—hundreds of people could see it—and then we tied on another roll, and it was out *beyond* Culver Road and still asking for more string.

I had an almost frightened feeling—I was holding directly on to something that was alive and flying and yet far away. Having thought my way out to the empty air where the kite was, I almost forgot how to balance as I stood on the grass of Cobbs Hill. Even the square knots that we had tied had risen out of sight—the string was getting more and more infinite every minute.

Then, as always, we ran out. But we wanted more. We wanted our bat to go a full mile out. Fred held the line as I gathered a length of scrap string that some departed fliers had left behind; I tied it on, even though it had a nested tangle in it that held a twig, and the kite kept pulling. I found another abandoned string, but here Fred and I were overhasty when we tied the knot, we were laughing crazily by now, we were tired, and neither of us was checking each other's work. We sent up the new string, but when it had gone just out of reach, I saw a tiny unpleasant movement in the knot. It was a writhing sort of furtive wiggle. I said, "No, bring it down!" and I grabbed the line, but the kite's pull was too strong, and the flawed knot shrugged off the rest of its loops—it had been, I now saw, a granny knot. The string that we held went limp, and the string on the other side of the failed knot went limp as well, and floated sideways.

Way off beyond Culver Road, the kite learned the truth all at once: it flung itself back some feet as if pushed or shot, and its bat wings flapped like loose sails, and then it slid down out of the sky into some trees that were beyond other trees, that were beyond houses, that were beyond trees.

We went looking for it, but it was gone. It had fallen somewhere in a neighborhood of short streets, in one of a hundred little back yards.

(2003)

# *Coins*

In 1973, when I was sixteen, I got a job in building maintenance at Midtown Plaza, Rochester's then flourishing downtown shopping mall. I spent a day pulling nails from two-by-fours—loudly whistling Ravel's *Boléro* while I worked, so that the secretaries would know that I knew a few things about French music—and then Rocky, the boss, a dapper man with a mustache, apprenticed me to the mall's odd-job man, Bradway. Bradway taught me the right way to move filing cabinets (you walk with them on alternating corners, as if you're slow dancing with them, and when you have one of them roughly in position in its row, just put the ball of your foot low against a corner and step down, and the cabinet will slide into place as if pulled there by a magnet); and he taught me how to snap a chalk line, how to cut curves in Sheetrock, how to dig a hole for a "No Parking" sign, how to adjust the hydraulic tension on an automatic door, the right way to use a sledgehammer, and how to change the fluorescent bulbs in the ceiling of the elevator. He wore funny-looking glasses, and he sang "Pretty, Pretty Paper Doll" to the secretaries, embarrassing them and me, but he was a decent person and a good teacher. For reasons I still don't understand he was disliked by one of the carpenters in the maintenance department, who referred to him as a "proctologist's delight."

One afternoon Bradway gave me a beeper and told me he was going to teach me how to sweep up the pennies in the fountain. Midtown Plaza's fountain had a fifteen-foot-high inward-curving spray, and there were four or five low mushroom fountains to one side, lit from below; the water went around and under a set of stairs rising up to the mall's second level. People threw pennies in from the landing on the stairs and while standing at the railing on the second level, but mostly they tossed them in as they walked past. I had thrown in pennies myself. The thing to do when you wished on a penny was to thumb-flip it very high—the more air time it had, the more opportunity it had to become an important penny, a singular good-luck penny—and then watch it plunge into the water and twirl down to the tiled bottom of the pool. You had to memorize where it landed. It was the penny with the two very tarnished pennies just to the left of it—or no, was it one of the ones in that very similar constellation a foot away? Every day you could check on your penny, or the penny you had decided must be your penny, to see how it was doing, whether it was accumulating wish-fulfilling powers.

So when Bradway said that I—a maintenance worker earning $2.50 an hour—was going to be sweeping up all the pennies, I experienced a magisterial shiver. We went down to the basement and got a pair of rubber fly-fishing boots, a black bucket with some holes in it, a dustpan, and a squeegee broom. Bradway showed me the switch that turned off the pump for the fountains. I pressed it. There was a clunk.

Back upstairs the water was almost still. I stepped over

the marble ledge and, handed the long pole of the squeegee, I began pushing around other people's good luck. The bottom of the pool was covered with small blue tiles, and it was somewhat slimy, so that the pennies, moved along by the squeegee, formed planar sheets of copper, arranging themselves to fit into one another's adjoining curves, until finally a row of pennies would push up, make peaks, and flip back, forming a second layer, and then another layer would form, and eventually there was a sunken reef of loose change—including some nickels and dimes, but no quarters—in one corner of the pool. "That's it, just keep sweeping them toward the pile," Bradway said. He gave me the black bucket with the holes in it, and, rolling up my sleeves as high as I could, I used the dustpan to scoop up the change and pour it, entirely underwater, into the bucket. The sound was of anchor chains at the bottom of the sea. By doing as much of it as possible below the surface, we kept the penny removal somewhat discreet.

Bradway went away while I swept farther afield, and I looked out with a haughty but weary look at the people walking by: I was the maintenance man, standing in the water; they were just pedestrians in a mall. "Are you going to keep all that money?" a man said to me. I said no, it was going to charity. "I'm a good charity, man," he said. The trickiest area to sweep was along the row of mushroom fountains (which were just stalks when the water was turned off), but even there it wasn't too hard, and when I got the strays out into the open tilework and scooted the change along in a cloud of pale, sluggish dust, I felt like a seasoned cowboy, bringing the herd home.

Bradway came back and together we pulled the black bucket out, letting the water pour from the holes. It was extremely heavy. We set it on a two-wheeled dolly. "Feel that slime?" said Bradway. I nodded. "The bank won't take the money this way." We went down the freight elevator to the basement and he showed me a room with an old yellow washing machine in it. Together we dumped the money in and Bradway turned the dial to regular wash; the coins went through a slushy-sounding cycle. After lunch, I scooped out the clean money and wheeled it to the bank. As told, I asked to see Diane. Diane led me back to the vault, and I slid the black bucket off the dolly next to some dirty sacks of quarters.

Every week that summer I cleaned the fountain. Every week there was new money there to sweep up. I flipped more coins in myself; one nickel I deliberately left in place for a few weeks while I maneuvered away all the pennies around it, so that my wish-money would have more time to gather momentum. The next time, though, I swept it along with the rest, trying, however, to follow its progress as a crowd of coins lined up like piglets on the sow of the rubber blade. There were momentary collisions and overturnings, and the wavelets of the water added a confusion. My coin slid over another coin and fell to the right, and then, as I pushed them all into the corner pile, a mass of money avalanched over it and it was lost to view.

Once I came across a penny that had lain in the water under the stairs, unswept, for a very long time—perhaps years. Black it was and full of power. I pushed it into the heap with the others, dumped it into the washing machine, and delivered it to Diane at the bank.

*(2001)*

# How I Met My Wife

She was walking up a flight of stairs in a college dorm; I was carrying my bicycle down the stairs. I could hear the ticking sound of the slowly revolving tire as I introduced myself.

I stood in her room with my hands in my pockets while she did her Italian homework. She sat on the floor, leaning against the bunk bed, wearing clean, wrinkly T-shirts of various colors. She was dissatisfied with her clothes, and she often changed several times a day. She moved her head almost imperceptibly when a song came on that she liked. She didn't own a bra, though her mother pleaded with her. She liked someone else who lived on the hall; I liked watching her blush when he dropped by. On our first date she wore a wonderful cashmere coat that she had bought at a thrift store. It had a shawl collar made of lambswool that went with her soft, thoughtful lips. I tried to get her to shoe-ski on the thin layer of snow on the sidewalk in front of the administration building, but she didn't want to. It was snowing big intermittent designer flakes that night. She told me about a kitten she had found in one of the forums in Rome, who grew up to be an enormous, arrogant, affable cat. Once, she said, it fell off the sixth-floor balcony of their apartment in the Piazza Paganica and broke its nose when it landed; its purr was especially loud and resonant after that fall.

(1993)

# La Mer

After school, when I was thirteen, my bassoon teacher told me that the Rochester Philharmonic, where he played second bassoon, was rehearsing a piece of music called *La Mer*. *Mer* didn't mean "mother," he said—it meant "sea," and the remarkable thing about *La Mer* was that it really and truly did sound like the sea. He played me some bits from the score while I put together my instrument. What he played didn't sound like the sea to me, but that wasn't surprising, because nothing sounds like the sea on the bassoon. A few months later, I bought a record of Pierre Boulez performing *La Mer* with the New York Philharmonic. I put on the heavy, padded headphones, that were like inflatable life rafts for each ear, and I heard Debussy's side-slipping water-slopes, with cold spray blown off their crests, and I saw the sudden immensity of the marine horizon that followed the storm, and I was amazed by how true to liquid life it all was. It was just as good as Joseph Conrad's "Typhoon," then one of my favorite stories—maybe even better.

Later, after I'd applied to music school, I bought the pocket score of *La Mer* and tried to figure out how Debussy did it, but the score didn't help much. What gave Debussy the confidence to pick up half a melody and then flip it away, like a torn piece of seaweed, after a moment's study? How did he turn an orchestra, a prickly ball of horsehair and old machinery, into something that splashed and surged, lost its balance and regained it? There may be things about *La Mer* that are slightly dissatisfying—there may be too much of the whole-tone scale in a few places (a novelty then, worn out by cop-show soundtracks now), and Debussy made a mistake, I think, when he revised the brass fanfare out of the ending— but this piece has so many natural wonders that you drive past the drab moments as if they were convenience stores, without paying attention to them, looking out at the tidal prodigies.

Debussy finished *La Mer*—adjusting its orchestration and correcting proofs—during a month in England in the summer of 1905, in Eastbourne, a late-Victorian summer resort where he had gone with Emma Bardac. Emma was married to a well-to-do banker at the time, and was very pregnant with Debussy's only child. A few years ago, paging through one of the biographies, I stopped at a picture of Debussy frowning down into the viewfinder of a camera, on the stone-parapeted balcony of the Grand Hotel Eastbourne. The camera was pointed out at the English Channel. I was living in Ely at the time, north of Cambridge, but it occurred to me, as I consulted a map and a schedule, that I could easily go to Eastbourne and return the same day.

I rode the screeching, battered local train out one March morning; I walked into town and stopped at a used book store, which had nothing about Debussy, and then at the tourist information center, where a kind woman pulled out a red notebook entitled "Famous People," with entries for Wordsworth, Tennyson, Swinburne (who wrote "To a Seamew" nearby, at Beachy Head), King Arthur, and Debussy. The woman pointed me in the direction of the Grand Hotel, and when I finally found it, after turning the wrong way on the shore road, I was told that room 277 was the Debussy Suite, but that they couldn't let me in to look out the windows of the suite because it was almost check-in time and that night's guests might arrive at any moment.

So I sat in the garden on a white bench, with my back to the sea, looking up at the balcony where Debussy and Emma had, not so many years ago, looked out over the channel toward an invisible France. The balcony was right over the main entrance, under the letters that spelled "Grand Hotel." In the pale sunlight, I sketched the facade of the hotel, with its eye-guiding beaux arts urns and scrolls (designed by R. K. Blessley in 1876); it seemed to me that Debussy, often penniless and foolish about money, had felt industriously rich here, perhaps for the last time, as he put the final touches on his ebullient sea poem. A few months later, back in Paris, his wife, abandoned and heartbroken, shot herself near the heart, and though she recovered, everyone's life was different afterward.

I went back inside the hotel and up the fire stairs to the second floor. (The stairs had nicely carved banister knobs.) It was one of those buildings in which the flights of stairs and the placement of windows are out of synchrony: in the stairwell, the top of the window frame was low to the floor, so that I had to bend way down, my head pounding, to get a proper view. I had only a minute or two before I needed to leave to catch the train back. There was dried rain-dust on the outside of the glass, but I looked out over the water and saw, near to shore, an unexpected play of green and gold and turquoise waves—not waves, really, because they were so small, but little manifestations of fluid under-energy. The clouds had the look that a glass of rinse water gets when you're doing a watercolor—slowly diluting black roilings which move under the white water that you made earlier when you rinsed the white paint from the brush. But the sea didn't choose to reflect the clouds that day; it had its own private mallard-neck palette, the fine gradations of which varied with the slopes of the wind-textured swells. Through the dirty window, I thought I saw, for a moment, what Debussy had seen.

*(2001)*

# Why I Like the Telephone

When I was little, I played with the phone a lot. I liked the physical sensation of dialing, of having my finger guided in its numerical hole (first it was black metal, then more comfortable clear plastic) along arcs of a perfect circle, as if it were a pen in a Spirograph. Sometimes I hurried it back around and felt the center gear strain slightly.

Also, for a period of several years while I was growing up, no member of my family wore a watch, and our house had no dependably working clock. (We had an antique clock on the mantel but we often let it wind down.) My job was to call, often several times a day, the time-and-temperature number, sponsored by Rochester Savings Bank, and find out what time it was. I was delighted to make these calls. The other phone numbers I had memorized merely reached people my own age (e.g., my friend Fred, GI2-1397, and my friend Maitland, CH4-4158), but the time-temperature number linked me to a realer, kitchenless world of atomic clocks and compound interest and absolute zero, to times and temperatures thrillingly beyond dispute, endorsed, it seemed, by the National Bureau of Standards and the FDIC.

The day after daylight savings, the time-and-temperature number was always busy, a sign of simultaneous citywide activity as definite as the drop in water pressure during the ad breaks in the Super Bowl.

Later I learned the trick of calling myself up: you dialed some short number (was it 811?), and you made a carefully timed click of the cradle, and, miraculously, your own phone, the phone you were touching, would ring—a result that seemed, in those years before the discovery of other solitary auto-dialed pleasures, exotic and shocking and worthwhile.

It isn't stretching things too much to say that in *Vox*, my phone-sex novel, I was performing the novelistic equivalent of these early telephonic diversions: I was calling up, or calling on, what I hoped were National-Bureau-of-Standards-level verities about the interests and flirtations of two representatively chatty single phoners, a pair who began as strangers to me and to each other and who thus had to move as mere voices from the absolute zero of their initial connection to the high-Fahrenheit range of their affectionate spoken orgasms. And at the same time, of course, I was making my own phone ring.

*(1994)*

# What Happened on April 29, 1994

A Contribution to *240 Ecrivains Racontent Une Journée du Monde,*
the *Nouvel Observateur*'s anthology of events for April 29, 1994

I took my daughter to school, and then, at my office, I wrote
an e-mail about library catalogs, although I was supposed
to be reviewing a novel. A fact-checker from a newspaper
called, wanting to know if I was thirty-seven, and whether it
was correct to say that a book of mine had been published on
a certain day in 1992. I had lunch at a Chinese restaurant with
my wife and sleeping five-month-old son. We talked about an
article on homelessness that she had read in the *New York
Review of Books.* Then I wrote about library catalogs some
more. When I got home, my daughter was wearing a new
Girl Scout Brownie uniform. She was proud of her long, blue-
tasseled socks, and her pride made my eyes fill with tears,
partly because I was tired from writing about libraries all day.

Outside on the back deck, we used strips of masking tape

to outline the dimensions of a possible second bathroom, to be installed in the laundry room. Chairs stood for the sink and the toilet; the space proved to be too small to accommodate a shower.

I bought hamburgers for dinner and rented *Arsenic and Old Lace* for us to watch as a family (never having seen it), but it frightened my daughter, so we stopped the tape. I made my son laugh by tickling the soles of his feet with my beard and making munching sounds at his ribs. When both children were asleep, my wife watched the rest of the movie while I, tipped sideways forty-five degrees, dozed on the couch. Then I went back to my office and sorted the mail I was supposed to answer into four piles. I didn't actually answer any letters, but I felt that I had moved forward by sorting them. One of the pieces of mail I came across was a fax from *Le Nouvel Observateur,* and I realized that this was the very day I was supposed to write about and that I had thus far taken no notes. So I took some notes on the margin of the fax, which smudged on the shiny paper but remained legible.

The last thing I did before I got in bed was to put a computer disk between the two halves of my wallet so that I wouldn't forget to take it with me to Phoenix, Arizona, where I was going the next morning to watch a friend get married to a tall woman who had appeared in a Jeep commercial. I went to sleep fondling my wife's engagement ring.

Now, several months later, the bathroom is built. The strips of masking tape, which we didn't bother to peel up when we finished our architectural planning that evening, have become ineffaceably baked onto the gray planks of the back deck. They are, in fact, the only tangible remains of that particular day.

*(1994)*

# Sunday at the Dump

It's a Sunday afternoon in South Berwick and I'm at the dump, sitting in a white plastic lawn chair. Dump days are Wednesday, Saturday, and Sunday; most people go on Sunday afternoons. The busiest time is just before six, when the dump closes: if you come too late, you're stuck with your trash until Wednesday, and when Wednesday comes around you're likely to forget. There are no garbage trucks in our town—everyone must make an appearance here. Just before election day, candidates for local office show up to shake hands and campaign—only here at the dump does a candidate have a chance of meeting a voter from every household. Many residents hardly set foot in the little stores on Main Street; they don't use the post office much; they shop for groceries in supermarkets across the border in another state; their children are bused to school. But everybody comes to the dump. "We get more business here than town hall," Jim told me. Jim is the dump's manager—a stocky man in his twenties with a deep sunburn. When I had been sitting in my white plastic chair for about half an hour, in a shady place to one side of the parking lot, Jim came over to be sure I wasn't trying to drop off some illegal toxic material in the bushes. I told him I was writing about the dump, because most people are happy when they come here. In fact, I'm smiling now, as I type this sentence, looking out at the sunlit cars and trucks, and the long rectilinear containers, each accepting a different kind of refuse. There is a beautiful red container, freshly painted, the size of a caboose, with a ladder up its side; in front of it there is a sign that says "Shingles Only."

Though we call it a dump, technically it isn't one: it used to be a landfill. Behind the main building there is a steep man-made hill, covered with yellow wildflowers, with two T-shaped structures poking up from it. These are vents; they release trapped gasses from the heap. Now all the trash that we bring goes in trucks to the nearby town of Biddeford, where they burn it. Biddeford residents complain of the smell; for unknown reasons, Biddefordians sited their incinerator in the center of town. I told Jim the Manager that our dump was looking very clean these days. When Jim took over a year ago, the place was a mess; now everything's in order, and there's no smell. "Every night we clean out all the recycling cans with a mixture of Simple Green, bleach, and water," Jim said. "We don't get any bees. When I got here, there were a lot of bees."

Agamenticus Road is the way to the dump. Agamenticus is the name of a mountain nearby; there are rare plants that grow only on Mount Agamenticus, but I've never seen them. There is a pile of rocks on top of Mount Agamenticus, too. Indians supposedly had a tradition of commemorating a sacred burial site by arranging a large pile of rocks; now visitors to the mountain bring their rocks as well. I've been to the top of Mount Agamenticus once; I've been to the dump hundreds of times, often with my son. You take a right at the Civil War statue onto Agamenticus Road; you drive past some houses and a cemetery; and then, just after the ice cream stand and potted plant store, you take a left and you're in a paved area in front of the dump's main building, a brown shed. Next to it is a yawning opening—a sort of double-high garage door—into which people toss their clear bags of trash. One of the pleasures here is in throwing: today I flung each bag underhand, so that it had a final airborne moment of multicolored spin before it fell into the compaction pit. Sometimes I overturn the whole garbage can (which I've brought in the back of my van) and shake out its contents, holding it high over my shoulder: the bags emerge slowly, hissing slightly, held by the vacuum I created several days earlier when I stuffed the bags down into the can in order to close the lid. The bags holding regular trash must be transparent, so that the dump attendants can verify that you're not throwing in something forbidden, like cat litter. Cat litter goes into another enormous container separate from the main one, a receptacle entirely devoted to mattresses, old couches, and cat litter.

There are three windows in the main building—one window is labeled "Brown," one says "Green," and one says "Clear." Formerly the windows were fitted with swinging flaps of Plexiglas, but the flaps have been removed now—an improvement. Into these windows we throw bottles and jars. When the bottles fall into the bins on the other side of the swinging flaps (or where the swinging flaps were when there were flaps), the clinks they make are painfully loud. When the bottles break it's a relief: shattering is noticeably less noisy than intact clinking. Why? Perhaps because some of the kinetic energy is used up in the breakage, and there are no broken inner bottle-hollows to muffle the radiating noise.

Down a slope and to the left of the main building are two dark-green containers, each the size of a mobile home. One holds newspapers and magazines, and one holds cardboard. You can flip pizza boxes like Frisbees into the container for cardboard, hoping to lodge them at the top of the pile, way back in the shadows. Often the boxes slide back out again. I took several bags of newspapers into the newspaper-and-magazine bin. There is a partition up halfway back, to hold the four-foot-high tide of paper from pouring forward. It's hushed and warm deep in this news-vessel; the shiny advertising inserts make slushy whispering noises as you release them from the bag.

The most exciting place in the dump is the little shack with a cement floor and a sign over it saying "Swap Shop," where people leave their serviceable junk. Today at the Swap Shop I noticed three toasters, two toaster ovens, a bike, a textbook of surgery, many pairs of shoes, two tape recorders, and an infant's car seat. A man with a large, high stomach dropped off a green and white poolside chair that he had no use for; half an hour later I saw a grandmother walking off with it, while her grandson left with a toy parking garage.

My son and my wife once brought me home a bicycle from the Swap Shop: it has two flat tires, but it's otherwise in good shape. Another time we found a pair of antique sleds there. Our friends the Remicks have gotten a treadmill, several extension cords, and an outdoor cooker, all from the Swap Shop. My prize was a complete set of the *Golden Book Encyclopedia,* with trompe l'oeil paintings on the covers—my beloved childhood encyclopedia. Since then, I've seen several more sets of this encyclopedia here—I suppose families must be getting rid of their copies all over the country at the moment. This afternoon, I selected a fifties paperback of

Lao Tzu and a book about Czechoslovakia in 1968. (Lao Tzu says: "Rule a large country as small fish are cooked.") The bookshelves are in the back of the shed—sometimes I take a strange pleasure in straightening up the rows of Reader's Digest Condensed Books.

Now a woman of eighty or so, with a fresh white perm, is walking with stocky but sometimes unsteady steps toward the dump-mouth. She is wearing blue easy-care pants and carrying a small clear bag of tidy aged-person's garbage. She tosses the bag in, watching it take its place in the pit among everyone else's contributions. Maybe it's the clearness of the bags that makes the dump seem like a place of confidences— everyone can see just what everyone doesn't want.

A few times every Sunday, one of the crew drives the toothed bucket of a backhoe deep into the container full of cardboard to compress it: as the motor strains, the drooping arm of the machine disappears into the welter of boxes, which are forced up as well as back, and then it withdraws, like a hand reaching into a basketful of tickets at a raffle to pick the winner.

*(2000)*

# Writing Wearing Earplugs

Some years ago I bought an industrial dispenser pack of two hundred pairs of Mack's earplugs from earplugstore.com. Mostly, though, I buy them from the drugstore. Recently, Mack's began offering them in orange, which is less disgusting than white.

I can sit anywhere, in any loud place, and work. Everything becomes twenty feet farther away than it really is. The chirping, barking, jingling cash drawer of a world is out of reach, and therefore more precious.

You must have a good seal. When you unstick your thumb from a jammed-in plug, your eardrum will make a tiny, silent cry of pain, like a word in Arabic. Then you know you have a good seal.

(2007)

## One Summer

One summer I lived in a house that was being renovated, in a bright yellow room, with a mattress on the floor. I woke up late and tried to type in bed. I was working on a story about a man who by chance runs into his brain on the street. His brain is wearing a jaunty hat and is in a hurry. It has some kind of a sales job. At night I walked to a restaurant called Gitsis Texas Hots and ordered two hot dogs and a cup of coffee and reviewed the day's work on "My Brain." The story was never finished.

One summer my family went on a boat in Georgian Bay with another family. There was a girl who slept on the boat with her eyes open.

One summer a friend and I went on a bicycle trip. In a small town in New York State, somebody opened a car door and we both collided with it and fell down on the street. And we were fine. Later a flock of birds gathered in the tree above our sleeping bags in the early morning.

One summer in California I owned a hundred shares of stock in Koss Corporation, the headphone company. I bought a newspaper and discovered that the stock had doubled in value. I sold all my shares and bought a Honda Passport motor scooter. My girlfriend rode on the back, wearing a red helmet, and I had a blue helmet, and it was lots of fun except that she burned her leg on the muffler and had to go to the emergency room.

One summer my girlfriend and I got engaged and we went to Jordan Marsh and bought a mattress and a box spring from a salesman named Sam. Sam said his wife liked a softer mattress, but he liked a firmer mattress. He led us to a mattress that was both firm and soft. The thing about this mattress, he explained, was that on it the two of us could "sleep to the edge." If you got a cheap queen-size mattress, he said, it was really like only getting a full-size mattress, because you couldn't sleep to the edge. We bought the mattress Sam recommended and twenty years later we are still sleeping to the edge on it.

One summer I painted the floor and ceiling of a room in the same day. The paint didn't stick very well to the floor, however.

One summer I tried to write about a man I'd interviewed named Pavel Moroz. Mr. Moroz had invented something he called a microcentrifuge. He took tiny spheres of liquid and spun them at the highest speed he could spin them at, using a dentist's drill. Nothing spins faster than a dentist's drill, apparently. Mr. Moroz believed that ultracentrifugation would transform matter into new states of purity and enlightenment. But nobody paid attention to him. When I talked to him he was taking classes to become a licensed masseur.

One summer I had a paddleboard and I went up the side of a big wave to the top. Then I was under the wave looking up at its sunlit crest. Then I was turned some more, and I saw sand and gravel doing a little polka on the bottom. I had no idea there was so much going on inside a wave.

One summer there were several cars with trick horns installed that played "La Cucaracha."

One summer I heard someone next door typing on an electric typewriter while I sat outside in the sun. I listened to the swatting of the keys and thought how rare that sound was now. I tore an article out of the newspaper about the bankruptcy of Smith Corona.

One summer I sat at a table with Donald Barthelme, the short-story writer, while he drank a Bloody Mary. He said he was planning to buy a new stereo system. I recommended that he go with Infinity loudspeakers.

One summer I worked for a company that made modems. I began working twelve hours a day. In the morning, driving to work, I held the coffee cup in my teeth when I was unwrapping a doughnut. Once, passing a truck, I forgot that the coffee cup was there and I whipped my head around to be sure a car wasn't in the next lane, sloshing coffee on my shirt and my seat belt. Another time a can of 7 UP exploded in the glove compartment. The car, a Dodge Colt, began to have a sweetish smell that I liked.

One summer my grandmother took us to visit a blind woman who lived by the sea. The woman told us that when she swam, she would listen for her dog, who barked whenever she drifted too far from shore. Once she went out to do errands and didn't come home till very late. Her dog had had a bathroom emergency under a knicknack shelf, away from where she would step, which she thought was very considerate. We agreed.

One summer I went on a bike trip through Quebec and Maine, eating four peanut butter and jelly sandwiches a day. The roads in Quebec are very straight and flat.

One summer I worked at a place where they stored old copying machines. I learned to drive a forklift, and I drove it around the old copying machines, beeping the horn, which made a plummy "meep meep." The second floor was filled with metal desks, and when it was break time, I would go up there to read spy novels. One of the people I worked with wandered around these desks drinking clear fluid from a bottle. That man sure drinks a lot of water, I thought. He opened and closed the drawers of the desks, checking to see if something of value had been left behind. I listened to the sound of drawers opening and closing, far away and nearer by, and fell asleep.

One summer a raisin stuck to a page I was writing on, so I drew an outline of it and wrote "A Raisin Stuck Here— Sunmaid."

One summer I went to Italy with my girlfriend and her family. My girlfriend's uncle brought a set of dissolvable capsules containing foam circus animals. Every night at cocktail hour we dropped one capsule into a glass of water. As each foam leg emerged, we would say, "There's another leg!"

One summer two of my friends and I found a loose door. We hauled it up to the top of the garage roof and positioned it there with some struts so that we could sit on the door and look out at the world. There wasn't much to do once we were up there except eat crackers, and the asphalt roof shingles were soft and easily torn, like pan pizza, we discovered. They overlapped unnecessarily, wastefully, so we tore off quite a number of them and flung them down. They glided like Frisbees. My parents were unhappy because they had to have the garage reroofed.

One summer my friend and I bought Corgi toys, about fifteen of them, and built a parking garage for them out of blocks. Then we had an argument, and my friend took the Corgis he owned back to his own house.

One summer I worked as a waiter in a fancy restaurant that had been owned by a reputed mobster. The mobster sold the restaurant to the head chef for a lot of money. But many of the people who'd gone to the restaurant had been friends and associates of the reputed mobster—when he stopped going, they stopped going. So business dropped, and I stood wearing a ruffle-fronted shirt with a black bow tie, looking out at the empty tables. Once a waitress told the chef that a patron wanted a simple chicken salad sandwich. The chef, whose speciality was veal dishes, was affronted. "Chicky salad?" he said. "Tell him to bring his dick in here, I'll make him some nice chicky salad."

One summer I converted all my old word processing files, written on a Kaypro computer, to DOS. And that was fun.

One summer a guy down the street got mad at the fact that people were allowing their dogs to poop every day in front of his yard. He took some white plastic forks and put them in the dog poops. They looked like little sailboats.

One summer we had four fans set up in the upstairs bedrooms. One fan started smoking and our alert dog barked to let us know. Then we had three fans.

One summer I read the Edmund Scientific catalog a lot of times and fantasized about owning a walkie-talkie and communicating with my friends with it. But they cost a hundred dollars.

One summer I was on the verge of making a baloney sandwich. I had the tomato in my hand and I'd opened the door of the refrigerator and I was looking down at the jar of mayonnaise on the bottom shelf, and then I thought, No, no baloney right now. And I closed the refrigerator door. I was able to resist that baloney and put it out of my mind.

One summer I read an old copy of *Confessions of an English Opium-Eater* with great fascination.

One summer my father put up a Tarzan swing in our back yard. My friend and I used an old refrigerator crate as the leaping-off point, with two smaller boxes on top of that for extra height. We swung so high that we could grab a branch in a spruce tree and hold on to it. Then one time the branch broke, and my friend fell. He lay on his back going "Orf orf." I was worried and got my mother. She said he'd had the wind knocked out of him, but that he would be fine. And he was fine.

One summer I got a crush on a girl who was eleven. I was eleven at the time as well.

One summer my father planted an herbaceous border in our yard. I helped him plant the *Santolina incana nana* and mix in the peat moss. On weekdays he would go out after dinner and water in the dark, so that if I went out to get him I could only see the spray from the hose reflecting the porch light, and hear his whistling.

One summer I went to see a new movie called *Annie Hall* with two women who played the harp. One harp player didn't like it, one harp player really didn't like it, and I liked it a lot.

One summer I spent a lot of time in my room trying to learn how to handstand. But one of my wrists was not flexible enough.

One summer a photographer was doing an ad for a bank and needed a woman to make a funny face. He called up my mother, because he had heard that she could make funny faces. The two of them went out onto the front porch, and he said to her, "Okay, now make a funny face." She grimaced, then laughed. He said, "Try not to laugh. Good. Now puff out your cheeks." So she puffed out her cheeks. The ad, announcing a higher interest rate on savings accounts, came out in the newspaper. The picture looked nothing like my mother. I spent a good deal of time making funny faces in the mirror in case a photographer called me.

One summer I went to a science camp called Camp Summersci. We were driven in a used hearse to places of scientific interest. In Herkimer, New York, we chiseled quartz crystals called Herkimer diamonds out of a rocky hillside. One of the campers was a kid who knew more about *The Lord of the Rings* than I did. We talked about *The Lord of the Rings* for many hours in the back of the hearse.

One summer my father and I put up a basketball hoop above the garage door, and I played basketball with myself for a week and then stopped.

One summer a new friend said we should learn taxidermy at home. He sent off for lesson one. The course instructed us to look around for dead squirrels to stuff. I told him I didn't know where any dead squirrels were. His voice was already changing and mine wasn't. He laughed: "Heh heh." I laughed nervously back. He shook his head and said, "See, I knew you'd laugh. All I have to do is pretend to laugh, and you laugh."

One summer my girlfriend was unhappy with me when we went out for dinner because I pulled the onions out of my salad with my fingers and put them on the bread plate along with a glob of salad dressing. Later I leapt up from the table to watch a brief fistfight between a waiter and a patron. I said I was sorry and she forgave me.

One summer my daughter learned how to read the word *misunderstanding*.

One summer I rode to the top of a hill and then coasted, and the wind came under the back of my neck and down in my shirt and cooled me down. It felt very good. This was somewhere in West Virginia, on my bike.

One summer my friend Steve and I went out to a movie. He was getting his medical degree then. He suggested we go buy some cheese at the Super Duper. That sounded like a good idea to me. We bought two large pieces of mozzarella cheese and got into his car and ate them, talking about the current state of science fiction.

One summer I worked at a job where we had to wash hundreds of venetian blinds in a tall metal tank that stood in a loud room next to the air circulation fans. We dipped the blinds in soapy water in the tank, and then we moved them up and down. The dipping was supposed to remove the dust from the slats, but the dust had bonded with the paint and it stayed. So the man said we had to wash the slats by hand, with a rag. This made the white paint come off. We put all the blinds back in the windows, although they were bent and peeling and sorry-looking. Later I used a sledgehammer on a big piece of cement.

One summer I went to a Nautilus Fitness Center at the Americana Hotel in Rochester. I did various strenuous things on the machines, and then I crossed the street to McDonald's and ordered two Big Macs. My hand trembled so much from the exercise that I could barely push the straw through the little cross in the plastic lid of my root beer.

One summer my son and I built a tree house near the compost pile. We painted it green. We ate dinner up there a few times.

One summer after my wife and I spent all day packing boxes I had a dream in which I'd grown a split personality that snarled and lunged at me like a police dog. I woke up and lay perfectly still, too afraid to close my eyes or click on the light. After several minutes of motionless nostalgia for the days when I had been a sane person, I finally touched my wife and said, "Dear one?" She made a questioning noise from deep in her sleep. I said, "I'm sorry to wake you but I'm having some kind of unusual panic attack." She said, "I'm so sorry, baby." I said, "It's really bad, I'm scared about everything, I'm even scared to turn on the light." She said, "I'll hold you. Everything is good. Go back to sleep now." She held me and I turned a different way in the bed and the fear dissolved and I went back to sleep. I woke up feeling fine.

One summer I dropped a bowl of hot fudge that I'd warmed up in a microwave onto the kitchen floor of a Howard Johnson's and burned myself.

One summer my friend and I dug in his back yard using a hose to blast holes deep in the dirt. We made a series of small ponds and bogs. My friend's mother was unhappy with us because the water bill was very high.

One summer my family and I ate dinner at a restaurant that had a machine that made saltwater taffy. The machine had two double-forked prongs that folded and stretched the taffy ball onto itself until there were unimaginable numbers of layers. When the taffy had been stretched and folded enough times a man rolled it into a loaf and mounted it in a machine that cut it and wrapped the cut pieces with waxed-paper wrappers. The device that twisted the wrapper ends moved too fast for the eye to see. The taffy man looked at us without acknowledging us or smiling. He had no privacy—he was like a zoo creature. He had a small mustache.

One summer we moved from Boston, Massachusetts, to New York State. I was driving the old brown car and my wife was driving the new red car down Routes 5 and 20. There was a big hot blue sky and enormous trees. I rolled my window all the way down. Immediately the wind sucked a map of New York State off my dashboard. In my rearview mirror I saw the pale creased shape float on air for a moment, as if deciding what to do. Then it plastered itself to my wife's windshield, where she pulled it inside. She waved.

One summer when I was fourteen I took care of an orange cat at a house owned by two minimalist painters. All their walls were flat white, and they had many of their paintings up—long, narrow paintings, with silver metallic paint sprayed in from the ends, dripping subtly. The lonely cat roamed this minimalist house, meowing. I read issues of *Artforum* neatly stacked on their coffee table. There was an article about an artist who created an empty room with a sloping wooden floor. The artist, whose name was Vito Acconci, "pleasured himself" under the sloping floor, while visitors walked around the room overhead. I fed the cat, pleasured myself, and rode my bike home.

One summer I wrote "Truth wears sunglasses" in my notebook.

*(2005)*

# Reading

# *Thorin Son of Thráin*

I learned how to read, in the sense of knowing how to follow a story with pleasure as it accumulates over many chapters, by being read to. My mother read us (my sister and me) the things she had liked as a child, with several additions—she took us through *The Hobbit, Mistress Masham's Repose,* Tove Jansson's Moominland books, Lear's "The Pelican Chorus," *The Wind in the Willows, Winnie-the-Pooh,* the Dr. Dolittle series, some Kipling, several Tintin books, and Hawthorne's *Wonder-Book.* She was an expert at the seamless substitution of a comprehensible phrase for the more involuted elegancies of Hawthornian diction, a fact I discovered only after I knew how to read by eye and could compare her version with the text. Her shoulder had a bone in it that was comfortable against my temple; I was under the impression that I was hearing some of each book through that shoulder-bone. And I was interested in how entertained she was by certain scenes: how much she liked, for example, the image of Toad sitting entranced by the side of the road near his overturned canary-yellow traveling wagon, murmuring "Poop-poop!" at the dwindling sight of the motorcar that had just zoomed past. It only became funny after she laughed.

But the most emotional early reading experience I had was the devastating death of Thorin Oakenshield in *The Hobbit*. I had no practice then with the conventions of character flaws and the plot signals that such flaws provide, and thus Thorin's greed and his brusque treatment of Bilbo didn't tip me off that he, Thorin son of Thráin, King under the Mountain, wasn't going to recover from the wounds of battle, even though my mother had gently tried to prepare me. I wept hard until I fell asleep. My mother wanted to abandon the book because it upset me so much, but the next night I convinced her that I could cry quietly, and she kept going until the end. It became one of my favorite books.

Two Tintin books—*The Secret of the Unicorn* and *Red Rackham's Treasure*—were the first things I truly liked reading by myself. Golden Books was the publisher of a few Tintin titles then, and they had Americanized the text slightly: Haddock's ancestral home was called Hudson Manor rather than the Marlinspike Hall of the other Tintins that we ordered later on from England like jars of marmalade. I loved the shark-shaped one-man submarine, and Tintin's shameless habit of talking to himself in his diving helmet while he was being stalked by the real shark, and the scene in which Thomson and Thompson, tired out, forget to keep cranking the air pump that leads below. Following a brief post-Tintin apprenticeship with some Freddy the Pig volumes, the first small-type reading I did was of *The Wonderful Adventures of Nils:* attractive because it was an ostentatiously thick edition and had a promising high-altitude goose-riding scene and concerned a person with a name similar to my own. After a chapter or two I could hardly follow what was going on, though, and I finished *Nils* joylessly, out of brute pride. The second thick book was *20,000 Leagues Under the Sea,* which we owned in an old translation with fancy marbled boards. Since the only other use of *leagues* that I knew of was in the story of the cat with the seven-league boots, the notion of descending a full 20,000 leagues seemed eerily grownup. And the phosphorescent undersea glow of the *Nautilus* as it approached or fled from a ship at night was a glow that I have been on the lookout for in reading ever since.

*(1996)*

# Narrow Ruled

When I come across something I really like in a book, I put a little dot in the margin. Not a check, not a double line—these would be pedantic—but a single nearly invisible tap or nudge of the pen tip, one that could almost be a dark fleck in the paper. In fact, sometimes as I've flipped through a book that I read closely years before, my eye has been caught by an actual paper-blemish that I have taken to be one of my own dots of approval, and I've stopped to read slowly through some undistinguished passage, prepared for beauty—and sometimes the beauty is discoverably there, and sometimes it isn't, and then, suspicious, I bring the page close to my eye and inspect the dot and find that I was misled.

It's best not to make too many dots—no more than, say, ten or fifteen for a single book. Compared with underlining, or highlighting in yellow or pink, the dot method is unobtrusive—that's one of its great advantages. I can reread a book that I have dotted here and there, and yet not be too distracted by the record of my earlier discoveries. And I can feel secure in the knowledge that if others idly open my books, they won't be able to see at a glance what interested me—they won't say to themselves, He thought *that* was good?

But my method is not only to mark the passages I like. I also write the number of the marked page in the back. Then—and this is the most important part—at some later date, sometimes years later, I refer to the page numbers, locate the dots, and copy out the passages that have awaited my return into a spiral-bound notebook. About fifteen years ago I fell behind—I have dozens, probably hundreds of books with a column of page numbers written in the endpapers whose appealing sentences or paragraphs I have not yet transcribed. Sometimes many months will go by without my adding anything to my copybook. But it is almost the only handwriting I do now, aside from writing checks, and whenever I take up the studious pen and begin, it makes me a happier person: my own bristling brain-urchins of worry melt in the strong solvent of other people's grammar.

My first notebook dates from 1982, when I was twenty-five. On page 2 is a sentence from Boswell's *Life of Johnson:* "I passed many hours with him, of which I find all in my memorial is, 'much laughing.'" Back then, I did a lot of the copying on lunch hours in Boston, and on weekends at a dark restaurant near Park Street Station called the Mug 'n Muffin, where I ordered a coffee and a blueberry muffin, which would arrive sizzling, after two full minutes in the industrial microwave, too hot to remove from its fluted wrapper, and which then, as I obliviously transcribed, would slowly turn to stone. At nearby tables, Bible students from Park Street Church would have long, hoarse conversations about God's love, shaking their heads over His mercy as they stubbed out their cigarettes. Every few months at the Mug 'n Muffin there was a rich, almost chocolatey smell of some comprehensive insecticide. It was the perfect place for longhand.

I've filled seven notebooks since then—not many, I admit, but they loom large. They are all spiral-bound: the spiral is itself inspirational, a bit of chromium cursiveness worming through and uniting otherwise easily scattered pages, just as handwritten script links together what is, on the book's page, an un-umbilicaled sequence of discrete letters. Over the years, I have stepped on some of the notebooks by mistake, so that their pages turn less freely than they once did: it is as difficult to restore a bent spiral binding as it is to repair an overstressed Slinky. In 1983, saline contact-lens solution leaked into the pages of one notebook in my briefcase, obliterating parts of passages from Bacon, Anthony Powell, Darwin, Johnson, and F. Scott Fitzgerald, as well as the word *Memory* in a sentence from Martin F. Tupper's *Proverbial Philosophy* (1852) that I had found reading the *OED*'s entry on *rote:* "Memory is not wisdom: idiots can rote volumes." Still, despite these injuries, the page-turning, and the reading, continues to be extremely satisfying.

As a rule I transcribe the work of people who wrote a long time ago. It is a way of momentarily reanimating them, slowly unwinding their sentential shrouds; it is the only sure way to sense their idiosyncrasies. Sometimes I whisper the words while I copy them. On December 5, 1994, I copied something from Richard Porson (1759–1808), a classical scholar who could recite much of Smollett's *Roderick Random* by heart, but who drank too much and wrecked his life. "Anyone might become as good a critic as I am," Porson says, "if he would only take the trouble to make himself so. I have made myself what I am by intense labour; sometimes in order to impress a thing on my memory I have read it a dozen times and transcribed it six." I was struck by this before I copied it over, but only by copying it over did I notice the unobtrusive poise of "make himself so." Porson spent years in poverty; from him I also transcribed this sentence: "I used often to lie awake through the whole night, and wish for a large pearl."

My notebooks are seven and three-quarter inches tall and five inches wide; they originally contained eighty sheets. (I've torn out pages in the back of some of them.) They are all "narrow ruled." The first one has a postcard from the National Gallery of Bellini's *St. Jerome* taped to the cover—I wanted to cover up the words "university note book" printed in eighties moderno-lowercase type. Bellini's Jerome is an old man in knotted rags reading a big red book in front of a superb thesaurus of rock formations. A lion sleeps nearby. A more recent copybook bears a postcard of Albrecht Dürer's *Saint Jerome*—the light through the bottle-glass windows in Dürer's interpretation of Jerome's study casts rows of shadows on the wall that resemble schematic drawings of plant cells, or softly spiraled cinnamon rolls arranged on trays, and there is a lordly gourd or squash presiding from an eyelet in a roof beam. The coiled feelers of this vegetable have nothing to entwine; they exult in their midair inflections and self-induced spiral bindings. My Dürer-decorated notebook begins with a vocabulary word, *phlyctenule*, that I found reading *Webster's New Collegiate Dictionary* (1975): a phlyctenule, for those who may be curious, is a small pustule on the cornea. I was interested in the disgusted "flick" that begins it, interested that it included its own revulsion—words with exotically unknowable foreign roots sometimes survive because we hear ordinary meanings in them.

On January 15, 1988, and then again on June 7, 1994 (forgetting that I'd already done it once), I transcribed

George Saintsbury's judgment of a certain work of Erasmus. It comes from a posthumous collection of Saintsbury entitled *A Last Vintage:*

> Perhaps the best thing in it [Saintsbury writes] comes from the mouth of the unblushingly illiterate and good-for-nothing abbot when he says, 'With immense labour learning is obtained: and then you have to die,' which is better still in its native Latin, '*Immensis laboribus comparatur eruditio: ac post moriendum est*'; and which, if not original, remains consummate and unanswerable.

"Consummate and unanswerable" (a phrase worth whispering to yourself three times slowly) has an autobiographical heartfeltishness: Saintsbury, more than most hard-reading garreteers, labored to accumulate and keep in good repair a productive enormity of book-memory. He consumed a French novel every morning before breakfast, but that was just warming up. All day his bookmarks were near at hand, finding pages to mark, and after dinner he was at it still, reading on, and writing with learnedly brimming charm and chattiness about what he read; with the result that there are few French, English, Greek, or Latin writers of more than antiquarian interest in whom he hasn't found some trait, or tag, or particularity, worth praising. He is the greatest praiser in the history of criticism—each thing he reads provokes him to written acknowledgment in the form of a review-essay thank-you note, and every encountered writer feeds his own genial style without misdirecting or overburdening it.

Lots of passages from George Saintsbury have gone into my copybooks, and a fair amount of William James, too; some Olivia Manning, some Iris Murdoch, some Dryden, some

Updike, some Philip Sidney. Here's a sample Olivia Manning passage, from *The Great Fortune:*

> They had been served with a rich goose-liver paté, dark with truffles and dressed with clarified butter. Inchcape swallowed this down in chunks, talking through it as though it were a flavourless impediment to self-expression.

Here's another Manning extract, from *The Spoilt City:*

> Yakimov, discomforted by a sense of lost advantage, stared into his empty glass for some moments before it occurred to him that he had in his possession the means of re-establishing interest in himself. He drew from his hip pocket the plan he had found in Guy's desk. 'Got something here,' he said. 'Give you an idea . . . not supposed to flash it about, but between old friends . . .'
>
> He handed the paper to Freddi, who took it smiling, looked at it and ceased to smile.

In copying these over (in 1985) I was forced to take stock of every hyphen, every observational glance. I became Olivia Manning's flunkey, her amanuensis, her temp worker, in effect saying to her, for however long it took to thread her words on the page, *Where you go, I follow.* Such labor is usefully humbling, because it delivers you back into the third grade, when you copied things off the board and had to pay attention to the little boat shape in the last stroke of the cursive capital *B*, but it isn't mechanical or fancy-cramping because the transcriber's mind can think its own pinstriped thoughts on the sly, betweentimes.

And, just as helpfully, every appealing highpoint that you read with transient delight can become, through commonplacing, merely average: it is no longer the jewel it was when you pried it from the dried salt marsh of its page, but has now itself been reduced to the primordial matter out of which only your own writing can lift and deliver you—you become, even textually, Sir Thomas Browne's Amphibian, "compelled to live in divided and distinguished worlds"—between the belly-squirming world of sedulous apprenticeship, and the nakedly leaping bipedal world of self-expression. Thus Bach copied out Buxtehude's and Vivaldi's music to learn its secrets, staying up late in his brother's latticed music library even though forbidden to do so; thus Wallace Stevens copied out in his commonplace book (entitled *Sur Plusieurs Beaux Sujets*) what D. J. Bach had to say about Schoenberg; thus E. M. Forster in middle age copied out Tennyson and Macaulay; and thus Gibbon copied over Pascal, and Giannone's *History of the Kingdom of Naples:*

> This various reading, which I now conducted with discretion, was digested, according to the precept and model of Mr. Locke, into a large commonplace-book; a practice, however, which I do not strenuously recommend. The action of the pen will doubtless imprint an idea on the mind as well as the paper; but I much question whether the benefits of this laborious method are adequate to the waste of time; and I must agree with Dr. Johnson (Idler, No. 74), 'that what is twice read is commonly better remembered than what is transcribed.'

But that's not true, is it? Gibbon couldn't have formed his style—that unique window display of teacups and sarcophagi—without having felt his way, word by word, at the artificially impeded speed of handwriting, through some of the poetry of Gray and Pope, for instance. Probably he remembered Johnson's *Idler* essay because he had once been moved to commonplace it himself.

*To commonplace*—is it a legal verb? It is, according to Samuel Johnson:

> *Commonplace-book*
> A book in which things to be remembered are ranged under general heads.
> I turned to my *common-place book* and found his case under the word *coquette. Tatler.*

> *To Commonplace*
> To reduce to general heads.
> I do not apprehend any difficulty in *commonplacing* an universal history. *Felton.*

"Felton" turns out to be one Henry Felton, D.D., who in *A Dissertation on the Classics* (1710) wasn't sure that the activity of reducing to general heads was always beneficial:

> *Common-Placing* the *Sense* of an Author, is such a stupid Undertaking, that, if I may be indulged in saying it, they *want common Sense* that practise it. What Heaps of this Rubbish have I seen! O the Pains and Labour to record what other People have said, that is taken by those, who have nothing to say themselves! . . . When I see a beautiful Building of exact Order and Proportion, taken down, and the different Materials laid together by themselves, it putteth me in mind of these *Common-Place Men.*

Felton may be right—you don't want to take it too far. Charles Reade, the nineteenth-century novelist, had so many commonplace books that "they completely filled one of the rooms in his house," according to Richard Le Gallienne. He devoted one full day out of each week "cataloguing the notes of his multifarious reading." Still, it worked for him. The big risk, if you accumulate a lot of chirographic bits and pieces, is that you will be tempted to quote more of them than you should. In a review of a book called *The Progress of the Intellect*, George Eliot criticizes the author (Robert William Mackay) for writing pages that "read like extracts from his common-place book, which must be, as Southey said of his own, an urn under the arm of a river-god, rather than like a digested result of study, intended to inform the general reader." Don't feel you must recirculate everything that you have found (so I tell myself); a recopied passage will urn its keep even if you never quote it anywhere.

There is good to be gained in signing someone else's mind-signature, in scribbling in tongues: the retracing of a series of long-lost authorial motions with your own present pen, if you do it in the proper spirit, out of a desire to stay delight's presence rather than out of autodidactic obligation, or even if you begin reluctantly, dutifully, troubled by feelings of self-pelf in the face of so many pressing university-press editions, can calm and steady your state, not to mention improve it, for while the transcribing may appear to be a form of close and exclusive concentration, it has an equally important element of peaceable meditative mindlessness as well, like playing with a paper clip. Reading is fast, but handwriting is slow—it retards thought's due process, it consumes irreplaceable scupperfuls of time, it pushes every competing utterance away—and that is its great virtue, in fact, over mere underlining, and even over an efficient laptop retyping of the passage: for in those secret interclausal tracts of cleared thought-space, in those extended dreaming blanks of fair-copying between the instant it took the eye to comprehend a writer's phrase, and the seeming eternity it then takes the hedgehog hand to negotiate that phrase again in legible, physical loops on the notebook page (especially on the verso side of the notebook page, when the spiral binding interferes annoyingly with the muscle of the little finger), during which all of your purplest hopes are compelled to idle, and you must pay attention to some common rhetorical turn that you had never until then deigned to think about, at the same time your constrained prose-aptitude is stimulated to higher rates of metabolism by what Johnson called "the contagion of diligence" and through its temporary forced conformity with another person's exhaust-system of expression—in this state of rubber-burning, clutch-smoking subservience, new quiet racemes will emerge from among the paving stones and foam greenly up in places they would never otherwise have prospered.

Just don't do it too much—and always use quotation marks.

*(2000)*

# Inky Burden

Preface to *A Book of Books*, by Abelardo Morell

In the old black-and-white TV series, Superman, when he needed to pass through a wall, would put his palms against it and lean, frowning. Gradually his caped form would merge with the plaster and pass through lath and two-by-fours, and then he would reappear in the next room. It wasn't as easy as flying, apparently, but it could be done. This became my childhood model of reading. You press your mind, your forehead, against the beginning of a book, the cool cover of it, appreciating its impenetrability. It is rectangular and thick, heavy enough to stop a bullet or press a leaf flat. It will, you think, never let you through. And then you begin to lean into it, applying a little attentive pressure, and the early pages begin to curl back with a soft, radish-slicing sound, and you're in. You're in the book. The thick, unitary clumps of chapters fan out into their component pages, and each turned page dematerializes itself, once read, into the fluent, cajoling voice its words carry, and then you're past the midpoint, and the book stretches out before you and behind you like a string of paper lanterns in a huge shadowy tent. Then you're almost done, and the pages begin to shrink and solidify once more. When you reach the last sentence, there rests under your left thumb a monolithic clump of paper through which, it seems, you could not possibly have traveled.

What unites all books, as Abelardo Morell is able to document in these magnificent photographs, and what is responsible for a good measure of their appeal, is their inter-dimensional ambiguity. Does the printed page inhabit two dimensions, or three, or four? As we read or look, we pretend that a page is an ideally flat and code-bearing plane, with a measurable height and width but no thickness and no curvature. But a page is almost never flat except when a book is closed; opened, its surface rises up slightly toward the inside margin and then veers south into the binding, like a mounding wave.

And of course each page has thickness. Your fingertips know this perfectly well: they inform you immediately when they have by mistake snagged two corners together, rather than one, in preparation for turning. The embossed letters in a book for the blind cast sharp shadows. Some paper is marvelously thin: the thickest books, the big dictionaries, for instance, whose bindings arch upward into mining tunnels when opened, sometimes have the flimsiest, rattliest pages. And into these towering cliffs of reference the publisher scoops out a series of alphabetic fingerholds as an aid to the word-hunter; crescent-moon notches that then become worn, so Morell's camera records, as if made of soft sandstone, by the impatient touch of many queries.

Bad things happen to books all the time, and then the books hold the record in their pages of those disasters, too. Books become water-soaked and writhe into the shapes of giant clams, and they wait in warehouses for dealers to cut pages out of them for piecemeal sale. Over many decades, paper changes color and becomes more fragile (though considerably less fragile than some paper-apocalyptists have claimed)—the particular fragility of an old volume is part of what it has to tell us.

Some of the most evocative photographs in this collection are the ones in which a book is allowed to fall open slightly, so that we glimpse some of the foreshortened secrets (an upward-glancing face, a colosseum) it may hold. Pages, for the most part, live out their long lives in the dark, keeping hidden what inky burdens they bear, pressed tightly against their neighbors, communicating nothing, until suddenly, like the lightbulb in the refrigerator that seems to be always on but almost never is, one of them is called upon to speak—and it does.

*(2002)*

# *No Step*

In 1994, I took a nap on an airplane. On waking, I pushed up the oval window shade and looked outside. The window was surprisingly hot to the touch: incoming sunlight had bounced off the closed shade, heating it up. And the wing looked hot, too, like something you would use to press a shirt. But it wasn't hot; volumes of freezing wind were flowing over and under it—invisibly wispy, top-of-Mount-Everest wind. Suddenly I felt an injustice in being so close to the wing, closer than any other passenger, and yet being unable to determine for myself, by touch, what temperature it was. Would my finger stick to it?

The plane turned, so that the long sickle-shape of sun-dazzle slid from the wing and fell to earth; and then, in the shadow of the fuselage, dozens of Phillips-head screws appeared, like stars coming out in an evening sky. Some of these wing screws surrounded a stenciled message, which I read. The message was: WARNING WET FUEL CELL DO NOT REMOVE.

A few months later, on a Boeing 757, I was given a window seat with an excellent view of the right engine. The engine was painted a dark glossy blue; it hung below the wing, shiny and huge, bobbling a little in the turbulence, like a large breast or a horse's testicle. There was a message on the engine. HOIST POINT, it said.

In April 1996 I looked out directly over another wing. Its leading edge was made of shiny naked metal, but the middle of the wing had been painted a pinky beige color. The painted part looked like a path—and because the wing tapered, the edges of the path angled in and converged at the far end, so that it seemed by a trick of perspective to extend for miles, disappearing finally at the blue horizon. If I climbed out the window and set off down that path, I'd have to walk carefully at first, with my knees bent to steady myself against the rush of the invisible, very cold wind, which would otherwise flip me off into the void. But I would get my wind legs soon enough. When I was a quarter of a mile down the wing, I'd turn and wave at the passengers. Then, shrugging my rucksack higher on my shoulders, I would set off again.

There were no words for me on that wing. But on the return flight I got a seat farther forward in the cabin, near the left engine. This engine said: CAUTION RELEASE UPPER FWD LATCH ON R.H. AND L.H. COWL BEFORE OPERATING. And it said: WARNING STAND CLEAR OF HAZARD AREAS WHILE ENGINE IS RUNNING. The hazard areas were diagrammed on a little picture—it was not difficult to heed this warning, since the areas were all out in empty space. I spent a long time looking at the engine. It was an impassive object, a dead weight. You know when propellers are turning, because you can see them turn, but this piece of machinery gave no sign that it was what was pushing us forward through the sky.

Usually I don't become interested in the wing until the plane has taken off. Before that there are plenty of other things to look at—the joking baggage handlers pulling back the curtain on the first car of a three-car suitcase train; the half-height service trucks lowering their conveyors; the beleaguered patches of dry grass making a go of it between two runways; the drooped windsock. As you turn onto the runway, you sometimes get a glimpse of it stretching ahead, and sometimes you can even see the plane that was in line ahead of you dipping up, lifting its neck as it begins to grab the air. Before the forward pull that begins a takeoff, the cabin lights and air pressure come on, as if the pilot has awakened to the full measure of his responsibility; and then, looking down, you see the black tire marks on the asphalt sliding past, traces of heavier-than-usual landings. (It still seems faintly worrisome that the same runway can be used for takeoffs and landings.) Some of the black rubber-marks are on a slight bias to the straightaway, and there are more and more of them, a sudden crowding of what looks like Japanese calligraphy, and then fewer again as you heave past the place where most incoming planes land. You're gaining speed now. Fat yellow lines swoop in and join the center yellow line of your runway, like the curves at the end of LP records. And finally you're up: you may see a clump of service buildings, or a lake, or many tiny blue swimming pools, or a long, straight bridge, and then you go higher until there is nothing but distant earth padded here and there with cloud. Then, out of a pleasant sort of loneliness, ignoring the person who is sitting next to you, you begin to want to get to know the wing and its engine.

In April 1998, sitting in an emergency exit row on the way to Denver, I was surprised by how sharp-edged some mountains were. I was used to the blunt mountains of three-dimensional plastic topographical maps, which are pleasing to the fingertips. But real mountains would scrape your palm if you tried to feel them that way. I passed a salt lake, perhaps the Great Salt Lake, which had a white deposit on its edges like a chemistry experiment. And then I gave up on the world and looked out at my new friend, the wing. It had nothing to say to me at first, no words that I could see; but then, when I put my head as close as I could to the window and looked down, I could make out two arrows. These were painted on a textured non-slip area near where the wing joined the fuselage. We passengers were not meant to see these arrows from our seats: they were there in case of a catastrophe, when we would hurry out the window and leap off the wing onto an inflatable rubber slide. How fast do you go down a slide? Fast enough to break a leg, I would think. I wouldn't want to leap onto that slide, but I like the arrows.

On the return from Denver, the wing, attached to an Airbus A-230, said DO NOT WALK OUTSIDE THIS AREA. I had no interest in walking outside that area. The clouds were enormous flat-bottomed patties resting heavily on an ocean of low-pressure air. A few days after that, on a Boeing 767—one of the ones with the mis-designed call buttons on the sides of the armrest which people press when they are trying to adjust the volume on their headphones, so that when the movie begins, the cabin is filled with unintended dinging calls for flight attendants—I had, just after takeoff, a quick, pleasing view of the neighborhood where I lived, visible just above the lump of the left engine, whose crest bore the words NO STEP. And then in June of that year I again saw NO STEP on the top of a jet engine, while the plane I was on was still on the ground. A man was leaning into the engine, so that only his legs were visible. On the wing there were faint wind-wear lines streaking like aurora borealises from behind one of a group of eight little flathead screws. Two weeks later, the engine of a Boeing 757 said: HOIST POINT SLEEVE ONLY, and THRUST REVERSE ACTUATOR ACCESS, and LEAVE 3 INCH MAXIMUM GAP BETWEEN FAIRINGS PRIOR TO SLIDING AFT AND LATCHING, and SAFETY LINE ATTACH POINT.

By 1999 I had become a collector of wing language. I copied the words down on folded pieces of paper, with arrows pointing out which words were stenciled in red paint and which in white. McDonnell Douglas planes were a pleasure to fly, because they were less common and offered different messages. Once when I was in an emergency exit row in a McDonnell Douglas MD-80, there were two pilots seated behind me. "This is an old plane," one of the pilots said, "but it's got new engines—you can hear the new engines." I listened for the note of newness in the engines but wasn't sure that I could hear it. On the wing there was an irregular area bounded with red paint, with NO STEP commands around the inside, and then in the middle it said ELECTRIC HEATER BLANKET 110 VOLTS.

In April 1999 I rode a little propeller plane called a Dash 8 to Seattle. The window looked out below the wing, leaving the landing gear, projecting from below the engine, spindledly visible from my seat, as if I were looking at someone's legs from under the dinner table. I watched the wheels as we began the surge down the runway, to see whether the tires (there were two tires on each side) would change shape at the moment of liftoff. They didn't, but the moment was marked by a sudden extension of the greased piston of the shock absorber, and by the appearance of the tire's crisp shadow against the asphalt. Then came a small surprise: the wheels kept turning, fast, as we rose a few hundred feet, and then the wheel struts folded and disappeared into the under-nacelle, and, with the wheels still going, the carapace flaps closed.

When the plane descended an hour later, I watched our shadow coming into focus on the blur of the skidmarked ground; and when the now motionless tire first touched the runway there was a beautiful puff of white smoke before it began to turn. As we drove to the gate, the rubber showed its whitish burned patch over and over; it was almost worn away by the time we reached the gate. I was so interested in the wheel struts and the smoke puff that I failed to note down the messages on the engine. Later, though, when I rode a Dash 8 propeller plane again, I recorded this from the engine cowling: WARNING HYDRAULIC SERVICES MAY OPERATE / CLEAR PERSONNEL FROM RUDDER FLAPS AND LANDING GEAR DOORS BEFORE CONNECTING.

On an Airbus A330 this past March, the engine said CAUTION—PRESS HERE ON LATCH TO ENSURE LOCKING, and there was a little set of gills next to which were the words FAN COMPARTMENT VENT AIR INTAKE. I copied down the cautionary words and then walked the aisles and galleys until I reached the curtain beyond which was the first-class cabin. Parting the curtain, I saw a man's shoulder and, beyond it, a small china plate on which there had been a bunch of grapes. Now the grapes were gone, but the fireworks display of green spent stems was there. I walked back down the coach-class aisle, allowing my eye to fall on the tableaus of sleeping passengers, each of whom arranged his or her blue blanket a different way. I kept thinking I was getting close to my row, but I wasn't—instead there was someone in a black sweater asleep with her head on a bunched blue blanket. I was one whole cabin section off, I realized. And then I saw a magazine with a clear plastic protective cover angled over a file folder, and the back of one of my shoes just visible on the floor. I was home. I slid into the window seat and looked outside. The window was cool to the nose. The engine, my engine, was still out there, toiling away, as inanimate and companionable as a thermos bottle. NO LIFT NO STEP NO LIFT NO STEP NO LIFT NO STEP, said the wing.

*(2001)*

# *I Said to Myself*

One day I saw a groundhog eating a clover blossom. It chewed it up quickly and then, in the quiet that follows a swallowed mouthful, it lifted its head up and froze, listening for danger. There wasn't any, so it moved forward to the next stalk. Its fur was kind of baggy, but sleek. I looked at its childishly ineffectual paws, and then I remembered that a month earlier I'd seen two big groundhogs sunning themselves in another part of the yard, down by the rhubarb. They'd had tails that looked like the handles of Revere saucepans. "I wonder if this one has a tail that looks like a Revere saucepan, too," I said to myself, waiting for the creature to turn a little so that I could see its hindquarters. In a minute, it did turn, and I was able to verify that the tail was black, whereas the rest of the animal was a light brown, and, yes, it had a curve that looked quite a lot like a saucepan handle, though without the little metal ring at the end.

"Ah, good, that's confirmed," I thought, turning away from the window. Or did I think that? For I hadn't actually said to myself, in an interior whisper, "Ah, good, that's confirmed." Really I'd just made a quick mental nod—not even a grunt, but just a sort of pleasant checking-off of the box next to a momentary visual curiosity directed at the groundhog's tail, conjoined with an image of a matte-finish handle in profile. Words had had little to do with it. Still, if someone had asked me what had gone through my mind just then, I would have gestured at the window and talked briefly about the groundhog anatomy, and then I would probably have translated the mental checking-off moment into spoken English as "Ah, good," etc.

It was cheating, in a sense, true—but what choice did I have? The gulf between words and thoughts is unbridgeable, and yet we must bridge it constantly. One way writers have developed to circumvent the problem is to report all thinking indirectly. Here is the sort of substitution you can make:

DIRECT: "I just don't know anymore," I thought.
INDIRECT: I was no longer entirely confident that I knew.

If you're a novelist and working in the third person, the change can work something like this:

DIRECT: "That hurts," Ed reflected.
INDIRECT: Nothing that Ed had ever experienced had
prepared him for the anguish of that syringe.

You see? A paraphrase acknowledges itself as close to but not identical with the thing (in this case the thought) that is phrased, and for some writers, a well-formed paraphrase is entirely sufficient.

It's more than movies offer, after all. The poor movie director: What does he have to work with? Things like grimaces and winks and head tosses of various kinds, and camera angles. A writer can say, "Hope died within him." The director, on the other hand, must have the actor sit on the floor and look desolate while the camera moves in—in movie code, the fact that the person is sitting on the floor signals that a low point has been reached, a point so low that even the comfort of a chair is unwelcome. Or a movie will have the despairer suddenly become enraged, which is more filmable: he sweeps some figurines off of a shelf and then, after this release, sinks to the floor. Or the hopeless person will bounce a ball expressionlessly against a garage door, or toss acorns into the river: the moviegoer translates this mechanically repeated activity as "the numbness that follows despair." The music helps a lot, too.

How clumsy, how broad, how expensive these cine-matographic sign-systems seem, when compared to the dental trays full of pryers and pickers and angled mirrors that are the fiction writer's rightful inheritance. Any mind Tolstoy wants to enter, he enters. It costs him nothing but a drop of ink. In fact, merely by using indirect thought-reportage, Tolstoy can enter two minds at the same time:

> But for all that, as is often the way with men who have chosen different callings, though in discussion each of them might justify the other's career, at heart he despised it. Each believed that the life he himself led was the only real life and the life led by his friend was nothing but an illusion.

All the camera angles in the world couldn't help you here.

And yet Tolstoy wasn't content merely to offer indirect thoughts. He was one of our very best introspectors, alert to uncatalogably fine gradations of moral compromise and motivic ambiguity, and sometimes he wanted us to *overhear* mental states rather than to read secondary paraphrases of them. So he has his characters think, "We shall see," or "Oh dear!" or "Where was I?" or "Can it really be true?" Sometimes their inner voices are quite chatty:

> 'If this is the case,' he said to himself, 'I ought to think it over and make up my mind, and not let myself be carried away like a boy by the impulse of the moment.'

Sometimes they are jealously chatty:

> 'I cannot be made unhappy because a despicable woman has committed a crime. I merely have to find the best way out of the painful situation in which she has placed me. And find it I shall,' he said to himself, his face growing darker and darker.

Did Tolstoy believe that his characters really said this sort of thing to themselves? I can't believe that he believed it, any more than Shakespeare believed that people make life-or-death decisions in blank verse, with one hand on their chest and the other held out sideways. I believe that if I were able to tap Tolstoy on the shoulder and ask him why he had written these particular lines this way, he would say to me, "Well, I was trying to record what my characters would have told me if I had been able to tap them on the shoulder and ask them at that instant what words were in them."

Actually, though, Tolstoy would probably say to me, "I have no patience for questions of this kind. Leave me now to walk barefoot among the birches."

In any event, Tolstoy is, fortunately, not the only writer to understand that the reader's bond of sympathy and intimacy with a character must be reinforced, goosed slightly, every so often, by a directly quoted brain-whisper. The character must say things that only we, and nobody else in the book, can hear. It doesn't have to happen much.

Some children's writers do it well, and there's pedagogy in this, perhaps: quoting thoughts is an efficient way of teaching how to match spoken language with invisible states of mind—it's like holding up an apple you can't see and saying "apple." Masters of the ghost story, too, rely on the technique to create a quick shudder, as in this from M. R. James:

> 'What should I do now,' he thought, 'if I looked back and caught sight of a black figure sharply defined against the yellow sky, and saw that it had horns and wings?'

Note the punctuation in these passages: they have quotation marks. These writers evidently felt that, as with real speech, psychic speech needs visible delimiters to set it off from its surroundings. (In the original Russian, Tolstoy used little «French-style brackets,» but the effect of enclosure is the same.) I have spent some hours recently foraging around in paperbacks, and I can report that practically all the big-name writers through 1930 or so—people, I mean, like Henry James, Edith Wharton, Virginia Woolf, E. M. Forster, Willa Cather, Theodore Dreiser, Joseph Conrad, Sherwood Anderson, and Sinclair Lewis—felt the need to put their characters' thoughts within quotes from time to time. (Sinclair Lewis: "She said to herself, 'As though I cared whether I'm seen with this fat phonograph!'" Willa Cather: "She remembered him and said to herself: 'I don't think I ever heard a nicer voice than that boy had.'")

Now writers don't do this. I asked a copy-editor friend

how the literary world was punctuating its thoughts these days, and he polled some copy-editor friends of his. One wrote back: "I haven't seen quotation marks on thoughts in at least five years."

Why did they die out? Joyce and Faulkner—they're at the root of it. *Ulysses* has great blobs of transcribed thought, but the quotation marks themselves are lacking:

> Mr Bloom moved forward raising his troubled eyes. Think no more about that. After one. Timeball on the ballast office is down. Dunsink time. Fascinating little book that is of sir Robert Ball's Parallax. I never exactly understood. There's a priest. Could ask him. Par it's Greek: parallel, parallax.

Not only are the quotation marks gone, but there is no obliging tag such as "he reflected" or "he said to himself" inserted after the first interior sentence to help us keep track of where we are. "Oh, good," said Joyce's readers to themselves, brushing Hi Ho cracker crumbs from their laps, "now all the artificial barriers can come down, and interior and exterior reality can ooze together into one sense-perceptual fondue."

But, again, did Mr. Bloom actually, literally think, "There's a priest," followed by, "Could ask him"? I can't imagine that he did. Mr. Bloom's eye lighted on a figure in clerical dress—a visual, not verbal, mind-event—and the possibility of asking the figure a question briefly arose and was dismissed within him. Joyce's way looked new, but he was doing what the traditional novelists did: hanging out raw, wet harvestings of visual and emotive protoplasm to dry on grammatical clotheslines, the only difference being that there is in *Ulysses* a great deal more dried protoplasm.

Bloom's thought-residues are (once you get into the swing of the book) sometimes startling and beautiful, but they aren't any less artificial than when, say, M. R. James has a character mentally scope out, within quotes, his evening plans. In fact, they're more artificial. Here's how M. R. James did it:

> 'I might walk home tonight along the beach,' he reflected—'yes, and take a look—there will be light enough for that—at the ruins of which Disney was talking.'

Joyce would twist off the knobs of the quotation marks and render the passage something like this:

> The beach way. Might walk home tonight. Disney said the ruins? Templars' preceptory. Knights in Jerusalem, looters, really. Cries of the maidens. Having their way. Light enough for that.

And then, while the literary classes were still chewing over this development, Faulkner began an aggressive program of italicizing. Here's a snip from *Light in August:*

> That was two years ago, two years behind them now, thinking *Perhaps that is where outrage lies. Perhaps I believe that I have been tricked, fooled.*

What was a modernist to do? There was simply no way to reconcile Joyce's austere depunctuation with the booming self-importance of Faulkner's typography. Both were excitingly modern, and yet they pointed in opposite directions. Thought transcription was thrown into a state of uncertainty from which it has not yet recovered. Some went naked—

I too have done my share of social climbing, he thought, with hauteur to spare, defying the Wasps. (Bellow, *Herzog*)

To the gallows I go, she said to herself, and had another large drink. (Drabble, *The Realms of Gold*)

—while the post-Faulknerians, such as Tom Clancy, reached for italics, which are punchier:

Julio stood and shouldered his weapon. There was a slight but annoying tinkle from the metal parts as he did so—the ammo belt, Ding thought. *Have to keep that in mind. (Clear and Present Danger)*

Sometimes, though, those urgent forward diagonals turned out to have a little too much punch, forcing the reader to interpret a shy, fleeting brain-state as if it were roared out in a hoarse whisper:

He fumbled his latchkey into its slot, thinking: *Now she'll ask me why I lock my door and I'll mumble and stumble around, looking for an answer, and seem like a fool.*

In roman type, within quotation marks, this thought-quote could easily be Tolstoy; in italics, however, it is from Stephen King's *The Stand,* page 516.

I suppose there's no single correct method, but I sometimes wish that the old way would come back. I miss the clarity, the lack of fuss, the innocence. So here's what I propose. Let's use quotes for spoken dialogue, as usual, and—once in a while, *if* it makes sense, *not* excessively—let's try using them for interior speech as well. Those who feel ambitious could experiment with double quotes for dialogue and single quotes for thought, since part of the problem is that double quotes sometimes look too heavy to fence off delicate interior states. But that distinction isn't necessary and it may actually cause further confusion—so, no, skip that. If the words in the thought really do have force and punch, by all means use italics, but if they don't, don't. And if you would prefer to use only indirect thought-discourse, fine. Just don't utterly rule out the blameless embrasure of those curlies. Here's something I came across in *Winnie-the-Pooh:*

> Sometimes he thought sadly to himself, "Why?" and sometimes he thought, "Wherefore?" and sometimes he thought, "Inasmuch as which?"—and sometimes he didn't know what he was thinking about.

I'm with Eeyore.

*(2002)*

# Defoe, Truthteller

I read Daniel Defoe's *A Journal of the Plague Year* on a train from Boston to New York. That's the truth. It's not a very interesting truth, but it's true. I could say that I read it sitting on a low green couch in the old smoking room of the Cincinnati Palladium, across from a rather glum-looking Henry Kissinger. Or that I found a beat-up Longman's 1895 edition of Defoe's *Plague Year* in a Dumpster near the Recycle-A-Bicycle shop on Pearl Street when I was high on Guinness and roxies, and I opened it and was drawn into its singular, fearful world, and I sat right down in my own vomit and read the book straight through. It would be easy for me to say these things. But if I did, I would be inventing—and, as John Hersey wrote, the sacred rule for the journalist (or the memoirist, or indeed for any nonfiction writer) is: Never Invent. That's what makes Daniel Defoe, the founder of English journalism, such a thorny shrub. The hoaxers and the embellishers, the fake autobiographers, look on Defoe as a kind of patron saint. Defoe lied a lot. But he also hated his lying habit, at least sometimes. He said the lying made a hole in the heart. About certain events he wanted truth told. And one event he really cared about was the great plague of 1665, which happened when he was around five years old.

*A Journal of the Plague Year* begins quietly, without any apparatus of learnedness. It doesn't try to connect this recent plague with past plagues. It draws no historical or classical or literary parallels. It just begins: "It was about the beginning of September, 1664, that I, among the rest of my neighbors, heard in ordinary discourse that the plague was returned again in Holland." The "I" is not Defoe, but an older proxy, somebody mysteriously named H.F., who says he is a saddler. H.F. lives halfway between Aldgate Church and Whitechapel, "on the left hand or north side of the street." That's all we know about him.

H.F. watches the bills of mortality mount—he keeps track—and he debates with himself whether to stay in town or flee. His brother tells him to save himself, get away. But no, H.F. decides to stay. He listens. He walks around. He sees a man race out of an alley, apparently singing and making clownish gestures, pursued by women and children—surgeons had been at work on his plague sores. "By laying strong caustics on them, the surgeons had, it seems, hopes to break them, which caustics were then upon him, burning his flesh as with a hot iron." H.F. hears screams—many different kinds of screams, and screeches, and shrieks. In an empty street in Lothbury, a window opens suddenly just over his head. "A woman gave three frightful screeches, and then cried, 'Oh! death, death, death!'" There was no other movement. The street was still. "For people had no curiosity now in any case."

At the plague's height, H.F. writes, there were no funerals, no wearing of black, no bells tolled, no coffins. "Whole streets seemed to be desolated," he says, "doors were left open, windows stood shattering with the wind in empty houses, for want of people to shut them; in a word, people began to give up themselves to their fears, and to think that all regulations and methods were in vain, and that there was nothing to be hoped for but an universal desolation."

What do we know about Defoe? Very little. He was one of the most prolific men ever to lift a pen, but he wrote almost nothing about himself. Not many letters have survived. Readers have been attributing and de-attributing Defoe's anonymous journalism ever since he died, broke, in Ropemaker's Alley, in 1731. He was almost always writing about someone else—or pretending to be someone else. There are a few engravings of him, and only one surviving prose description. It's unfriendly—in fact it was a sort of warrant for his arrest, printed in a newspaper when Defoe was wanted by the government on a charge of seditious libel. "He is a middle-sized, spare man," said the description, "about forty years old, of a brown complexion, and dark brown-colored hair, but wears a wig; a hooked nose, a sharp chin, grey eyes, and a large mole near his mouth." Anyone who could furnish information leading to his apprehension by her majesty's justices of the peace, said the notice, would receive a reward of fifty pounds.

We know that Defoe, late in life, wrote the first English novels—*Robinson Crusoe* in 1719, about a lonely sailor who sees a man's naked footprint on the beach, and *Moll Flanders* in January 1722, about a woman who was "twelve year a whore." We know that he was born about 1660, the son of a London butcher or candlemaker named James Foe. In his twenties, Daniel went into business as a hosier—that is, as a seller of women's stockings. Trade and speculation went well for a while, then less well, and then he had to hide from his creditors, to whom he owed seventeen thousand pounds. He was rescued by friends on high, and began writing pamphlets and poetry. Soon he was running a large company that made roofing tiles—and the pamphleteering was surprisingly successful. He added a Frenchifying "de" to his name. In 1701 he produced the most-selling poem up to that time, "The True-Born Englishman," which hymned his native land as a motley nation of immigrants: "Thus, from a mixture of all kinds began / That het'rogenous thing, an Englishman." Another pamphlet—in which, several decades before Swift's "Modest Proposal," he pretended to be a rabid high-churchman who advocated the deportation or hanging of nonconformists—got him clamped in a pillory in 1703 and sent to Newgate Prison.

While in prison he started a newspaper, the *Review*, an antecedent to Addison and Steele's *Tatler* and *Spectator*. Besides essays and opinion pieces, the *Review* had an early advice column, and a "weekly history of Nonsense, Impertinence, Vice, and Debauchery." That same year, still in prison, he gathered intelligence on a disaster that had visited parts of England. His book *The Storm*—about what he called "the greatest and the longest storm that ever the world saw"—is one of the earliest extended journalistic narratives in English.

For a faker, Defoe had an enormous appetite for truth and life and bloody specificity. He wanted to know everything knowable about trade, about royalty, about low life, about the customs of other countries, about ships, about folk remedies and quack doctors, about disasters, about scientific advances, and about the shops and streets of London. He listened to stories people told him. "In this way of Talk I was always upon the Inquiry," one of his characters says, "asking questions of things done in Publick, as well as in Private." But his desire to impersonate and playact kept surging up and getting him into trouble. He wanted to pass as someone he wasn't—as a Swedish king, as a fallen woman, as a person who'd seen a ghost, as a pre-Dickensian pickpocket. He was an especially industrious first-person crime writer. Once he ghost-wrote the story of a thief and jailbreaker named Jack Sheppard. To promote its publication, Defoe had Sheppard pause at the gallows and, before a huge crowd, hand out the freshly printed pamphlet as his last testament—or so the story goes. "The rapidity with which this book sold is probably unparalleled," writes an early biographer, William Lee.

*Robinson Crusoe* is Defoe's most famous hoax. We now describe it as a novel, of course, but it wasn't born that way. On its 1719 title page, the book was billed as the strange, surprising adventures of a mariner who lived all alone for eight-and-twenty years on an uninhabited island, "Written by H I M S E L F"—and people at first took this claim for truth and bought thousands of copies. This prompted an enemy satirist, Charles Gildon, to rush out a pamphlet, "The Life and Strange Surprising Adventures of Daniel de Foe, Formerly of London, Hosier, Who has lived above fifty Years all alone by himself, in the Kingdoms of North and South Britain."

Addison called Defoe "a false, shuffling, prevaricating rascal." Another contemporary said he was a master of "forging a story and imposing it on the world as truth." One of Defoe's nineteenth-century biographers, William Minto, wrote: "He was a great, a truly great liar, perhaps the greatest liar that ever lived."

And yet that's not wholly fair. A number of the things that people later took to be Defoe's dazzlingly colorful tapestries of fabrication, weren't. In 1718, in *Mist's Journal*, Defoe gave a detailed account of the volcanic explosion of the island of St. Vincent, relying, he said, on letters he had received about it. A century passed, and doubts crept in. One Defoe scholar said that the St. Vincent story was imaginary; a second said it was tomfoolery; a third said it was "make-believe" and "entirely of Defoe's invention." But the island of St. Vincent had actually blown up, and it had made a lot of noise as it blew. Defoe had done his journalistic best to report this prodigy.

Something similar happened in the case of *A Journal of the Plague Year*. When Defoe published it, he, as usual, left himself off the title page, ascribing the story to H.F. "Written by a Citizen," the title page falsely, sales-boostingly claimed, "Who Continued All the While in London." People believed that for a while, but by 1780, at least, it was generally known that Defoe was the book's author. Then someone did some arithmetic and realized that Defoe had been a young child when the plague struck London—whereupon they began calling the book a historical novel, unequaled in vividness and circumstantiality. Walter Raleigh, in his late-nineteenth-century history of the English novel, called the book "sham history." In a study of "pseudofactual" fiction, Barbara Foley says that the *Plague Year* "creates the majority of its particulars." And John Hollowell, investigating the literary origins of the New Journalism, writes that Defoe's book is "fiction masquerading as fact." Is it?

One night H.F. visits the forty-foot burial trench in Aldgate Churchyard, near where he lives. "A terrible pit it was," he writes, "and I could not resist my curiosity to go and see it." He watches the dead-cart dip and the bodies fall "promiscuously" into the pit, while a father stands silently by. Then the father, beside himself with grief, suddenly lets out a cry. Another time, H.F. describes the butchers' market. "People used all possible precaution," he says. "When any one bought a joint of meat in the market, they would not take it out of the butcher's hand, but took it off the hooks themselves. On the other hand, the butcher would not touch the money, but have it put into a pot full of vinegar, which he kept for that purpose."

A *Journal of the Plague Year* is an astounding performance. It's shocking, it's messy, it's moving, it sobs aloud with its losses, it's got all the urgency and loopingly prolix insistence of a man of sympathy who has lived through an urban catastrophe and wants to tell you what it was like. The fear of death, notes H.F., "took away all Bowels of love, all concern for one another." But not universally: "There were many instances of immovable affection, pity and duty." And Defoe's narrator is at pains to discount some of the stories that he hears. He is told, for example, of nurses smothering plague victims with wet cloths to hasten their end. But the particulars are suspiciously unvarying, and in every version, no matter where he encounters it, the event is said to have happened on the opposite side of town. There is, H.F. judges, "more of tale than of truth" in these accounts.

Still, there's the false frame. The story isn't really being told by H.F., it's being told by Defoe. That's clearly a forgery—although more understandable when you learn that Defoe had an uncle with those initials, Henry Foe. Henry was in fact a saddler, who lived in Aldgate near the burial pit. In order to launch himself into the telling of this overwhelmingly complex story of London's ordeal, Defoe needed to think and write in his uncle's voice. The "I" is more than a bit of commercial-minded artifice. The ventriloquism, the fictional first-person premise, helped Defoe to unspool and make sequential sense of what he knew. He sifted through and used a mass of contemporary published sources, as any journalist would, and he enlivened that printed store with anecdotes that people had told him over the years. (His father could have been a source for the butcher's vinegar pot.) The book feels like something heartfelt, that grew out of decades of accumulated notes and memories—although written with impressive speed. It doesn't feel like an artificial swizzle of falsifications.

In 1919, a young scholar, Watson Nicholson, wrote a book on the sources of Defoe's *Journal of the Plague Year*. He was quite upset by the notion that the Journal was now, without qualification, being called a novel. In his book Nicholson claimed to have established "overwhelming evidence of the complete authenticity of Defoe's 'masterpiece of the imagination.'" There was not, Nicholson said, "a single essential statement in the *Journal* not based on historic fact." True, Defoe had a way of embroidering, but even so, "the employment of the first person in the narrative in no sense interferes with the authenticity of the facts recorded."

Other critics agreed. In 1965, Frank Bastian cross-checked what Defoe said in the *Journal* against Pepys's *Diary*, which Defoe couldn't have seen because it wasn't decoded until a century later. "Characters and incidents once confidently asserted to be the products of Defoe's fertile imagination," wrote Bastian in 1965, "repeatedly prove to have been factual." Introducing the Penguin edition of the *Plague Year* in 1966, Anthony Burgess wrote: "Defoe was our first great novelist because he was our first great journalist."

Six thousand people a month died in London's plague, most of them poor. The locations of many burial pits passed from memory. One was later used, according to Defoe, as a "yard for keeping hogs"; another pit was rediscovered when the foundation of a grand house was being dug: "The women's sculls were quite distinguished by their long hair." Is the author being a reporter here, or a novelist? We don't know. We want to know.

Daniel Defoe seems to have needed a pocketful of passports to get where he was going. But the moral of his story, at least for the nonfictionist, still is: Never Invent. People love hoaxes in theory—from a distance—but they also hate being tricked. If you make sad things up and insist that they're true, nobody afterward will fully trust what you write.

*(2009)*

# From A to Zyxt

Ammon Shea, a sometime furniture mover, gondolier, and word collector, has written an oddly inspiring book about reading the whole of the *Oxford English Dictionary* in one go. Shea's book resurrects many lost, misshapen, beautifully unlucky words—words that spiraled out, like fast-decaying muons, after their tiny moment in the cloud chamber of English usage. There's *hypergelast* (a person who won't stop laughing), *lant* (to add urine to ale to give it more kick), *obmutescence* (willful speechlessness), and *ploiter* (to work to little purpose)—all good words to have on the tip of your tongue when, for example, you're stopped for speeding.

Shea's book, *Reading the* OED: *One Man, One Year, 21,730 Pages,* offers more than exotic word lists, though. It also has a plot. "I feel as though I am eating the alphabet," he writes halfway through, and you want him to make it to the end. This is the *Super Size Me* of lexicography.

Shea is well equipped for the task he has set himself. He owns about a thousand dictionaries, which he keeps on shelves in the apartment he shares with his girlfriend, Alix, who teaches psychology courses at Barnard. Some of the dictionaries he bought from a book dealer named Madeline, who lives in a loft in Lower Manhattan. Madeline owns twenty thousand dictionaries. She taught Shea, he says, "the ineffable joy that can be had in pursuing the absurd."

Back in the '90s, Shea read Webster's *Second* from beginning to end—no easy feat. Did doing so help him in any way? No. It didn't make him a better or smarter person, or improve his test scores. In fact, it seems to have hindered his capacity for self-expression. "My head was so full of words that I often had trouble forming simple sentences out loud," he writes, "and my speech became a curious jumble of obscure words and improper syntax." But Shea seems to have loved this experience of verbal overspill—he underwent the prolonged brain-shiver that comes when thousands of unfamiliar meanings pour in without stopping. "It felt wonderful," he says.

The logical next step was to read the *OED*, but here Shea hesitated. The *OED* is huge, as everyone knows. It's monstrously deep and serious and maddeningly detailed, each entry a miniature etymological seminar. It's the one that, in one incarnation, came with a rectangular magnifying glass; the one that the polymathic Simon Winchester wrote about in *The Professor and the Madman*. Could Shea really make his witting way through twenty heavy volumes of tri-columnated type, all of it twinkling and squirming with abbreviations, small caps, foreign derivations, and archaic spellings? Could one man read, in one year's time, 59 million consecutive words—the equivalent of one John Grisham novel per day—of definitional "prose"? Or would Shea fail and be forever known as the guy who read through to the letter N and couldn't go on?

Shea decided to make the attempt and to record his

progress in this book. Each letter gets its own chapter. In Chapter A the volumes arrive, wrapped in the "regal and chitinous gloss" of their dust jackets. Shea sits near the window, his feet up on an ottoman, and begins to read. Difficulties ensue. He gets pulsing headaches and sees gray patches on the edges of his vision. His back bothers him. His neighbors make salt cod, and the odor is distracting. He's tempted to look things up in his other dictionaries, comparing definitions, which slows his progress.

So he ventures out into the city, reading on park benches and in public libraries. No place is right. Finally he settles on a location in the basement of the Hunter College library, among books in French that don't tempt him away from the task at hand. He drinks many thermosfuls of coffee. He gets eyeglasses and finds, much to his surprise, that they help him see better. His headaches continue.

And the lovely-ugly words, words that Shea didn't know existed, leap up to his hand. *Acnestis*—the part of an animal's back that the animal can't reach to scratch. And *bespawl*—to splatter with saliva. In Chapter D, Shea encounters *deipnophobia,* the fear of dinner parties; Chapter K brings *kankedort*, an awkward situation.

Months in, Shea arrives—back aching, crabby, page-blind—at Chapter N. "Some days I feel as if I do not actually speak the English language," he writes, his verbal cortex overflowing. "It is," he observes, "like trying to remember all the trees one sees through the window of a train." Once he stares for a while, amazed, at the word *glove*. "I find myself wondering why I've never seen this odd term that describes such a common article of clothing."

By Chapter O there is evidence of further disintegration. Is he turning into, he wonders, one of the "Library People"—

the bag-toters and mutterers who spend all their time there? "Sometimes I get angry at the dictionary and let loose with a muffled yell." At night he hears a deep, disembodied voice slowly intoning definitions.

But then, thank goodness, he breaks through into sunlight. In Chapter P he finds a rich harvest of words, including one, *petrichor,* that refers to the loamy smell that rises from the dry ground after a rain, and a nicely dense indivisible word, *prend,* that signifies a mended crack. He notes these down in his big ledger book. He attends a lexicographical congress in Chicago, where he is misunderstood by his colleagues, and returns to the Hunter library basement with renewed vigor. He tells his tolerant girlfriend about a rare P word and then wonders aloud if he is boring her. "The point at which I became bored has long since passed," Alix replies.

Shea arrives at another bad patch partway through Chapter U, with the "un-" section—more than four hundred pages of words of self-evident meaning. "I am near catatonic," he writes, "bored out of my mind." But he doesn't skip; he is lashed to the tiller, unthimbled and unthrashed.

Théophile Gautier read the dictionary to enrich and exoticize his poetry. Walter Pater read the dictionary to keep his prose pure and marmoreal—to learn what words to avoid. Shea has no interest in purity or poetry. His style is simple. He just wants to identify and savor, for their own sweet sakes, malocclusive Greek and Latin hybrids that are difficult to figure out how to pronounce. He is fond of polysyllabic near-homonyms—words like *incompetible* (outside the range of competency) and *repertitious* (found accidentally), which are quickly swallowed up in the sonic gravitation of familiar words. And a number of Shea's finds deserve prompt resurrection: *vicambulist,* for instance—a person who wanders city streets.

The effect of this book on me was to make me like Ammon Shea and, briefly, to hate English. What a choking, God-awful mash it is! Surely French is better. Then I recovered and saw its greatness afresh. The *OED,* Shea notes, is "a catalog of the foibles of the human condition." Shea has walked the wildwood of our gnarled, ancient speech and returned singing incomprehensible sounds in a language that turns out to be our own.

*(2008)*

# The Nod

Read at the Kennedy Library's "Tribute to John Updike"

I heard a little chirp come from my computer—it was like the beep of a hospital heart monitor except that there was only one of them. It was software telling me that an e-mail had arrived. And then, a second later, there appeared, fading in, a little ghostly rectangle down on the right-hand corner, which named the sender of the e-mail and gave its subject line. It was from a man I didn't know very well but who sent me many e-mails, about his own dislikes and his health troubles and his political opinions. But the subject line, which appeared and then faded, caught my eye. It said something incomprehensible, that wasn't in English but was in some horrible language of euphemism. It said: "Condolences on Updike's Passing." I thought, Passing? What does that mean? Are we talking about death, about the death of John Updike? He's not dead, he's very much in the middle

89

of things. He's just had a book out, as always—as would always be true. But I checked and it said he'd been sick and apparently he had very politely, and without making any sort of public scene, without any forewarning to people outside his closest circle, died.

Sitting there at the desk I did what you do when you've lost your glasses or your wallet or some crucially important document that you need—a note to the principal—I felt around on the desktop of my mind for what I had of John Updike, what I could substitute for the livingness of the man. And I didn't have anything that would serve, because the tremendous thing about him was that he was alive and writing and revising and reviewing some big wrongheaded biography and releasing another small piece of his own remembered past, perhaps slightly disguised and fictionalized—he was in the midst of being a writing person, as well of course as being a human being who has a wife and a former wife and children and editors and fans. That's what I wanted from him, and that's what I didn't have: evidence of his ongoingness.

The computer started chirping again and there were editors who wanted me to write something about him immediately, a remembrance, an obituary, because a long time ago I published a book that was about him, sort of, and therefore I guess I was thought of as an expert on Updike, when I wasn't, I was just a mourner like anyone else. So I said, No, I'm sorry, I'm just sad. That's all I have to offer, just my own sadness.

What I think of now, though, is a time more than twenty years ago, when I saw him in the Boston Public Garden. It was a cold, overcast late afternoon, and there was a man walking toward me on the path. I knew who it was. It was the famous John Updike. We were over past the statue of

George Washington, in a part of the garden that has fewer trees, that's always colder and windier than other parts—and I had to figure out what to do. He was wearing a tweedish jacket buttoned up and a scarf and a hat and he obviously had somewhere to go, as I didn't, really. If I stopped and I said "Mr. Updike?" he would of course politely stop and we would have a brief conversation. I would maybe say that I liked his writing and that he'd signed one of his books for me once and that I'd sent him a fan letter once that I hadn't put a return address on because I didn't want to compel him to answer it and that in the letter I'd told him that my girlfriend, who had since become my fiancée, had dug out of a wicker basket of *New Yorkers* a story of his and given it to me to read and I'd read two-thirds of it and had decided, walking under the awning of a tuxedo shop in a moment of passing shade, that I wanted very much to write him and tell him about how happy it made me to *know* that he was out there working. But I couldn't stop him on his path and tell him all that. He was on his way somewhere. So I decided instead that I would just nod. I would pack in everything I knew about him in my nod, all the memories I had of reading about packed dirt and thimbles and psoriasis and stuttering and Shillington, Pennsylvania, and the *Harvard Lampoon* and the drawing class at Oxford, and his little office upstairs in Ipswich—and the letters that he and Katharine White had exchanged when he was writing his early stories for *The New Yorker* that I'd seen behind glass in a display case at Bryn Mawr College— all that knowledge of him I would cram into one smiling, knowing nod. And that's what I did. And he nodded back, a little uncertainly, I think. He wasn't sure: Maybe he knew me?

And then later, in a letter, he said, Didn't we meet once on Arlington Street? He remembered my nod.

What a memory on that man.

His very best book, I think, is his memoir, called *Self-Consciousness*. He was best when he was truest. And the most amazing thing about his truthfulness is its level of finish. Of polish. Because we all have thoughts. They're slumped on the couch and they are not at their very best, in fact they aren't completely shaven and they aren't all that clean, necessarily. They're living in the halfway house of what you have to say. What Updike does is he sends them an invitation—it's tasteful, understated, but beautifully engraved. He says to his thoughts: the favor of your reply is requested—please accompany John Updike to the official writing of his next piece on whatever it is—on the car radio, on the monuments of the United States, on William Dean Howells, who, he said, "served his time too well"—please attend this essay. And then at the bottom it says, very quietly: black tie. Formal wear. That's what you want from an essay, is you want these thoughts to have done their very best to at least rent their outfits and present themselves to the world in their best guises.

Don't come as you are, Updike said, come in black tie, put on your best punctuational studs—and they, his ideas, obliged him, repeatedly. They said, Okay, RSVP, we will be there.

We had, I guess you could say, a correspondence over the years. He wrote Dear Nick and I wrote Dear John. I love his reserve. He didn't really want to have a cup of coffee with me, in fact I think he'd much rather have written me a letter than have a cup of coffee—and who can blame him? But there was one thing I wanted to write him in a letter for years, and never did. One time I read one of his stories aloud to my daughter. She was then about thirteen. I read her a story called "The City." It's about a man who is on a business trip—and he has a spot of indigestion that then turns out to be excruciatingly painful—and he goes to the hospital and it's his appendix and the whole story is just the very simple but well-described account of his hospital stay in a city that he never ends up seeing. And as I was reading it to my daughter, I came to the moment in the story that I remembered from when I first read it. The man is lying in his hospital room in the middle of the night and he hears people moaning on either side of him and then there's a sound of "tidy retching," and then comes the sentence: "Carson was comforted by these evidences that at least he had penetrated into a circle of acknowledged ruin." The word *ruin* there was so amazingly good and well placed—"acknowledged ruin." And maybe it was that I gave it a special inflection as I read it aloud, but I don't think so. My daughter said, "Oh, *that's* good." Right at that moment. She liked and she was excited by the very same phrase in the story that I'd been excited by. It seemed so reassuring to know that there is sometimes an absolute moment in a story that many people will independently discover and remember, even across generations, and that this may have been one of those moments. I wished I had told him that in a letter. And now I'll never get to tell him that. So I tell it to you. With sorrow. Thank you.

*(2009)*

# David Remnick

David Remnick is fifty-two. He's got all of his hair, which is black, and he's got an office with quiet brown carpeting and a desk made of a slab of grainy black wood and a fat-rimmed yellow ceramic cup that holds his pens and his pair of scissors. He's smart and quick to laugh, and if you sit in one of the square soft chairs in his office, he remembers things about your life that you barely remember. He likes baseball and *The Wire* and A. J. Liebling and spaghetti with squid ink sauce. You might feel jealous of him except that he works too hard and nobody else would want that kind of constant hellish weekly pressure. His wife, Esther Fein, is a writer, and he's got three kids. He's the fifth editor of *The New Yorker,* which may be the best magazine ever published.

I've met Remnick a few times, briefly. Once was at a party where he was chatting about boxing to the novelist Joyce Carol Oates. Another time was in 2001, at the National Magazine Awards. That year his magazine won four awards, including the award for general excellence. Remnick kept striding up to the podium as we applauded him, wearing an impeccable blue suit and David Mamet-style glasses, and each time he found some new way to be abashed and thankful, as he was handed yet another copper-colored trophy designed by Alexander Calder, the mobile-maker. (It's called an Ellie and it looks like several modernist boomerangs glued together.)

The awards are deserved, but they don't convey how consistently good his magazine is. Remember, it's a weekly. Every Monday it's in the mail, or in the newsstand, or on a little flat screen, reassuring a million subscribers that things are still pretty much under control in the transatlantic world of letters. There are always at least a few funny cartoons, and one absorbing piece about something or another, and perhaps a brilliantly dismissive movie review by Anthony Lane, who sharpened his pencil at the *Independent* before Tina Brown, Remnick's predecessor, lured him away. I confess I don't read it all—few can—but let me just say it right now: *The New Yorker* is one of the three great contributions the United States has made to world civilization. The other two are, of course, *Some Like It Hot* and the iPhone. Maybe you have your own list. But it's likely *The New Yorker* will be on it somewhere, because the magazine has been sharp and witty since the 1920s, angling unexpected adjectives in place with winning exactitude.

Its tone, from the outset, was, as John Updike described it in an onstage interview with Remnick, "big-town folksy." E. B. White was one of the early sources of the style—along with James Thurber and Joseph Mitchell, and an alcoholic named John McNulty, who wrote stories about regulars at a bar on Third Avenue. Later there was Maeve Brennan, from Ireland, who wrote beautiful unfurling paragraphs about living in cheap hotels in the city, using as her byline "The Long-Winded Lady." Brennan was evidently a little crazy toward the end, as writers tend to be, but in her "Talk of the Town" prose she is extremely sane and full of kind attentiveness.

And there were the cartoonists—Peter Arno, who liked drawing high-breasted showgirls, and Saul Steinberg, who made surreal black-and-white rainbows, and William Steig, whose trembly pencil seemed never to want to leave the paper, and George Booth, master of quizzically frowning brindle-eyed dogs. There were storytellers, too—J. D. Salinger, John Cheever, Updike, William Trevor, Alice Munro, and John O'Hara, who in his prime could tell a tight, bitter tale of private woe in 1,800 words. A magazine that has been around for this long pulls its own history behind it like a battered Brio train. At the front is David Remnick, gently drawing it forward, helping it over the next little blond wooden hill, hoping that the shiny domelike magnets don't detach.

I was in the *New Yorker* offices, on the twentieth glass-sheathed floor of the Condé Nast building in Times Square, one Friday in April. The week's issue had just closed, and the place was quiet. People stared at their screens, catching up with all the things they had put off during the recent editorial flurry. Remnick was having his picture taken, so I said hello to Pam McCarthy, the magazine's deputy editor, whose office is next to Remnick's. What is he like to work with? I asked her.

"He's easygoing, and he's not," said McCarthy. "He likes to keep his finger on every detail. He really pushes until it's right. He's a great floorwalker. He circles the floor several times a day and talks to people."

Just then Remnick came in with Alexa Cassanos, the director of publicity, and the four of us talked about earphones and earplugs. "In Maine why would you need earplugs?"

Remnick asked me. (I live in Maine.) "When I'm out of the city," he continued, "I'm up till four in the morning because it's so damned quiet. I think somebody's going to jump in and strangle me. It's not relaxing."

We walked a few blocks to a seafood restaurant, Esca, on Forty-third Street, where Remnick goes once in a while. Mark Singer, one of the magazine's best-known writers of profiles, wrote a piece on Esca's owner, Dave Pasternack, who does his own fishing around Long Island and knows how to cut mahi-mahi into raw tidbits.

Pasternack himself came by the table soon after we'd sat down and told us that he'd opened up a new business—a seafood concession in center field of the Mets' baseball stadium, where he sells crabcakes, fish sandwiches, lobster rolls, and chowders. Jeff Wilpon, the general manager of the Mets, lost a lot of money several years ago to Bernie Madoff's Ponzi scheme, but, according to Pasternack, Wilpon was upbeat about his life. "I was at a party the other day," Pasternack said, "and I go, 'How're you doing?' Wilpon goes, 'I was rich and miserable and now I'm poor and happy.'"

"Are you sure about the latter?" asked Remnick.

Suddenly I had a strange and not unpleasant sensation. I'd entered the printed pages of *The New Yorker*; I was physically inhabiting a Mark Singer profile, as edited by David Remnick.

Pasternack said, of Wilpon, "This is a guy who came to me to ask if I wanted to do a concession. I said, 'I'll make a couple of things for you.' I bring a lobster roll down— beautiful lobster roll, toasted bun, nice and buttery the way it's supposed to be. He looks at me and he says, 'I don't like toast.' All I could think about is: when you're born they give you toast, and on your deathbed they give you toast. Who in this world doesn't like toast? When you're sick they give you toast!"

"I get cartoons about toast every week," said Remnick.

"Yeah?" said Pasternack.

"I got a cartoon," said Remnick, "it was a toaster the size of the restaurant." He turned to me. "Do you waste your time watching baseball?"

I said no, not really, I'm out of it.

Remnick said, "I'm sure that when I'm on my deathbed . . ."

"You're going to have toast," said Pasternack, with finality. Then he went away to fillet more fish.

I asked Remnick what his dining room was like when he was a kid. "Lots of mirrors," he said. "We didn't eat in the dining room." He grew up in Hillsdale, New Jersey—"Springsteen Jersey, without the shore"—and his mother got multiple sclerosis when he was six. Some years later, his father, a dentist, became ill with Parkinson's disease. "To be a Parkinsonian dentist is like a Buster Keaton movie," Remnick told me. "It's funny unless you're living it." In high school he edited the school paper, *The Smoke Signal*, writing articles for it under several pseudonyms. He wasn't a devoted *New Yorker* reader then. "*Guitar Player* magazine meant more to me in high school than *The New Yorker*," he said. "There were no chord diagrams in *The New Yorker*."

He studied comparative literature at Princeton and took a class with the *New Yorker* writer John McPhee, who taught him that you have to be willing to seem stupid when you interview people. He spent a semester in Japan, teaching English and feeling lonely. He also went to Paris, where he wore a Leon Russell T-shirt and nine-dollar Converse sneakers and made money singing Bob Dylan songs in the

Metro. His Princeton classmates were all getting jobs as investment bankers; he got a job at the *Washington Post,* as the night crime reporter. He covered boxing for a while, and then, as he limbered up, he interviewed celebrities in their hotel rooms. He was good, something of a prodigy in fact—a natural reporter, nimble and prompt with copy.

The *Washington Post* sent him to Russia in 1988, with his new wife, where he covered, with astonishing fecundity, every phase of the disintegration of the Soviet empire. He wrote somewhere between three hundred and four hundred stories a year, watching and learning from Bill Keller, the fast-fingered Russian correspondent for the *New York Times,* later its editor-in-chief. Framed in Remnick's office is the front page of the *Washington Post* for August 24, 1991, which has two Remnick stories. The top one begins: "Communist rule collapsed tonight in the Soviet Union after seven decades as President Mikhail Gorbachev resigned as Communist Party general secretary and ordered the government to seize all party property."

Out of that heady period grew Remnick's first book, *Lenin's Tomb.* There's a characteristic scene early in the book where he is trying to interview the last living member of Stalin's cabinet—an old man named Kaganovich. Remnick finds out that Kaganovich, by a strange coincidence, lives downstairs from him, and he knocks on the door. He knocks for a long time. There's no answer. Every day he knocks. He finds Kaganovich's number and calls it. No answer. He lets it ring for dozens of rings. Finally he reaches Kaganovich's wife, who says her husband isn't going to talk. He keeps calling; he wants to see, he says, "what an evil man looked like." He learns there's a secret telephone code: let it ring twice, then hang up and call again. Kaganovich answers. Remnick identifies himself. Kaganovich says, "No interviews! That's it!" He dies soon after. But Remnick had at least heard the voice of the last of Stalin's inner circle. There are dozens of scenes of poignancy and loss and upheaval in *Lenin's Tomb;* it won a Pulitzer Prize in 1994.

By then Remnick was freelancing for *Esquire* and *Vanity Fair,* and then staff-writing for Tina Brown's *New Yorker*, writing one telling profile after another—on Don DeLillo, on Mike Tyson, on Benjamin Netanyahu. Netanyahu's father, Remnick wrote, "has little white tufts of hair and weary, narrow eyes, the eyes of a Chinese scholar." On Tyson's fight with Evander Holyfield: "Incredibly, Tyson once more nuzzled his way into Holyfield's sweaty neck, almost tenderly, purposefully, as if he were snuffling for truffles. He found the left ear and bit." Remnick is modest about these writing successes, which he attributes chiefly to "sitzfleisch"—the capacity to sit in a chair until the work is done. "A lot of what I do is just the mental illness of persistence," he told me.

In 1998, Remnick published his second book, *King of the World,* about one of the heroes of his youth, Muhammad Ali. Then something momentous happened: Tina Brown suddenly left her job in order to found a new magazine, *Talk*. ("Tina is more of a comet than a planet," said Remnick. "She shines brilliantly and moves from thing to thing.") S.I. Newhouse, *The New Yorker's* owner, asked David to take over. When the staff heard the news they stood and applauded for five minutes. "It was an applause of relief," according to Remnick. "It was like the inner applause when you go to the neurologist and you find out that you don't have a brain tumor." The job wasn't easy at first—he lost ten pounds in the first couple of months. It still isn't easy. "You have to understand," he said, "for me to be at this magazine is preposterous. I feel like a pretender."

Actually, though, he's the real thing: a great, omnivorous editor. He takes *The New Yorker*'s history seriously—he's edited a series of anthologies of themed *New Yorker* pieces from earlier eras—but he is just as determined that, in the era of iPads and bloggery, he won't be the last of the magazine's masters of ceremonies. One of his biggest hits came in 2004: Seymour Hersh's reporting on abuse in Abu Ghraib. He also brought Ian Frazier, a comic genius, back into the fold—Frazier had been on strike, more or less, during Tina's tumultuous tenure—and he found and encouraged some good new writers, among them Ben McGrath, who can write deftly about anything, including football concussions and theorists of dystopian collapse.

After 9/11 Remnick had an odd (to me) burst of militancy, as so many did, writing with approval on the attack on Afghanistan, and, in a famous comment piece in "Talk of the Town," endorsing the invasion of Iraq. "I was wrong," he told me, about Iraq. He wants his magazine to get truths out. I asked him what he would have done if Julian Assange had offered him a basketful of WikiLeaks documents. Of course he would publish them, he said—he'd let the courts sort it out later. "I think the world is better off knowing than not knowing."

Last year he published an enormous book about the civil rights movement and the rise of Barack Obama. He wrote it early in the morning, before leaving for work, and late at night. "Sitting next to him, if I hadn't known he was writing a book, I wouldn't have been able to tell," Pam McCarthy told me. "I don't mean to sound hagiographic, but actually he really is quite amazing. And exhausting."

Remnick left me in his office while he did an afternoon circle of the twentieth floor. I took some pictures of his bookshelves—hundreds of works by *New Yorker* contributors past and present, books in Russian, a well-thumbed copy of the poems of Walt Whitman, and a recent run of the magazine bound in black and gold. Then I looked out of the window at a sign that said "Toshiba" in big letters, and another sign for Thomson Reuters. Down the street was the tarnished green roofline of the old *New York Times* building, one of the seemingly few structures in the neighborhood that was there when the magazine began. I looked at a snapshot of Remnick's wife and children, at a small plastic windup radio, at a framed photograph of Updike, at another of Ornette Coleman, at hundreds of CDs, and at a nesting doll of Vladimir Putin, whose profile Remnick wrote in 2003. On his desk was "the long"—the single big piece of paper with all the stories on it that were in the hopper, ready to go into future *New Yorkers*. I felt like a trespasser, like a spy, too high up in the Manhattan skyline for my own good. I heard the discreet bong of a ringing phone. Remnick walked me to the elevators. "Remember what Barbara Walters said at the end of the Jimmy Carter interview?" he asked.

"No," I said.

"Be kind to us, Mr. President."

*(2011)*

# Libraries
## and
# Newspapers

# Truckin' for the Future

I got a call from the Rochester Public Library, the library I used most as a child. They were getting rid of their card catalog; I had written about card catalogs at some length in *The New Yorker*. Did I want it? If I paid for shipping, they would mail it from Rochester to Berkeley—minus the cabinets, which had resale value. I said no, I didn't want it, I wanted them to keep it. So they threw it out.

About a year later, I got some unhappy e-mails from librarians at the San Francisco Public Library. The SFPL had just moved to a new building, and the press was responding with prolonged, ecstatic coverage. Robert Hass, U.S. poet laureate, wrote that "the interior of the library is a marvel, so deeply delicious you forget your previous ideas of what a library is"; Allan Temko, architecture critic for the *San Francisco Chronicle*, likened its several inner bridges to "the visionary architecture of Piranesi." The old card catalog, however, was, according to the librarians who wrote me, going to be destroyed—the cards recycled, the cabinets auctioned off. For now it still sat intact in the old building: an ornately carved summation of the contents of a great urban public library, "frozen" (i.e., not filed into or updated) as of

1991. "You are the only one who can save it now," a librarian wrote me.

Because I felt I had shirked my duty as a preservationist in my hometown, I agreed to try to keep it intact. On May 21, 1996, I made a formal request under the Public Records Act to inspect the card catalog. (The Public Records Act is California's version of the federal Freedom of Information Act.) This legalistic demarche would, I hoped, define the catalog as a public document, and temporarily prevent the administration from treating it as surplus property. The request was not unreasonable: the database conversion project wasn't finished, and there were thousands of cards in the card catalog for books held in closed-stack areas of the library that had no match yet in the online system. (More than half the library's collection was in closed, unbrowsable stacks.) The request was, however, denied, in a letter from the city librarian, Kenneth E. Dowlin: "We are unable to allow this at this time."

So, inspired by the library's own letterhead, which reads: "Access, Discover, Empower," I sued for legal access. On June 26, 1996, eighteen drawers from the old card catalog were brought over to the new building, where I was allowed to use them. Meanwhile, the San Francisco Board of Supervisors proposed and passed a nonbinding resolution "urging the Library Commission to preserve the card catalog at the Main Library and make it available to the public." On September 3, 1996, after hours of public testimony, the Library Commission voted to find a way to keep it.

But by the time I was successfully looking up names like Walter Benjamin, John Milton, and J. K. Huysmans on paper cards—and noticing that there were substantially fewer books in the online catalog by these writers than there were in the card catalog—I had spent over a month talking to members of the library staff. I knew the real story, which is only incidentally about catalogs.

The real story is about what happens—what to a greater or lesser degree is happening in a number of cities around the country—when telecommunications enthusiasts take over big old research libraries and attempt to remake them, with corporate help, as high-traffic showplaces for information technology. Such transformations consume unforecastably large sums of money, which is why the SFPL found itself, just then—despite receiving a goodly percentage of the city budget every year as part of Proposition E's "Preserving Libraries Fund"—essentially broke, with a one-million-dollar deficit in its operating budget, its new building annotated and beflagged with the names of major benefactors who enabled it, just barely, to open its doors in April.

One of these benefactors is the Pacific Telesis Group (parent to Pacific Bell, the phone company), a corporation that wants to become a "content provider" in the growing fee-for-service information business. Steven Coulter, a vice president at Pacific Telesis, is the president of the Library Commission; he is a proponent of the virtues of informational connectivity and public-private partnerships, and he is a masterful fund-raiser for the library. Kenneth Dowlin, the city librarian—hired away from Colorado Springs, where, as the head of the Pikes Peak Library District, he developed an early dial-up-access catalog called Maggie's Place—also wants SFPL to become a sort of telecommunications utility: he told members of the American Library Association in 1992 that he envisions the library offering "electronic access to each home, school, and office by the year 2000," and added, "We intend to generate revenue off of this pipeline." He also said, "I will let the planning department ship documents for building permits over my system, but I get my five percent."

The pipeline metaphor is a useful one, and it exerts an understandably powerful hold on the minds of many library managers these days, as everyone, in and out of the stacks, tries to figure out who gets to adjust the valves and calibrate the pressure gauges, and who will have the privilege of setting tariffs on the ideational flow. Last year, the entrepreneurial SFPL launched Library Express, a service that charged sixty dollars an hour to clients who needed, and could afford, a higher level of research assistance and document retrieval than the unpaying patron.

Not all observers like the privatizing tendencies in the public-library world, but it would be mere churlishness to point out the shortcomings of this self-proclaimed "library of the future," the outcome of so extraordinary an outpouring of civic spirit and generosity, were it not for one thing: under Dowlin and his A-team (as he calls his cadre of chiefs and special assistants), the SFPL has, by a conservative estimate, sent more than two hundred thousand books to a landfill— many of them old, hard to find, out of print, and valuable.

"I'm sure that at least that many are gone," one librarian told me. "I would guess that maybe a quarter of them, fifty thousand, should have been thrown out. But I would guess that at least a hundred thousand shouldn't have been. And another fifty thousand that I just can't guess. . . . I personally saw at least twenty or thirty thousand books when we were still in the old building that were boxed up and never made it back into the collection." This man, like most of the staff members I talked to, doesn't want me to quote him by name, since Dowlin has a way, some assert, of punishing dissidents by exiling them to branch duty (a charge the administration has denied). What the employees wanted me to know was that the library was undergoing a kind of brain surgery. In the words of one woman I interviewed, "Its EEG is going flat."

The worst period of book dumping happened late last year, in the months before the library's move to the New Main, as it is called—a large gray structure with a hole in the middle where the stacks should be. The construction was financed with more than a hundred million dollars in public money; the voters approved this munificent bond issue because the Old Main, they were told, couldn't hold what it was being asked to hold—a research-level general collection, thousands of specialized periodicals, the Grabhorn Collection on the History of Printing and the Development of the Book, the Schmulowitz Collection of Wit and Humor, city archives, newspaper archives, photo archives, and so on. When appeals went out for money to furnish and outfit the new building, more than thirty million dollars flowed in from private donors and "affinity groups," representing gays and lesbians, several ethnic communities, and environmentalists.

From the outside, the building looks enormous— and inside, too, the visitor can enjoy sweeping expanses of carpeting, vistas of distant gift shops and security checkpoints, multi-story works of public art, the Chevron Corporation Teen Center, the BankAmerica Foundation Jobs and Careers Center, and uninterrupted sight lines in almost every direction. Throw back your head, and you stare upward through a "glittering void" (as its principal architect, James Ingo Freed, describes it) that extends to a conical cornea of white glass eighty-six feet above you. But space, from the point of view of an existing collection of books, means something quite different from floor space, or atrium space, or bandwidth in a telecommunications cable, all of which the

New Main has in relative abundance. Space, to a book, means shelves: the departments of the library were supposed to get enough shelves to hold their collections, with plenty of room to grow. And yet most of the departments still do not have enough shelf space to hold what they have.

Even before the influx of hundreds of thousands of new books, bought with Proposition E money, some staff members had serious doubts about the building's capacity. In 1991, when the administration passed around plans for the New Main, thirty-one library employees signed a letter contending that "of the 375,000 square feet promised, much of it will be all but useless. . . . Obviously the current plan for the new building is not meeting the needs set forth to voters to justify the expenditure." But the gravity of the problem only began to dawn on the A-team late in 1995, when individual librarians began mapping potential book arrangements prior to the move. Tape measures came out, calculators were turned on, rules of thumb were invoked. Suddenly it was abundantly clear: the collection in the Old Main Library was not going to fit in the New Main Library. Kathy Page, chief of the Main, wrote in Progress Report No. 34, dated December 1995, "Several surprises and errors were discovered that are proceeding to be solved or mitigated." How were the errors solved or mitigated? The collection itself was hastily reduced in volume. It was "weeded."

*Weeding* is a term of art in librarianship, and it is a necessary part of what librarians do. If you have five copies of an old edition of Samuelson's *Economics*, or of Booth Tarkington's *The Gentleman from Indiana*, your librarianly obligation may be to reduce the number, so that there will be space for other books. The library sells them or gives them away—or even throws them away, if nobody wants them—so as not to be choked by the foliage of what was once heavily in demand but is no longer. But beyond such obvious examples, weeding a rich old collection such as San Francisco's takes time and careful thought. If your potential weed is a little out of your main area of knowledge, you have to look it up in standard bibliographies. You must be mindful of the traditional strengths and weaknesses of your library, and the myriad secondary ways in which an out-of-date book may enlighten the historically curious. If the book under your eye is an old edition of something that has been republished, you have to ask yourself whether that old edition has some intrinsic merit—something about its annotation, or the eminence of its editor—that the new one may lack. And even then there are differences of opinion, of course. To quote from a book called *Garden Friends and Foes,* by Richard Headstrom, "If you were asked to prepare a list of weeds and compare it with one prepared by someone else, they would probably not be in complete agreement."

Kenneth Dowlin himself offered a defensible theory of discarding to a questioner at a meeting in 1992. He said, "We have many books where we may buy two hundred copies of that book because there are thousands of people who want to read it. It makes no sense to keep all two hundred copies for the rest of our life. So at the time that the usage of that particular book drops, we will retain one, two, five, whatever the appropriate number is." Except for the inflated figure of two hundred, that is a fair description of what went on before Dowlin took command, when the volume of junked books was relatively small. But what has gone on at the San Francisco Public Library over the last year was not weeding in this specialized sense. I found *Garden Friends and Foes* this spring, in a room near the shipping-and-receiving entrance in the Old Main Library—a windowless, high-ceilinged room, measuring maybe ten by twelve feet. It's called the Discard Room. On most Tuesdays, until this past January, a Department of Public Works truck—a five-ton flatbed truck with wooden sides of the kind used to pick up brush and old washing machines—drove down to the Discard Room and two, sometimes three men threw the books, which were often tied with string in bundles of eight or ten, into the back. Sometimes the truck held other things, too, like an old chair or a shopping cart left on library property by a street person or hundreds of out-of-print phonograph records, and sometimes it just held books. When it was loaded (and it could hold perhaps 2,500 bundled volumes), the truck drove to a transfer station, where the books were shifted to big rigs, along with the rest of the day's garbage, and then taken to a landfill. In fairness to the current administration, book dumping, on a much smaller scale, has gone on for decades. (The administration sometimes says that a surplus-property law forced them to throw away all discards until 1989, but it is also correct to say that it was not until 1989 that the library sought official permission from the city to sell some of its surplus books through the Friends of the Library bookstore.) Things got especially bad this past winter, however, when Kathy Page put out the call to all stations: *Weed*. Sometimes the crew arriving from the DPW would crack open the door of the Discard Room and close it fast, afraid that an eight-foot-high pile of books would collapse on them.

Here is what two librarians who had been part of a weeding team told me one Sunday at a coffee shop:

LIBRARIAN A: They said, "Get rid of as much as possible."
And they said, "Anything that doesn't look like we should
have it in the New Main Library, if it doesn't look good,
if it needs to be repaired . . ." And then there was the
question whether when you sent things to be repaired,
was it actually being repaired, or were they tossing it?

LIBRARIAN B: There seemed to be a reluctance to send
things to Repair because they [in Repair] were
"overwhelmed."

LIBRARIAN A: People were beginning to think, "Wait a
second, these are just being tossed."

LIBRARIAN B: Actually, we don't know what happened,
because the librarians weeded their areas but a senior
librarian had the final word. We don't know what she did.

LIBRARIAN A: She started putting everything on the same
truck, and I said, "This is not to be thrown away, it's not
to be discarded." She said, "No, just put it on."

There are now no copies of *Garden Friends and Foes* on
the shelves of the San Francisco Public Library. There are no
duplicates of it at the University of California at Berkeley, or
at Davis, Stanford, or UCLA. There are copies of a number
of Headstrom's other books in SFPL's collection—he has
written about spiders, lizards, birds, insects, and even a
*Complete Field Guide to Nests in the United States*—but this
sole copy of his work on weeds was weeded. Why? Its binding
was slightly torn, and the weeders, as they are called, have
at times been urged to weed quickly and in quantity, basing
their decisions in large part on looks.

I hasten to say that many of the books in the Discard
Room which I have personally checked do have duplicates
on the shelves, or at least are represented by later editions of
the same work. The *1983 Arco Civil Service Exam Book for*

*Sanitation Workers,* of which the library has twenty copies—I found it in the Discard Room two months ago under ten books about ethics and a mint Clarendon Press edition of Leibniz's *Logical Papers*—makes sense to discard. (Question 67 on page 90 of *Sanitation Workers* asks you to choose the last phrase of the following jumbled sentence: "the book / the top shelf / of the bookcase / wanted was on / which she." The answer is "of the bookcase": "The book which she wanted was on the top shelf of the bookcase." Not in the back of a DPW truck.) But here are some of the other books I left with, after one unannounced visit, which either have no record online at all, or say "Ask librarian for holdings information," a phrase that is often, especially in the case of older circulating books, code for "I am a last copy, and I have been purged." There is *Crumbling Idols,* by Hamlin Garland; a lovely little Knickerbocker Press book with color plates called *The Way to Study Birds,* from 1917; a 1907 edition of *Rivers of North America,* by Israel Russell, with a complete chemical analysis of a water sample taken from a hydrant in Los Angeles on September 8, 1878, along with similar results for other samples from the Hudson, the Cumberland Reservoir, the Mohawk River, and the Rio Grande; and *Handbook for the Woman Driver,* by Charlotte Montgomery, which devotes a whole chapter to "Clothes and Beauty En Route." ("Dark glasses are a *must.*") *Studies of Abnormal Behavior in the Rat,* by Norman Maier, was another last copy. (On page 19: "An electrified grill was interposed between the jumping platform and the canvas net. Now the rat was punished not only for staying on the platform, but also for jumping from the platform. As a control the same grill was used in the case of the female rat. This technique failed to produce neurotic attacks in either animal." Give it time.)

Although the weeding continues, the good news is that since this past January no more books have been dumped. On January 29, the *San Francisco Chronicle*'s Andrew Ross and Phillip Matier published a front-page story headlined SF LIBRARY TOSSING THOUSANDS OF BOOKS and a picture of the Discard Room. "The ongoing crime was so apparent by then," one staff member told me. "The blood was seeping under the door." Since then, no book, to my knowledge, has been thrown away. (True, many thousands of recent unbound periodicals to which the library subscribes—serials with titles like *Welding Design & Fabrication, Nutrition Reviews, Journal of Tribology, The Canadian Journal of Soil Science, Car and Driver,* and *Bee Culture*—were secretly tossed into recycling bins this past February, March, and April; but no *books* were.) Instead, nonprofit and community groups are invited to tour a large room in the basement of the Old Main; the last public giveaway got rid of five thousand books. They have gone to other libraries, here and abroad, and to schools, prisons, and villages in Madagascar and Armenia. Every Friday this month the general public will have a chance to take whatever the charities don't want. Deetje Boler, of the Gray Panthers, left this summer with about twenty boxes of books: works on labor history and birds; books by McPhee, Malamud, Herb Caen, and a first-edition Elizabeth Bishop. (They are holding them in trust, waiting for the library to come to its senses.) At least we can be thankful that the newer rejects will continue their lives somewhere, and not make up a semi-sentient layer in the ultimate closed stack— the sanitary landfill.

Dowlin, who is a respected figure among library managers, has announced that he is running for the presidency of the American Library Association next year. He narrowly lost his first race for the ALA presidency, in 1987: "TRUCKIN' FOR THE FUTURE: Ken Dowlin for ALA President," his campaign stickers said. In his role as ALA luminary, Dowlin (who spent six years in the Marine Corps before a part-time job driving a bookmobile diverted his interest toward library administration) sometimes quotes business theorists like Everett M. Rogers, whom he has called "my guru for change." One of Rogers's books lists four ways to transform an organization—by destroying it, by restructuring it, by changing the individuals within it, and by introducing new technology. In a 1992 ALA talk (part of a forum entitled "Electronic Reference in the 21st Century: Innovation Through People, Money, and Imagination"), after citing Rogers's four ways, Dowlin went on to offer a fifth: "I can tell you what happens when you get an earthquake that puts five hundred thousand books on the floor. It's a perfect opportunity to rearrange them."

The Loma Prieta earthquake of October 1989 allowed Dowlin and the department managers, after closing the stacks to the public (in part for safety reasons), to combine departments, forming a template for the New Main. The literature and history departments were fused first. By the time the new building opened, the administration had, in spite of a petition signed by twenty-seven librarians, folded sports, recreation, and most of the sciences into a catch-all category now known as General Collections and Humanities. Cell biology, tree books, Elizabethan poetry, cookery, model trains, and pets were now all in the same group, and reshuffled librarians no longer necessarily had a close familiarity with the collection they oversaw.

Following the earthquake, Dowlin kept the library closed for two and a half months in order to complete this reorganization, even though some of his staff told him that they were prepared to open with at least partial services much earlier. Meanwhile large numbers of books were moving all over the place. A branch information memo, dated December 7, 1989, advised, "There will be no discard pick-ups until the discard room at the Main Library can be cleared. It is so full it has become a fire hazard." Between 150,000 and 200,000 infrequently checked-out books (including a nice collection of old travel books) went to an abandoned medical building, where they were stored in hospital rooms. Some of the rooms had broken windows; most were without shades or curtains. Some three thousand books were damaged beyond repair from mold and water and were thrown away. Back at the library, thousands of books that had never been entered into the computer were taken to a room on the third floor in the north wing. They sat there for several months; then every department was asked to go through these "Not On File"s, or NOFs, and make decisions about whether they ought to be kept or "deselected." The room thus came to be known as the Deselection Chamber. For a brief time during this period, according to one librarian, the DPW trucks were leaving with loads of books several times a week.

The NOFs that survived remained boxed for about five years, inaccessible, as cardboard sagged and collapsed, and bindings within gave way. They could have been reshelved, but they weren't. They weren't in the computer; they were "out-of-date material"—why spend money to reshelve them? Dowlin had already signaled his intention before the earthquake, when he told a reporter for the *Bay Guardian* that he planned to clean out what he called the "Augean stables" of the library. King Augeus, remember, had a problem with a backlog of ox dung, and Hercules managed

117

this situation by redirecting the flow of a convenient river. One of Dowlin's labors was to channel the river of federal earthquake-relief money toward his library. The FEMA grant application that his staff prepared requested money for (among other sensible things like physical repairs and book rebinding) a new computer system, in order to inventory earthquake-dislocated books. FEMA obliged with a large sum. The card catalog was frozen in 1991, and the library, with additional municipal and private funding, signed a multimillion-dollar lease agreement with Digital Equipment and brought its new catalog online.

Some books were repaired with FEMA money; others were simply thrown away. It wasn't until a few months before the move to the New Main that thousands of damaged books—many of them rare—stored since the earthquake in a low-ceilinged nook known as the Mouse House, about a block from the library, went out for repairs. Rather than actually repairing these books, according to one librarian, the library devoted its resources to the routine repair of circulating books damaged after the earthquake.

Repairing old books in-house would take a more sophisticated preservation program than the library is willing to commit to, even though Dowlin has served on an ALA president's committee on book preservation. An ensemble of new equipment for preserving manuscript pages—including an ultrasonic welder and a water-filtration and de-ionization system—remains unused (except for the welder, which is occasionally employed to make signs for the library), and many nineteenth-century works are shipped to a commercial service that shears off the decorated publisher's bindings and encases the books' interiors in plain cloth.

In the sixties, William Holman, then the city librarian, began an ambitious program of book buying (out-of-print as well as new books), with the intention of turning SFPL into a high-level research library—not quite as high-level as the New York Public, but worthy even so of San Francisco's literary past, with pockets of eccentric comprehensiveness. Subsequent city librarians built on Holman's hoard, until Dowlin arrived with an alternative vision. "First and foremost," Dowlin wrote in a letter to the *Chronicle* not long ago, "SFPL is a public library, not a research facility." It's both, of course, and the books and scholarly journals stored in Brooks Hall—a vast, dusty space under the street which the library borrowed recently to store its overflow—belie Dowlin's claim. The entire McComas Collection of Science Fiction and Fantasy—including unbound copies of *Amazing Stories* going back to 1929—resides in this offsite mega-crypt, as do the locked-case books, each with an acid-free identifying tag, that used to be kept behind glass in the old history-and-social-sciences department: John Gould's eight-volume *Birds of Australia* (a set of which sold at auction last March for over a quarter of a million dollars), for instance, and Bligh's *A Voyage to the South Sea*. (Patrons who want to consult these materials must make a special request, and wait until the next day.) A librarian was surprised to discover Athanasius Kircher's beautifully engraved fantasia on the Roman countryside, published in 1671, on a high shelf down in Brooks Hall. This is a book dealer's paradise, sitting unprotected in the squalor of a storage area, near carpet remnants and construction debris.

Brooks Hall holds what it holds partly because there isn't enough room in the New Main. But partly, too, its contents simply don't accord with the altered conception—fashionable now among some circulation-sensitive library managers—of the public library's true mission. In August 1992, Dowlin introduced the concept of "leveled access" in the humanities to the San Francisco Planning Commission. Leveled access involves offering the public, in Mr. Dowlin's words, "a large, generally accessible collection that is designed essentially to be current material—if you will, a mass selection." This mass of material would be supplemented by "focus collections" in selected areas, such as art and music. What nobody outside the library quite understood was that the leveling implicit in leveled access was apparently meant to be retroactive; in other words, that Dowlin's plan would involve downsizing what had already been achieved, at considerable expense, by his predecessors.

The staff understood, though. Some approved; many didn't. On December 6, 1989, William Ramirez, then chief of the Main Library, wrote a memo to Mr. Dowlin describing staff concerns over the events that followed the earthquake. Staff members, he wrote, "believe that current and planned actions will: Decimate the collection [through] weeding, discarding materials from the collections—both circulating and reference—which make this library unique." The staff believes that these actions will, Ramirez went on, "move us in the direction of changing this library from a strong reference, research resource and service center to an undistinguished 'popular library.'" Ramirez retired the next year. But a number of Dowlin's employees have continued to resist his vision. When asked to sort books in their departments into those that circulated within the past two years, and those that had not, they did not sort. When asked to weed, they have not weeded. A branch librarian wrote me that she sometimes goes around with a due-date stamp, furtively stamping into currency books that she feels are imperiled. Employees have saved thousands of books on the sly, quietly transferring them from one department to another, and hiding them in their lockers. They reintroduce these books when the danger has passed. They call it "guerrilla librarianship."

One day last May, after a few hours of note-taking in Brooks Hall (nobody challenged me when I came and went, but I took nothing, for the books I was looking at weren't discards), I went back to the New Main building, negotiated its catwalks and stairways, and entered a staff-only door on the lower level. (The door was slightly ajar, foiling its magnetically actuated lock.) Under several Plexiglas ceiling bubbles that held surveillance cameras, I hurried through the hallways until I came to what I was looking for—the all-important sorting room of the library of the future. In the old library, returned books slid down a chute into the sorting room in plastic bins: a simple, durable system. In the new library, a motorized conveyor belt pulls the books down the chute one at a time, and when they jam, they get hurt. It's as if you sent your clothes down to the luggage handlers in the airport without putting them in a suitcase. Hundreds of books have been torn and injured this way. Someone has taped up a postcard of a pained-looking Ezra Pound right over the opening out of which the books slide; the staff must poke the chute with a broom handle to keep the flow going.

The old sorting room could hold tens of thousands of books on its shelves; the new sorting room has no installed shelving. It was supposed to work on the "Federal Express model": everything would absolutely, positively get reshelved overnight. But because the plan depended on the creation of a new, lower-paid class of employee called a "shelver," which the union has opposed, and because there is no money at the moment anyway, books can take more than a month to get put back where they belong. (In staff areas, book trucks line the halls; at least forty thousand books currently await reshelving.) Hard-pressed book handlers until recently took the books that poured off the conveyor belt and flung them, as if they were dealing cards, into one of several mounds on the floor. I looked in and saw a sign taped to the wall that said "800s," which in the Dewey system means books of literature: under it was an enormous spreading berm of books. Then I was gently and politely reprimanded by a security guard for being in a restricted area.

The sorting room is like the entire new building, in that it has built into it a contempt for, or at least an indifference to, literary culture and its requirements. As one staff member told me: "De facto, this is not a good book building. There's not enough room for books, there's not enough staff to get the books back on the shelves, there's not enough staff to check the books out—however it happened, it's an absolute disaster."

I first told this story in the auditorium of the New Main Library last May. (I spoke at the invitation of the Intellectual Freedom Committee of the Librarians' Guild.) Since then the library has responded to my at-times intemperate criticisms, and to the resultant coverage in the press, in a variety of ways. In the August issue of *Library Journal*, Dowlin is quoted as saying, "The building is doing exactly what I wanted it to do." At a Library Commission meeting in July, Kathy Page, chief of the Main, said that the library had withdrawn more than a hundred thousand books from the entire system—the branches as well as the Main—in the period from January 1995 to June 1996, but she contended that the weeding was standard procedure. (Indeed, she said much weeding has yet to be done.) Librarians had been asked to do a thorough weed before the move, she said, but only so that the movers wouldn't have to carry things no one wanted. She said that all last-copy discards were now reviewed by a Main Library subject specialist, and complied with what she called "the bible"—the library's Collection Development Plan, which assigns a rank from 0 (not collected) through 6 (comprehensive) to every area of the library's holdings. (For example, subjects like life sciences, general philosophy, and Italian literature are assigned a Level 2, "introductory material" rating, which may explain why I found so many old books about birds and ethics in the Discard Room, and why old Italian novels were in discard piles last month.)

A few days after I gave the speech, a member of the board of the Library Foundation told me I was a pawn of the employees' union; later, when the San Francisco press picked up on the story, I became a sort of weirdo cultist, a "ringleader" who, in the company of a band of converts, was launching an attack on the library for personal glory. ("With some Rogaine and a few weeks' more growth of his salt-and-pepper beard, the 39-year-old Baker might pass for Rasputin in tweed," wrote a journalist for *SF Weekly*. "Soft-spoken, tall, and intense, Baker seems to hold an almost mystical sway over a ragtag collection of feisty librarians and disgruntled activists.") In July, a letter signed by representatives of a number of the fund-raising affinity groups went out to every member of the library staff. The letter accused one librarian,

Toba Singer—who had written an op-ed piece for the *Examiner* critical of the library's corporate sponsorship—of homophobia and racism, and it accused me of anti-Semitism, because I had used what were, the letter charged, Holocaust references by mentioning the so-called Deselection Chamber and by calling the book purge a "hate crime directed at the past." I and the audience that "cheered [me] on" were, according to the letter, "intellectually dishonest, disrespectful to the library staff, and insulting to all Jewish, gay and lesbian, and other individuals who suffered the actual Holocaust." Over the next several weeks, this letter began to appear on the desks of newspaper and radio editors.

Late in August, two librarians decided to measure the shelves of the old library in order to get a more accurate number for the oft-disparaged old building's capacity. Walter Biller (a historian) and I came along, tape measures a-dangle: it was impossible to resist this last chance to tour the old floors. We measured the card catalog, and we read the legend high on the wall to the right of the entrance to the catalog room: HANDLE A BOOK / AS A BEE DOES A / FLOWER / EXTRACT / ITS SWEETS BUT / DO NOT / INJURE IT.

The four of us spent several hours at our work, nervously listening for footsteps, and then we locked up and left. Unfortunately, the librarian in charge of coming up with the spreadsheet didn't, in her haste, note down one of the crucial numbers for the seven floors of the north stacks and relied instead on a faulty diagram that was taped on the wall; her newsworthily high preliminary numbers were then immediately leaked to a reporter. OLD LIBRARY HELD MORE BOOKS, SAY CRITICS, read the headline of the front-page article in the *Examiner;* and then, a few days later, FOUR CRITICS OF LIBRARY MUST EAT THEIR WORDS. Mortifying though it was, the episode had the unforeseen effect of prompting Kathy Page to write a constructive memo to all employees, which said, among other things, "The unhappy fact remains that we have less storage capacity in the new building than we had planned for and less than we need."

I have been able to speak only a few words to Dowlin, Page's boss, directly. At the end of May, he consented to an interview with me, provided I sent him, three days in advance, a list of questions. I mailed off the list; then, a few days before we were to meet, he (understandably) canceled the appointment, because, in the words of his likable secretary, "we are being sued." In the *Library Journal* piece, Dowlin is quoted as saying, "I'm not convinced Mr. Baker understands the people of San Francisco and what they want. There are some people who disagree with what I wanted to do, but they're about six years too late." Dowlin told the reporter for *SF Weekly* that my account of the library's extreme weeding was "bullshit," and that my writing was "crap."


Long ago, the library kept a "Withdrawal Register"—it appears on a WPA list of city records in the '40s—but nothing like that is available now. (In the words of one librarian, "The card catalog is the mute witness to all of this destruction.") As part of another public-records request, now Exhibit D of *Baker v. San Francisco Public Library,* I asked for "all records, including lists, card files . . . computer records and printouts thereof, of books withdrawn, discarded, dumped, weeded, given away, sold, pulped, or otherwise removed from the library's collections from 1987 to the present." In the same letter I wrote, "Surely there is a record of the disposition of millions of dollars' worth of city property." The library administration's official response, via the city attorney's office, was "No list or compilation exists for books discarded or destroyed since 1987." There was, however, a thirty-two-megabyte computer report entitled "Purge of Items Declared Withdrawn," which principally covers items removed from the collection between January 1, 1995, and April 1, 1996. That report has never been printed out, for it would fill almost five thousand large-format computer-paper pages. It includes only things that were deliberately withdrawn, nothing missing or stolen; and it does not include NOFs, which were never in the computer. It took me two and a half hours to download it from the library's file server. Kassim Visram, a systems analyst, ran some frequency analyses, which indicate that there are about 146,000 non-paperback books in the file—along with many phono disks, periodicals, cassettes, and so on. Amazingly, there are columns in the report headed "Last Copy" and "Last Main," under each of which there appears either a "yes" or a "no" for each book; Visram could thus produce a file made up entirely of last-copy discards. I downloaded that smaller list of more than 17,000 books and sorted it again several ways myself. Some of the discards are not troubling—the departure of yet another edition of *Gone with the Wind* doesn't represent an irreplaceable loss. But the last copy of Darwin's *The Movements and Habits of Climbing Plants* (in a 1901 edition) caught my eye; and I saw more than a thousand Chinese books, hundreds of books in German and Italian, and an appalling number of research-level monographs in the sciences. History was hit particularly hard in my sample, especially (for some reason) history published by the Cambridge University Press: listed were the last copies of works by Sir Herbert Butterfield, Henry

St. John Bolingbroke, William Stubbs, C. V. Wedgwood, and Lewis Namier. There were last copies of hard-to-find books by Muriel Spark, Goethe, and William Dean Howells.

According to the Automation Services Department, there was at least one earlier purge report, run in 1995, covering discards from some point in the past through the end of 1994. That purge report was itself purged, however; it doesn't exist on any backup tape or disk. "That's a report that hasn't existed on the system for a long time," I was told. "We did do a purge of withdrawals in May of 1995, but generally we don't keep those files around for very long, because once they're withdrawn and gone, there's really no need to keep a history of that."

I can't agree.

*(1996)*

# *If Libraries Don't Do It, Who Will?*

Remarks Delivered at the Ribbon-Cutting Ceremony for the
Library Service Center, Duke University Libraries

T hank you, and good afternoon, everyone. I've never commemorated the opening of a building before, and I must say it's an enormous pleasure and an honor to be here, standing in front of this large beige building, to talk about the storage of paper. Paper storage has been on my mind a great deal lately, because last year I started a little library that has in it twenty or thirty tons of bound newspapers, all sold off by the British Library. When the sale actually went through—I didn't want it to go through, I wanted the library to keep the papers—but when it did, I began to have yearning thoughts about storage. I would drive by some undistinguished steel-sided building, painted some shocking color, and I'd spot those beautiful words FOR LEASE on it, and it would call out to me: *storage*. I saw a FOR LEASE sign on a converted mill one day and I called the number; the developer said, "I can show you the mill, but I've got something better for you. I want to show you something that is a dream space, top of the line, and I know it may be more than you can do costwise, but I just want you to see this and I want you to think about it." I said okay, and my wife and I took a drive with the developer to a navy base, and we parked in front of an enormous stone building with towers and parapets. It looked like a gigantic medieval fortress. What was it? It was the navy prison. There was a vast rusting cell block with prison cages that went up many stories, and a crumbling men's room that in its bleak ruination stretched back into the shadows, with maybe thirty sinks along one wall, none of which worked. I was very tempted—but in the end, it just didn't seem like the right place to keep the last surviving twentieth-century runs of the *Chicago Tribune,* the *New York Herald Tribune,* and the New York *World.*

So I now know, more than I ever did before, about the deep and abiding joy that comes from having enough space—and even now I sometimes feel a slight envious resentment rising within when I cruise down a big highway near New York City and I see buildings that have fifty truck bays. What are they holding? They're holding cheese products, or truck parts, or Happy Meal toys, or Pentium computers that will be scrap in five years. They're not holding books. One tank depot or tire warehouse would hold everything that our national library has been sent, free, by publishers and has rejected every year. Our national library says that they don't have enough space, and they are unwilling to lease space, even though they're willing to budget 94 million dollars for digital projects.

So here we have a building that has one purpose—to

store books—books that we can carry around, flip through, and read just as they were meant to be read by their creators. There's a cherry picker machine inside, a state-of-the-art cherry picker, that lifts a book retriever up thirty-two feet, where he or she gets the book out of a cardboard tray and comes down with it. And there will be two and a half million books in here. The cost was seven and a half million dollars—so this brand-new place cost about three dollars a book to build. Very few of the books that are going in here have been digitally scanned—and here's the dramatic comparison. To store a nineteenth-century book, it costs three dollars a book, plus an estimated seventeen cents a book in maintenance and staffing; to scan a nineteenth-century book, it costs a hundred dollars a book. And the book doesn't even need batteries! Not that it's a bad thing to take digital pictures of books, as long as the picture-taking doesn't require that the book be cut out of its binding—the electronic versions can be extraordinarily useful. The point is that offsite book storage, even traditional storage in call number order, is cheap, and any scanning or microfilming we do should be done with the expectation that the original book go back into the collection when the copying is done. And it's compact, too—2.5 million books go in here, and across the street, an even bigger building is devoted to doing the laundry. Besides being things of intrinsic beauty and interest, books are marvelously compact.

Now there are some futurists, some central planners, who don't agree with any of what I've just said. There's a man named Michael Lesk, of the National Science Foundation in Washington, who is in charge of giving away millions of dollars in federal grants for digital library projects, who told me that he routinely says to libraries, hey, maybe you shouldn't repair your library building, you could scan everything in that building, and let the building fall down, and you would save money. Lesk refers to an analysis by a library director from Minnesota who claims that libraries would save about 44 billion dollars over the next one hundred years if they digitally scanned about twenty million books and got rid of more than four hundred million duplicate books. Our libraries would be better off, in other words, if they dismantled about 95 percent of their accumulated collections, according to this analysis. Many—not all, but many—in the digital library world believe that the destruction of local research collections will help hurry us toward the far digital shore. They inflate the cost of keeping things, and they denigrate the durability of paper, because it's distressing to them that it is so inexpensive to store what was long ago bought, cataloged, and shelved.

Research library collections grow. That's what this fine building recognizes. Your children's feet grow, and you buy them new shoes—the bigger feet do not represent a "growth problem" but a developmental fact, something to be proud of. For the past half century or more, though, growth has been an embarrassment to some Washington visionaries. They were swept by a kind of Cold War fervor of informational reform, and they wanted all growth to stop. Libraries would reach a certain fixed size, a few million volumes, and then the weeding parties would gather and the microcopying would crunch down the excess, and when the microfilm spools themselves took up too much room, then they could microcopy the microcopies at ultra-high resolution, and crunch things down more, and the stacks would function like a vast trash compactor, squeezing the words. Because words were squeezable, weren't they? They were disembodied astral presences that had nothing to do with the ink that formed them or the paper that they were printed on or the bindings that held the paper together; they could be "reformatted"—preserved by being destroyed—because they were immaterial; the books would still exist, they would just not exist; they would be there, but they wouldn't be there; you could hold your head high and say you had the finest U.S. newspaper collection in the world, when in fact you had gotten rid of 90 percent of it and replaced it with microfilm, much of it unchecked for quality.

What was the source of this thinking? There was one especially influential person some of you may have heard about. His name was Fremont Rider, head librarian at Wesleyan. Rider's first book, published in 1909, was about the amazing discoveries of spirit rappings and table turnings and levitation—he felt these things deserved serious study and that the tables did in fact turn. He wrote pulp fiction and he was the managing editor of *Library Journal*, and when he went bankrupt in 1929 after a manic episode in which he spent a small fortune founding a high-society supper club on Long Island, he wrote an indignant pamphlet in which he said that people were fed up with being indebted to banks, and they wanted a new deal. He sent the pamphlet to Franklin D. Roosevelt, and Roosevelt shot him back a letter with a handwritten note saying you're right—keep it up!—and then a few months later Roosevelt, in his nomination speech, pledged himself to a New Deal for the American People. So Fremont Rider was an influential person—and his new deal for librarians was this: make or buy microcopies of your book collection, sell off the book collection to dealers at scrap prices, and you will make, in his words, "an actual cash profit on the substitution." You'll enrich your library by getting rid of its books. Rider got the Librarian of Congress and the Deputy Librarian of Congress and the head librarian at Michigan and the head librarian at Harvard and other big-time leaders all over the library world to blurb his book and serve on his Microcard committee. It's a mathematical fact that book collections double every sixteen years, Rider said (he was wrong about that), and if we didn't start buying Fremont Rider's Microcard reading machines and selling off the collections, the stacks were going to overrun the entire square footage of New Jersey. Building a storage warehouse was, according to Rider, "a confession of past failure"—it was unmanly, somehow.

This way of thinking continues in some circles, and it was very powerful in the 1980s, when the Library of Congress had high hopes for its optical disk pilot project, which could, according to the Deputy Librarian, squeeze down the library's three buildings to one. But the optical disk pilot program didn't work out—nobody uses those big platters anymore—and over the past decade or so, some enlightened librarians have begun to accept the fact that the easiest way to keep a research collection is to keep the research collection. There is no shame in growth—it is not a confession of failure. Putting up shelves sufficient to hold what's there is the crucially important primary task that research libraries must fulfill—they must do this because no other institutions, public or private, can be depended on to keep these things— the obscure things, the cumbersome things that even though they're used only once in ten years or thirty years or fifty years are valuable because they are what people published and read. To a researcher, the fact that something is little used is a positive attribute—if a photo editor for a documentary on, say, Ellis Island pages through a forgotten autobiography and finds a picture that has never been reproduced before, she is overjoyed, because the picture is interesting, *and* because it is unused. We till around in great collections looking for things that have lain unnoticed—the urge to search through obscurity is basic to scholarship. And if the research libraries don't keep it—don't keep copies of the stuff that we as a people publish—nobody else is going to do it. It just won't happen. We can't depend on businesses to save our past. The *New York Times* has kept no run of its own paper, for instance.

We understand why fragile old flags and old presidential letters are valuable as things—we don't believe that taking a snapshot of Plymouth Rock amounts to a "reformatting" of Plymouth Rock, and after some long and painful decades of urban renewal we're doing better with old mills and train stations. There are very nice postcards of Whistler's painting of a woman in a white dress for sale in museum giftshops, but Whistler's woman in white is still on the wall. Storage! That's what this building is about. Keep it cool, keep it dry, but above all—keep it. Nice going, Duke.

*(2001)*

# Reading the Paper

An Address Delivered at the Annual Meeting
of the Bibliographical Society of America

Early one morning not long ago, I put on my coat over my pajamas and went out to the end of the driveway to get the paper. It was in a blue bag that said "The New York Times Home Delivery Service," and "Warning: Keep This Plastic Bag Away From Children." The bag's knot was untiable—tied by the deliveryman in the knowledge that each recipient would tear it open and pour out the newspaper, which I did when I got inside. The paper was curled around itself, and when I opened it and began paging through it I could feel in every section the timed-release coolness that is always associated with newsprint. You keep getting outside air on your hands as you read. Newsprint is its own insulation. A single page makes a rattling sound when you turn it, but the whole issue is quiet, muffled by its own layered pulp.

Because newspapers are such patchworks of visual miscellaneousness, we read them differently than we read books, which are, except for an occasional excursion to check a footnote, linear experiences. The newspaper's front page is both binding and title page at once, and it offers its above-the-fold headlines first, so big, often, that you take them in without even knowing you're reading them—and then the underworld below the fold comes up out of the shadows into view with a quick turn of the wrist. Next the unfolding begins, and once you open up a section and hear the rattly sounds of the singled-out pages, the rest of the world falls away—the newspaper is so big now that it becomes the landscape. Your eye loops and leaps, lighting on a photo and then dropping to read the caption and then circling to find the article that is associated with it; and you jump from page one to an inner page to finish the article, and then hop across to the adjacent page while you're there, where you notice an ad with a funny image and an article that looks interesting that is continued from page one, and so you return to page one. And when you turn the page, you don't turn it as you would turn a book page—you close the whole paper and hand off the right-hand page to the left hand—and then you open the paper again. And at the top of every page is the date: all this happened now.

That constant assertion of nowness is precisely what is so appealing and instructive about old newspapers, yellowing and fragile though they may be. Great libraries turned the newspapers into books—big, heavy books with, in some cases, vellum corners and marbled boards—by binding fifteen or thirty consecutive todays in one. And then the policy changed, beginning in the '50s, and the libraries got rid of most of their twentieth-century newspaper collections—meaning that the remaining runs are unspeakably rare, rarer than early Chaucers or Dantes. We are very close to losing our own twentieth century. So what I've been doing is opening volumes up and taking pictures of pages that interest me. Like a microfilmer of the 1930s, I've set up a digital imaging workstation, which consists of a wooden pallet on the floor over which I've put a sheet of plywood and some foam core and some white banner paper from Staples. For lighting I use the clamp-on utility lights that you can buy for five dollars apiece at the hardware store; these are supported by an old coat tree and a cast-off intravenous drip-bag stand on rollers. I could use the tripod to steady the camera, but I don't, because you have to be able to make tiny angle adjustments that are clumsy with a tripod. I just bend over the open volume and frame the picture and hold my breath and try not to quiver at the wrong moment and I end up with a reasonably good four-megapixel digital picture. Now, a four-megapixel picture is better than a three-megapixel picture, and it is in color, but the resolution isn't as good as 1940s black-and-white microfilm. But even if I had a four-hundred-megapixel camera, and could record from five feet up the ink-slippage marks on each Linotyped line, and the faint fuzz of paper-hairs that fringe a tiny tear in the margin, would I feel that I had successfully reformatted the pages and could now throw them away? Of course not. I like old things because they are old—their oldness and their fragility is part of what they have to say. They hold the record of the time in which they were printed, and the record of the years that have passed between that time and now. The copying of an old thing is, or should be, like the publishing of a scholarly edition, an act of homage to the physical source from which one is working—a way of saying thank you for holding the riches you hold.

So anyway, I've been taking lots of pictures; I enjoy doing it, because when you take a picture of something, you are forced to think about only it for a little while. You draw a mental frame around it, with the help of the camera's viewfinder, and everything else recedes, and after a minute or two, the thing that you're photographing takes on a fetching particularity—one page in a universe of possible pages. As a result of this camerawork, I have done a great deal of a certain kind of newspaper reading, and I am full of little ill-digested snippets of knowledge about 1898 and 1903 and 1939—and a feeling has grown in me that is difficult to convey. It's a sort of primitive amazement at how incredibly much has gone on. So much has happened. Massive numbers of named people have done an enormous number of things— some good, some horrible—and each good or horrible thing is potentially interesting. My head is crawling with old headlines—SUSAN B. ANTHONY SAYS THERE ARE WORSE THINGS THAN POLYGAMY, from the front page of the New York *World* at the turn of the century, or ONE WOMAN AND A THOUSAND RATS, also from the *World*, about a woman who raised rats and guinea pigs to sell to laboratories. And from the *Chicago Tribune* in 1909, HOW SUFFRAGE MADE ME BEAUTIFUL. Around 1900 there was a tiny, two-paragraph article entitled WILD EYED MAN ATE STAMPS. A man became deranged and ate some stamps—that was the article.

I have read articles on opium dens in New York and on how John D. Rockefeller acted in church, and I've come across stories by P. G. Wodehouse and F. Scott Fitzgerald, poems by Rudyard Kipling and Robert Frost and Dorothy Parker, essays by Mark Twain and H. L. Mencken, war dispatches by Stephen Crane, and I have a better notion of the grain of the past, the texture and rhythm of events, which is, I think, a prerequisite to doing many kinds of history. But I'm not a historian. I'm just someone who thinks that what historians do is important, and that they ought to be able to consult, if they have a mind to, what we as a nation published and read, and read in huge numbers.

Is there any publication that has had so wide a readership—that has entered so many people's lives at precisely the same time? Somewhere between half a million and a million copies of a big-city paper like Pulitzer's *World,* or the *Chicago Tribune,* went out every day. A million people read the *Tribune*'s headline from 1945, BOMB FOUR DOOMED JAP CITIES, and saw its front-page color cartoons, with their drawings of the Jap Buster Bomb. If you look at that page on microfilm, it seems to come from very long ago. It is lost in a rainstorm of scratches. Its words are heard through static, its immediacy is destroyed, and you think therefore that the people who read that paper must have been entirely different creatures than we are. But they weren't.

Again, think of the number of copies. *Life* magazine had a huge circulation at midcentury—five million—but that was five million copies per month. The *Chicago Tribune* printed six times that many copies every month. And each daily issue had much more in it—more brute wordage, more advertising, more miscellaneousness, more rough edges—than *Life.* Not that *Life* isn't fascinating, of course. But there are hundreds of bound runs of *Life* magazine in research libraries today. No long runs of the *Chicago Tribune* survive in libraries, and none of the twentieth-century New York *World,* and even the *New York Times,* especially the real *Times,* and not the rag-paper library edition, which though it cost more for libraries to subscribe to wasn't nearly as well printed, is on the edge of total oblivion. Hands placed all those tiny want ads, each representing some particular human want, the stories were typeset piecemeal by hundreds of compositors, and when they heard "Give it away" they knew to space out the remaining lines of Linotype so as to use up the rest of the column, and when the composing was done, the compositors clamped their three-hundred-pound forms tight and watched them roll away. All the editors and composers could proofread at high speed upside down and backward. Pulpy paper squashed over the forms, making a mold for more molten lead, and the curved plates were clamped to the presses and the paper began writhing through, twenty million or more sheets cut and folded each day, leaving those softly fluted edges that a newspaper has, and then bundlers tied them and truckers drove off into the city with them and they went out, hitting the sidewalk near the newsstand with a whoomp of something heavy—a big cube of todayness. Every day it happened. No matter what is in a newspaper, even if every word is untrue, we know for sure that these particular words and drawings and pictures happened— were published—on that day—and that is a precious sort of elementary knowledge to have.

(2002)

# *The* Times *in 1951*

Written for the 150th-Anniversary Issue of the *New York Times*

Being a backward-looking person, I was curious to know what the *New York Times* was like in 1951, on its last big birthday. I happen to have handy an original bound run of the newspaper from that era, in all its wood-pulp bulk and glory—a set of daily papers which once looped and cavorted through the groaning machines that dwelled in the basement of Forty-third Street, in an atmosphere heavy with ink mist and paper dust. I pulled out some of the old volumes, set them on a long table and began turning my way through them.

1951's pages are bigger than today's by about the width of a current column. The passage of time has dyed them a champagney hue; as they slowly rise and fall they bring to mind the intermittent wingstrokes of some great hovering bird. There are fewer photographs and more monochrome

Lord & Taylor fashion watercolors, signed by now-forgotten commercial artists like Karnoff and Hood: these are deftly blurry, like Japanese sumi paintings of twigs and birds. Only in the magazine section, in the ads, are there four-color illustrations: "It's HELLMANN'S the WHOLE-EGG Mayonnaise!"

But what strikes one first about the publication of fifty years ago is how much it looks like what we read now. The delivery trucks and printing presses have disappeared from Forty-third Street (the New York edition is now printed in stylishly automated factories in Queens and New Jersey); reporters no longer chain-smoke at their Underwoods, or shout "Copy!", or play cards, or place bets with Frenchie, the in-house bookie (who wore a beret and an ascot), or slip over to Gough's, the bar across the street. But the Sulzbergers' broadsheet has nonetheless remained faithful to its typographical traditions. And Al Hirschfeld's pen, I was pleased to see, was there on the theater pages—precise, frolicsome, full of genius, then as now.

What was the news in 1951? Well, there was the Korean War. Lists of killed and wounded appeared on page three in small type; in April, after General Douglas MacArthur made one too many unauthorized remarks about the necessity of bombing China, President Truman relieved him of his command in the Far East. The uproar was immediate. The Daughters of the American Revolution were deeply troubled; there was talk of impeachment; private citizens took out ads protesting the president's shameless act. The *Times's* editorialist, however, sided with Truman. "In this controversy this newspaper has taken an unequivocal stand in favor of the Government and against General MacArthur," it said on April 17; there was no need for another world war, and Truman was right to assert "the supremacy of the civil government over any military authority."

MacArthur's farewell speech to Congress, though, was good—the *Times* found it "eloquent and deeply moving." Lots of people saw it live, thanks to all those Emerson and Philco and Magnavox TVs that were advertised every day in the paper. "It was extraordinary television, whatever a viewer's political feelings," wrote Jack Gould, the *Times*'s TV critic. Gould was particularly struck by MacArthur's forceful comb-over: "He parted his hair low on the right side and had brushed it almost directly across his forehead."

Whether MacArthur was in charge or not, the Korean War had to continue, many at the paper believed. The alternative was withdrawal, "throwing in the sponge before the knockdown," and that would have "intolerable political, moral and psychological consequences," according to a military analyst for the *Times*. Couldn't nuclear weapons help somehow? In an article headlined ATOMIC DEATH BELT URGED FOR KOREA, the paper quoted from a letter to Harry Truman from Congressman Albert Gore Sr. The congressman suggested that the United States "dehumanize a belt across the Korean peninsula by surface radiological contamination." The belt, Gore said, could be "regularly recontaminated" until the Korean problem was solved; such a show of nuclear force would be, according to Gore, "morally justifiable under the circumstances."

In September the U.S. Army announced plans to test tactical atomic weapons on front-line combat troops at Frenchman Flat, Nevada. Following up, the *Times*'s science writer, William Laurence (who had been an observer on the Nagasaki bombing mission) wrote a story entitled A

HYDROGEN BOMB NOW SEEN AS SURE. Some well-placed fusion bombs could "blanket an army in the field," Laurence said, "and raise havoc with its personnel and equipment, as well as with its morale." The weapons, properly used, could nullify a superiority in manpower, "such as, for example, the hordes of Russia." By November a labor union was complaining that its members had been shut out of work on the billion-dollar hydrogen-bomb factory ("the largest construction project the world has ever known," according to one of its managers) that DuPont was building near Augusta, Georgia.

DuPont had other big launches that year as well. At a press event, a company representative showed off a suit made of a new miracle fiber, Dacron. The suit had been worn by a businessman for sixty-seven straight summer days without needing pressing. "To keep it clean," reported the *Times,* "the owner went swimming in it twice and at thirty-two days of wear it was washed in a home washing machine." A men's clothing store, John David, advertised a tie made of 100 percent Dacron: "DACRON is rated, along with cellophane, Nylon and neoprene rubber as one of DuPont's greatest technological achievements," said the ad. The tie was, according to the ad, "a sure conversation starter."

A conversation of sorts had started between the United States and the Soviet Union, but it wasn't going all that well. At a November United Nations conference in Paris, the Russians, trailing badly despite some bomb secrets obtained through the Rosenbergs (who had been sentenced to death in April), condemned the "mad armaments race." Vishinsky, the Soviet foreign minister, proposed a ban on all nuclear weapons and the destruction of existing stocks. Secretary of State Dean Acheson offered some halfhearted counterproposals, saying however that the Atlantic community was "building its strength." This prompted the *Times*'s James Reston, wise in the ways of diplomacy, to conclude that the practical purpose of the U.S. proposals was "not to end the 'cold war,' as the Allies proclaimed, but to wage the 'cold war' more effectively."

With increasing bomb-consciousness came civil defense. The Trucking Industry National Defense Committee ran a full-pager to point out that if the United States were attacked, railroads would be a primary target. "The Trucking Industry can't be bombed out of existence because it doesn't move over fixed road beds. Because it isn't concentrated. Because it is instantaneously mobile!" Armed men in jeeps began a round-the-clock protection of New York City's reservoirs, equipped with "two mobile laboratories in which quick water analyses will be made in the event of an atomic bomb attack." An NYU professor of psychology suggested that hymn singing would help allay panic among bomb survivors. At 7:30 p.m. on November 14, over a hundred thousand participants staged a gigantic civil defense drill. Two atom bombs were assumed to have gone off—one over Bushwick and Myrtle Avenues in Brooklyn, and one near the Manhattan-Bronx line, "devastating a large area of both boroughs."

But in the event, no bombs fell, and New Yorkers carried on as they had. In four out of seven of the new model rooms in the furniture department at Bloomingdale's, designers had chosen "restful pale blond color schemes." Peacock feathers and the color green were back in women's hats. Rachel Carson's first book, *The Sea Around Us,* was an up-from-the-deeps best-seller. Salinger's first novel, *Catcher in the Rye,* was "rambunctiously fresh and alive," in the opinion of a *Times* book reviewer. A movie called *I Was a Communist for the F.B.I.* contained "ugly bugaboos" and "reckless 'red' smears," said a *Times* critic; another critic liked Howard Hawks's monster movie *The Thing*, warning however that parents "should think twice before letting their children see this film if their emotions are not properly conditioned."

"Let Me Greet You Personally At My Restaurant," said Jack Dempsey, at the bottom of page two, on April 20; in June, Jake LaMotta, fighting as a light heavyweight, was "battered into a sick and gory spectacle" at Yankee Stadium—General MacArthur was in the audience. "Do you ever wish your child were going to a *nudist* camp?" was Macy's attention-grabber, promoting its extensive summer-camp outfittery. Two women ran unsuccessfully for seats on the AT&T board—there were "a number of Rip Van Winkles" in the company, according to one stockholder. Automatic ten-number dialing, using area codes, was introduced in New Jersey. Bus stops moved to the far sides of city intersections, and parking meters appeared in Manhattan. The Yonkers Police Department hired ten women to serve as traffic officers at school crossings at a rate of four dollars a day. Ex-King Zog paid for an estate in Syosset with a bucket of diamonds and rubies. The runoff from Long Island duck farms was killing beds of bluepoint oysters. Dashiell Hammett got six months in jail for refusing to reveal who had contributed to a pro-Communist bail-bond fund; "I think I dealt with him in an extremely lenient manner," said the sentencing judge. When a ring slipped from the finger of the daughter of the governor of Assam, in India, and fell into a lake, the governor had the lake drained in an attempt to recover the ring, causing "a storm of protest."

Someone stole four thousand ball bearings. There was a surplus of sweet potatoes in New Jersey; the Department of Agriculture was advising housewives to serve them often. An inedible cake in the shape of Winged Victory atop a

Roman temple was a prizewinner at the Salon of Culinary Art. Stopping Joseph McCarthy was "the most important single political job that has faced Wisconsin in many years," said Henry S. Reuss, a Milwaukee lawyer and Democrat who wanted a seat in the Senate. An intentionally soporific phonograph record called "Time to Sleep" was determined to fall within the control of the Pure Food and Drug Act. An ad announced a free home trial of the sensational new Polaroid camera—"Takes and Prints Finished Pictures in One Minute!" Ten cases of major psychiatric illness were observed to follow heavy doses of certain steriods. Roy M. Cohn, the assistant United States attorney, arrested some dealers in "hot tea"—marijuana. Attorney Cohn said that one marine with a distinguished war record "fell into the hands of these people so that his health and his entire life has been ruined"; the accompanying picture showed Police Commissioner Murphy dumping a shovelful of drug packets into the furnace in the basement of the police headquarters annex.

Old newspapers can pull you in deep very quickly. For a little while, as I turned the pages, the headlines and columns expanded and pushed aside all the rest of history— ungeneralizably rich and busy and full of telling confusions. On January 1, 1951, Anne O'Hare McCormick, the foreign affairs columnist, wrote, "News is the destroyer of illusions and the ultimate policy maker." I found myself agreeing with her.

The newspaper covered its own birthday, of course. On September 18, 1951, the *Times,* in a forgivable burst of pride, printed dozens of congratulatory messages—President Truman praised the newspaper for its "generally fair and accurate" reporting, the City Council passed a laudatory resolution, the American Polar Society cheered, and Cuba's *Diario de la Marina* wrote: "May you continue your brilliant and efficient life as the pride of the American Press." Even the archrival *Herald Tribune* paid tribute to the *Times*'s "high standards of dignity, thoroughness and accuracy."

There was more the next day: MESSAGES OF CONGRATULATION CONTINUE POURING IN ON 100TH ANNIVERSARY, reads one headline. The *New York Post* offered a "warm typewriter toast": "You would not want us to pretend that we always love you but as Americans and as journalists we can hardly imagine living without you." Fifty years on, the *Post* is still right.

*(2001)*

# Take a Look at This Airship!

Introduction to *The World on Sunday*,
by Nicholson Baker and Margaret Brentano

J oseph Pulitzer, the fretful, sleepless, Hungarian-born genius who, at the close of the nineteenth century, created the modern newspaper, understood Sundays better than most people.

When you got up on Sunday a hundred years ago, in the age of the six-day workweek, and you had a moment to rest and to feel the restlessness that attends rest, what did you want? News? Did you want headlines about Washington and Tammany Hall and Albany? Well, some, but not so much. You definitely wanted a newspaper: you wanted the comfort of a fresh floppy creation that had required the permanent marriage of tankfuls of ink and elephantine rolls of white paper in order to proclaim the elemental but somehow thrilling fact that this very morning in which you found yourself, despite its familiar features, was incontrovertibly, datably, new.

So, yes, you wanted a Sunday newspaper, but what you wanted from it wasn't really news—it was life. You wanted romance, awe, a close scrape, a prophecy, advice on how to tip or shoplift or gamble, new fashions from Paris, a song to sing, a scissors project for the children, theories about Martians or advanced weaponry, maybe a new job. You wanted to be told over and over again that your city was a city of marvels like no other, but you also wanted to escape for a few minutes to the North Pole or South Dakota or the St. Louis World's Fair, or to take a boat trip down the Mississippi. You wanted something with many sections that you could dole out to people in the room with you. And you wanted imagery—cartoons, caricatures, "gems of pictorial beauty"—layouts and hand-inked headlines that made your eyeballs bustle and bounce around the department-store display of every page. And that's what you got when you spent a nickel and bought Joseph Pulitzer's Sunday *World*.

The *World*—the self-described "greatest newspaper on earth"—was actually three newspapers, the morning *World* (published Monday through Saturday, often with a political cartoon by Walt McDougall or C. G. Bush on the front page), the *Evening World* (carrying boxing news and sports scores, with a more raffish flavor throughout), and "THE GREAT SUNDAY WORLD," which weighed as much as a small roast beef. Together these three *World*s were, in their days of triumph, seen simultaneously by more people than any other publication, with the possible exception of the Bible. Mornings and evenings, hundreds of thousands of fresh *World* issues groaned out from the basement levels of Pulitzer's imposingly gold-domed skyscraper onto every

New York street corner and trolley stop; in 1899, despite some competition from interloper William Randolph Hearst, the *World* claimed on its front page, believably, that it had achieved the "largest circulation ever reached in one year by any newspaper."

The Sunday *World* was the real prodigy of physical dissemination: it sometimes sold half a million or more copies, and it went all over the country. In 1908 Adolph Ochs, publisher of the smaller, soberer *New York Times,* wrote admiringly of the *World's* "phenomenal and prodigious success"; another newspaperman, Frank Munsey, said of Pulitzer: "He came here as a whirlwind out of the West, and overturned and routed the conservativism then in vogue as a cyclone sweeps all before it."

The peculiar thing, however, is that out of all this cyclonic activity, next to nothing survives. Libraries, suspicious of low and pandering art, collected and bound for safekeeping only a few complete original runs of mass-circulation newspapers such as the *World*—they preferred the *New York Times* and the *Evening Post,* papers that carried "real" news with less splash and dash. And then, in the '50s, intrigued by new techniques of photographic miniaturization, libraries began to replace the few runs of popular papers that they did possess with monochromatic copies made on inch-and-a-half-wide strips of clear plastic: microfilm. (You can see reproductions from a microfilm copy of the *Evening World* used as wallpaper in many Subway sandwich shops.) Almost every American library that could afford to swapped a new plastic copy for the heavy, space-consuming wood-pulp original—even two of the greatest, the Library of Congress and the New York Public Library. They threw out the bound volumes or, later, sold them to scrap dealers who razored out cartoons, automobile ads, and historical dates, and used the rest as quarry for the "original Newspaper of the Day You Were Born."

So the reproductions that you see in this book—the art by Bush, J. Campbell Cory, Richard Felton Outcault, Charles Saalburg, George McManus, Marius de Zayas, Dan Smith, and Louis Biedermann; the writing by Mark Twain, Robert Peary, and others—come from what is one of the very last, perhaps the last, set of original copies of the turn-of-the-century New York *World* in existence—certainly the last in such pristine condition. The set came from England: lucky for us, the British Library, in 1898, as the Spanish-American War loomed, felt that Pulitzer's *World* was an essential source of opinion and reportage, and librarians there began subscribing to the *World* and (just as important) began binding it into durable, red-spined, gold-lettered volumes. For decades, foresightedly, through various financial upheavals and geopolitical reshufflements, they kept these volumes safe on shelves. Then, in 1999, feeling the pinch after opening an expensive new building, the library's managers made quiet plans to offer much of its foreign (i.e., North and South American and Continental European) newspaper collection to other libraries, and to auction off the unwanted residue to dealers. I was in the midst of writing a book about the particulars of the losses attributable to microfilm—the crudity of the microcopying itself, the perishability of early acetate film, the bogus science predicting acidic paper's imminent doom—when I learned of the British Library's disposal plans. So I went to England and asked them to keep the American papers. I said that they were rich and rare—which they certainly are—and that I knew that they held, for example, true "first editions" of the writings of Stephen

Crane, O. Henry, Robert Benchley, John Steinbeck, H. G. Wells, Thomas Edison, William Faulkner, and hundreds of other writers, some named, some anonymous. I said that their foreign newspaper collection was just as valuable as, and considerably rarer than, just about any acknowledged rarity in their possession—rarer, for example, than the justly treasured output of Renaissance printers such as Aldus, Plantin, and Wynkyn de Worde. A century ago, newspapers like the *World,* the *Chicago Tribune,* the *New-York Tribune,* and many others were everywhere and were read by everyone; now they are almost nowhere: their historico-artifactual resplendence and indispensability was, it seemed to me, beyond dispute. Not only that—so I argued—but if we ever wanted to make better reproductions of the newspapers than microfilming offered—if we wanted to make digital or even old-fashioned analog reproductions in color, for instance—we would need the original pages to work from: you can't make a sharp, continuous-tone color photograph out of a fuzzy, high-contrast black-and-white microcopy. So I said to the librarians in England.

But my anti-sales pitch wasn't successful—the British librarians had gotten some interesting faxed-in bids from a Pennsylvanian dealer by the time I visited, and, it seemed, they simply wanted his money. And I knew what that meant. It meant box-cutter butchery and plastic-sheathed, issue-by-issue dispersal, and I concluded that the only way to save the collection was to raise the money to buy it and ship it to leased quarters in the United States. So my wife and I—my wife being Margaret Brentano, the editor and caption writer of this book—formed a nonprofit organization, grandiosely named the American Newspaper Repository, though it was really just the two of us overseen by some kindly advisers, and we bought more than six thousand volumes of American newspapers (a volume being anywhere from two weeks' to three months' worth of daily issues), plus another thousand wrapped bundles, most in extraordinarily good condition, all formerly owned by the British government. The cost, including two long runs that we ended up buying from a dealer who had outbid us, was approximately $150,000; the collection arrived in several shipments in 2000.

And that's how we came to be standing at tables in a large chilly brick mill building in Rollinsford, New Hampshire, paging with wonderment through Pulitzer's almost-lost *World*. The mill space we had rented, for two thousand dollars a month, was the size of two, maybe three, tennis courts, with rows of battered, factory-blue metal columns running down it and an inflatable black bat strung near a fire door at the far end. In Pulitzer's day, and well before, the building had held enormous, noisy, oil-dripping looms (which looked somewhat like newspaper printing presses), but when we got there the place had become extremely quiet. Over near the loading dock, the Humpty Dumpty Potato Chip Company stored boxes of barbecue-flavored snacks in metal cages; above us was the ever-shrinking presence of Damart, the French maker of silk underwear, latterly brought low by Asian competition. One of the mill's upper floors was jammed with cast-off hospital equipment—evil-looking gurneys and examination tables, failed heart monitors, vintage monster-movie X-ray machines—all trucked there by a man of mystery and energy who purportedly assembled medical clinics in third-world countries.

A former Damart employee volunteered to build a wall for us and install lights: suddenly we found that we had a huge still expanse with a sign on the door that said AMERICAN

NEWSPAPER REPOSITORY. I put up a few dozen extra-long window shades, because newsprint is better off in the dark, but the late-afternoon sun slipped in along the edges of the window frames and striped the floor with long, dusty blades that crumpled over the backs of volunteers—students, teachers, librarians, my own children—as they unloaded pallet after pallet of newspaper volumes and sorted them into yearly piles by title and date. (The British Library had shipped them to us in semi-random order.) We bought ten-foot-high industrial shelving till we ran out of money. Our shelved run of the *New York Times* was impressive; like a steam locomotive and its tender, it ran down much of the length of the room. Occasionally, students of history or journalism would come and browse through issues, taking notes, sitting on old hospital chairs, or some scholar would visit in search of a specific article or image or theme.

And the *World*? We loved its heavy, vellum-cornered volumes, which smelled faintly of acid paper: 1898 began on the upper left of the shelving, at the very top; one range over, there were the fat monthly tomes from 1903 and 1906 (for some reason I became particularly fond of the year 1906), and then the teens, and then on the other side of the shelves (near windows that, if you peeked under the shades, looked down on the Salmon Falls River), the run ran on through the *World*'s more sophisticated, literary period, when it invented the crossword puzzle, published Dorothy Parker and A. J. Liebling, and exposed the misdeeds of the Ku Klux Klan. Over several months, Margaret went through every *World* volume from 1898 to 1911, the year of Pulitzer's death. "Take a look at this airship!" she called. "You've got to see this Biedermann!" She found scenic wonders and oddities everywhere, marking them with strips of paper, but especially in the Sunday issues, where the *World's* editors and illustrators and writers were obviously having a fantastic time—cackling to themselves, we imagined, as every week they published another vaudeville revue of urban urges and preoccupations. The world should know about the *World,* we felt. Why should an artist such as Dan McCarthy, who gave us "The American Sky-Scraper Is a Modern Tower of Babel," be totally forgotten? You can go to a museum to see the paintings of Ashcan School artist George Luks, but his disturbing newspaper drawings of 1898, "The Persecution Mania" and "All Is Lost Save Honor," exist only on microfilm, as far as I can tell, apart from these pages. The *World's* innovations in page design, in color "electrogravure" printing, in puzzles and children's illustration, in teasingly elaborate charts, and in swervy, swoopy typography are everywhere evident to a modern eye; perhaps it's time to take a preliminary step toward restoring the Sunday paper to its rightful place in the history of American vernacular art.

In the fall of 2003 David Ferriero, then librarian at Duke University, offered to take the entire collection to Duke, where it now safely resides under the care of the Rare Book, Manuscript, and Special Collections Library. But before we packed it back up onto pallets and loaded it onto trucks (five tractor-trailer loads, as it turned out, a hefty gift), we wanted, like proud parents who send their grown child off to college, to take some pictures—not just digital snapshots, either, but real pictures. I first rented, then bought, a view camera and a lens, and I rigged a five-foot-high copy stand out of an old tripod and some cast-iron pipe, and Margaret and I began photographing the pages from the *World* that you see here. We have left the papers exactly as they were originally arranged, that is, in strict chronological order, because one of the delights of the *World*, as of all newspapers, is that it is as utterly miscellaneous as it is date-bound. We have not cut anything out, needless to say—the pages emerge from their respective volumes just where they were sewn by the British Library (then called the British Museum) a century ago. It's time to call an end to the razoring-out of beautiful things for the sake of copying them.

Joseph Pulitzer was all but blind when the art in these pages was first published: the more his own sight dimmed, the more imploringly colorful his paper became. He was too high-strung to appear in public—he was never seen at the *World*'s ornate offices, overlooking City Hall—and he lived mostly on his yacht, where he could get around by feel, traveling from port to port and managing the newspaper via a team of readers and abstractors and long-suffering plenipotentiaries. Through them he kept a close hand on his beloved creation, giving it, he said, every moment of his waking time. In 1898, when the reproductions in this book commence, Pulitzer had just bought a new high-speed color printing press from Richard Hoe & Company. The new press was "all important," Pulitzer wrote; he ordered his editors to "impress this novelty on the public mind as the greatest progress in Sunday journalism." Which they did. "Like rainbow tints in the spray are the hues that splash and pour from its lightning cylinders," said one ad announcing the coming of the new press. It was, said another, "THE MOST MARVELOUS MECHANISM OF THE AGE"—and in some ways it was, for it allowed each citizen, rich or poor, to gain entrance, every Sunday, into a private museum.

So the pictures in this book begin in 1898, with the Spanish-American War. And they close in 1911, the year that Pulitzer died. The Sunday *World* always wanted to surprise:

it exaggerated and sought the bizarre angle and turned small news into big news—but its exaggerations now have truths of their own to tell us. We hope you will find, as we did, that looking at these time-tanned pages gives a sense of the exuberance and modernness and strangeness of the turn-of-the-century city that no history book can easily supply.

*(2005)*

# Sex and the City, Circa 1840

On April 9, 1842, the *Whip*, a weekly New York newspaper that pledged to "keep a watchful eye on all brothels and their frail inmates," carried an article about chambermaids. Chambermaids were women of flesh and blood, according to the article, "with the same instinctive desires as their masters, and much of their time is necessarily passed alone, in remote apartments, which usually contain beds." Accompanying the article was a drawing: a chambermaid gripped the long wooden handle of a warming pan that projected rudely from between a tailcoated gentleman's legs.

The *Whip* was, along with three other newspapers—the *Flash*, the *Rake*, and the *Libertine*—part of what is now called the "flash press": a short-lived public outburst of suggestive talk, threatened blackmail, bare-knuckle boxing, and ornate vituperation that swept through New York in the early 1840s. For nearly 150 years, the flash press was all but forgotten

A review of *The Flash Press: Sporting Male Weeklies in 1840s New York*, by Patricia Cline Cohen, Timothy J. Gilfoyle, and Helen Lefkowitz Horowitz, in association with the American Antiquarian Society (University of Chicago Press, 2008).

by historians—before it was rediscovered by Patricia Cline Cohen, of the University of California, Santa Barbara.

In the late 1980s, Cohen was at the American Antiquarian Society, in Worcester, Massachusetts, researching a book about the sensational murder of Helen Jewett, a nineteenth-century courtesan. The antiquarian society had, as it happened, just bought a large private collection of flash papers from the son of a sportswriter and boxing promoter. Cohen, fascinated, began paging through the issues, taking notes. She told another scholar, Timothy J. Gilfoyle, now of Loyola University in Chicago, about what she'd found, and Gilfoyle cited the papers in *City of Eros,* his 1992 history of New York prostitution. Soon word got out in academia, and now, as the historiography of paid sex has come into vogue, the flash collection is one of the more heavily used holdings in the society's priceless antebellum hoard.

Cohen, Gilfoyle, and a third writer, Helen Lefkowitz Horowitz—a historian at Smith College and the author of *Rereading Sex,* a study of erotica—have together produced *The Flash Press,* the first book-length survey of this strange rock-pool of 1840s profligacy. Readers of Kurt Andersen's recent historical novel *Heyday*—and indeed everyone interested in knowing what New York City was like before the Civil War—will want to have a peek. The authors have managed to unearth and collate a remarkable amount of enriching detail about a curiously fleshy moment in the history of New York publishing.

The primogenitor of the flash press was a brilliant, doomed wretch from Boston named William J. Snelling. Snelling's mother died when he was six; his father was a war hero and a heavy drinker. After dropping out of West Point,

Snelling spent some time living among the Dakota Indians, later writing about them with affection and sympathy in *Tales of the Northwest.* He returned to Boston, went to prison for public drunkenness, worked up that experience into a book—and then, fired by literary ambition, attempted to create the great American *Dunciad:* a long poem called *Truth,* in heroic couplets, attacking many of the minor poets of the day and praising a few. After fifty pages of sharply turned iambic insults, Snelling exhaustedly wrote:

> Now have I thump'd each lout I meant to thump,
> And my worn pen exhibits but a stump.

After *Truth,* what? Versifying, Snelling wrote an editor, had gone flat for him. "I can only write in the excitement of strong feeling," he said. He was living in New York by then, still drinking heavily and spending too much time in the Five Points neighborhood north of City Hall, where members of the frail sisterhood were to be found. Out of this experience he and another editor created *Polyanthos,* in imitation of scandal sheets from Britain.

And then, in the summer of 1841, came Snelling's great innovation, the *Flash*. It was a normal-size weekly newspaper of four pages, set in the usual (i.e., absurdly, illegibly, rag-paper-conservingly tiny) type of the day, with a fancy masthead depicting a dogfight, a leggy ballet dancer, and other racy tropes. (In the back of Cohen, Gilfoyle, and Horowitz's book, you can see a foldout reproduction in miniature of the front page of one issue.) The paper was edited by Snelling, under the pen name Scorpion, along with two other men, Startle and Sly. Startle was George

Wilkes, a snappy dresser and man-about-town who had been arrested for bawdy-house rowdiness in 1836. Sly was George Wooldridge, who ran the Elssler Saloon at 300 Broadway, which sold pickled meats and other delicacies—these could be had in private rooms, "where visitors can sit without observation." Startle and Sly supplied the gossip and tips on brothel life, and Scorpion worked his caustic belletristic magic to produce a paper that was devoted, as it proclaimed, to "Awful Developments, Dreadful Accidents and Unexpected Exposures."

The weekly—sold for six cents by vocal newsboys and carrying advertisements for the Grotto and the Climax eating houses, cheap dress coats, midwifery, and antisyphilitic nostrums like Hunter's Red Drop—was an immediate success, and almost immediately it got into trouble. In the issue of October 17, 1841, appeared one in a series of articles called "Lives of the Nymphs." The article told the story of a rich, successful courtesan, Amanda Green—the tall, full-formed daughter of a dressmaker, who was abducted by a man in a coach and plied with champagne. "At the crowing of the cock she was no more a maid," said the article. Abandoned by her gentleman abuser, she took up with a German piano tuner—after which there was no recourse but a life of open shame. "May those who have not yet sinned, take warning by her example," the *Flash* reporter piously wrote. "She is very handsome. She resides at Mrs. Shannon's, No. 74 West Broadway."

In the same issue as Amanda Green's memoir—the details of which were furnished by "Sly" Wooldridge—was an attack written by Snelling on a Wall Street merchant named Myer Levy. Levy had an enemy, a stockbroker named Emanuel Hart, who fed Wooldridge some specifics of Levy's past, which Wooldridge passed on to Snelling, who dashed off a long, calumnious piece alleging that Levy had worked as a "fancy man" for a prostitute and asserting that he was, among other things, lascivious, sordid, and crapulous.

Levy complained to the New York district attorney, who promptly charged the three proprietors of the *Flash* with criminal libel and, in a separate charge, with obscenity. Wooldridge turned state's evidence and got off. He soon founded a new paper called the *True Flash*, which attacked Snelling: "His best effusions now are the mumblings of a sot," said the article. "What has he left but to crawl his way through the world, leaving his slime behind him." Snelling went to jail briefly on the obscenity charge (the ramifications of which are nicely elucidated in *The Flash Press*), and then, remarkably, when he emerged a few months later, he and Wooldridge made up and joined forces again in a new paper, the *Whip*—which was like the *Flash* but slightly racier and a little more careful about libel.

The burst of published indecorum reached its peak in the summer of 1842—indeed, as the authors of *The Flash Press* show, the use of the very words "licentious" and "licentiousness" in American periodicals rose from about 1,500 instances in 1830 to 3,000 in 1842, plummeting again thereafter. By that summer, there were two more flash rags, the *Rake* and the *Libertine,* and a printer and cartoonist named Robinson was busy selling dirty drawings with titles like "Do You Like This Sort of Thing?" It was all too much for James Whiting, the district attorney, who began issuing indictments right and left. The *Flash* and the *Whip* managed to continue in the face of legal troubles and editorial turnover until 1843, threatening malefactors with exposure, interviewing half-naked women in the park, excoriating sodomites, and writing up the beauties and the dress designs to be found in the richest bordellos. (One personality, Mary Walker, wore crimson embroidered silk: "Praxiteles never chiseled a more exquisite form, and Canova would have died in the vain endeavour to mould a bust like her own," the *Whip* reported.)

Then it was all over. Snelling left for Boston, where he rejoined his third wife and became editor of the *Boston Herald*. He was "the father of the smutty papers," said a writer in the *Rake*. "What would any of us have been without him?" Snelling died broke but legitimate in 1848, mourned as a pillar of the Boston scene.

Recently I drove to Worcester to see these papers in the original. There they were: large, light-brown scholarly objects, protected by acid-free folders, stored on cool shelves with brass rollers—full of strange lost scandal. In some fragile issues—those saved by the Queens College professor Leo Hershkowitz from masses of historical documents discarded by the City of New York in the 1970s—there are notations and cartoonish pointing fingers drawn by District Attorney Whiting himself, as he contemplated possible grounds for indictment. In one issue I read an editorial: "The Flash is known all over the Union," it said; "at the South it goes like wildfire." Like Al Goldstein's weekly *Screw*, which flourished more than a century later, the flash papers told a nervous young reader what was out there—where to go, how to act, and what to expect. "The Sunday *Flash* and its successors gave male readers paths to navigate the city without being conned or embarrassed as a greenhorn," Cohen, Gilfoyle, and Horowitz write. "Even a shy fellow who stayed in his boardinghouse could imagine himself as a blade making a sophisticated entry into a brothel parlor."

Thanks to the preservation efforts of the American Antiquarian Society and the meticulous research of these three scholars, we once again have a way of looking through a tiny, smudged window into New York's long-past illicit life. Oh, and the drawing of the chambermaid and her warming pan is on page 101.

*(2008)*

# Technology

# Grab Me a Gondola

Twelve years ago, I stood on the steps of the church of the Gesuati with a ceremonial handkerchief in my suit pocket, and watched my soon-to-be wife set out with her father from the far side of Venice's widest and deepest-dredged waterway, the Giudecca Canal. The sky was the color of Istrian stone—i.e., white—and the water looked choppy. Their boat leaned to one side (all gondolas lean, but I didn't know that then): sunk low among the silk-tufted cushions of their Byzantine conveyance, the passengers seemed to have their heads almost at water level. I worried that a large swell might slosh in unexpectedly from the side and capsize them.

The oarsman at the stern, Bruno Palmarin, had been endorsed by the local grocer. His grandfathers, his father, his older brother, and various uncles and cousins were gondoliers before him; members of the Palmarin family have rowed continuously since at least 1740. Nowadays, when Bruno does weddings, his nineteen-year-old son, Giacomo, is usually the second rower. Their boat is black, of course, in compliance with ancient decree (there is in fact a paint color called nero gondola), the oar blades are red-and-white-striped, matching the rowers' wedding shirts, and over the sleeves of their white jackets they wear red armbands bearing the Palmarin family emblem (lion and palm tree) in four-inch lozenges of brass. Embellishing the gunwales are gilded cherubs that tug at bridles of black spiraling silk—these replicate the fittings of the state gondola owned by King Victor Emmanuel III. Most gondolas have a proverb cast in a decorative ribbon of brass just in front of the passenger well. Bruno's was written for his grandfather, Ambrogio Palmarin, by Gabriele d'Annunzio, the poet: *Ogni alba a il suo tramonto* ("Every dawn to its dusk").

Bruno doesn't row out onto the Giudecca Canal anymore unless a job like our wedding specifically requires it. When he was a boy, traffic on the canal was light enough that he could swim all the way across, returning on the *traghetto,* or two-oared gondola shuttle, that operated into the 1960s; but in recent years it has become a major thoroughfare, a sort of truck route, and its water is abob with the cross-purposed wakes of a vast range of boats: mid-sized motor-launches, ramp-prowed car ferries, crane barges, tugboats, tiny fiberglass speed-wedges banging from one swell to the next with a sound of lawn mowers, eight-story Greek cruise vessels thrumming past like insurance companies that have come laterally adrift, and oval, flat-roofed *vaporetti* swerving in loose S-shapes from shore to shore. Each spreading wave-system is reflected from the quaysides back into the central confusion. You may see ten boats, but you know that the water is mumblingly remembering the previous twenty-five. Only very late at night does the surface revert to its pre-propellerine calm.

This abundance of manufactured chop—known to Venetians by the ominous name of *moto ondoso*—accelerates the decay of the city's foundational stonework. And it makes life difficult for the venturesome gondolier, who stands upright on a bit of carpet high on the upcurving tailpiece of a half-ton craft without a keel, trying, as he and his counterweighted, steel-pronged prow seesaw unrestrainedly, to propel it forward with one oar levered against a gnarl of polished walnut. His boat, with its sinuous, side-rocking way of proceeding by self-correctingly veering off course, is a curiosity, maybe even a marvel, of evolved hydrodynamics, but its peculiar nautical graces and efficiencies only assert themselves when it moves over relatively smooth water. A number of gondoliers say that the Giudecca Canal is dangerous. Bruno Palmarin avoids it not because it frightens him but because he thinks he looks out of place there. "In the choppy water, when you are struggling, when you are *distrait,* you feel ridiculous," he said to me. "You feel like a clown."

But on our wedding day, my veiled *fidanzata*—a gutsier import-word perhaps than the prissy-sounding *fiancée*—had a good time going across. "Out in the middle of the canal it was perfect," she says now. "Everything looked silver, or lead-colored, and misty. I don't remember its being choppy at all." We got married, walked out the front door through a spray of rice, and stepped into life's long boat together. It was dark by then; the red carpet in the passenger well glowed. The backboard behind our two seats was carved with some gold-leaf mermaids; its peaked shape, and the tapering form of the bow reaching ahead of us into the shadows, made me think of the Batmobile. There were two small gilded chairs for the best man (my father) and the maid of honor, Minette, with her beautiful smile. We began to move. We surged in the dark up a narrow canal, the San Vio, going surprisingly fast. At the Grand Canal, my father said, "If you're going to go, this is definitely the way to go." As a partial wedding present he gave us a plastic model of a gondola with a little red lightbulb in its gold cabin. We proudly displayed it on a side table in our first apartment, and then, when we moved, it got packed away in a box marked "Toys," and I didn't give gondolas another thought for a long time.

A year ago, we returned to Venice for the summer, to stay in my wife's parents' apartment on the island of the Giudecca. The first week, we did a lot of walking in the crowded trinket-lanes near the Rialto and San Marco, which are difficult to maneuver in with a three-year-old. A man walked into me, holding me momentarily by both arms, and immediately afterward my wife discovered that her wallet had been stolen; later I scolded a teenager on the piazza for luring a pigeon close to him with a handful of corn and then kicking it like a soccer ball. (The pigeon seemed all right afterward.) The second week, my wife had a dream in which her tongue was a large black dog that she had to take out for a walk. It was a sign. We were doing too much walking. The next day, we went on our first family gondola ride. The experience was startlingly pleasant—like sinking down in a warm bathtub, except drier, and with more interesting scenery. In aquatic shade, we turned tight corners in our long manual limousine, clearing edges of powdery brick by a quarter of an inch, admiring an occasional commemorative plaque (Byron is still big), with sunlight and strangely inverted conical chimneys and life-evincing laundry high overhead. There was no bad smell. My three-year-old son put his head in my lap and went to sleep; my nine-year-old daughter pointed out that the disintegrating doorways and passing tableaux were like Disney's *Pirates of the Caribbean*. Some French women on a bridge flirtatiously chided the gondolier, who had a fluffy ponytail and wraparound sunglasses, about his lack of a hat. Occasionally a thirties-looking wood-paneled water taxi disturbed our Edwardian trance as it dieseled by with the ruminative sound of toilets flushing. The people on it detached their faces from the rubber flanges of their video cameras for an instant and looked at us wistfully. They had thought they were being very clever by hiring a water taxi, since you can go so much farther in one; but now, seeing our silent, artful, blissful progress, our movement at the ideal speed of architectural self-disclosure, they were less sure: maybe they, too, should have gone for the gondola.

Without warning, I felt the sob-of-family-happiness-welling-up-during-an-expensive-vacation feeling. *We had gone for the gondola.* It wasn't a tritely touristic boat, though its steel spaghetti-fork of a *ferro* intrudes in every etching; it was an ancient and noble boat, which summed up many lost beautiful things, and Venice itself seemed worth all the guidebooked fuss. Any means of transportation that could produce that much joy in fifty minutes, for a cost of a little over a hundred dollars, including tip, deserved further study.

In the Palladian library at San Giorgio Maggiore I read "The Evolution of the Venetian Gondola," by G. B. Rubin de Cervin, which attributes the boat's un-Palladian asymmetry—its "deviation from the curvature of the central line"—to the increasing use of one rower, rather than two, in the poorer times that followed Napoleon's subjugation of the Venetian Republic. And I read "The Energy Cost of the Venetian Rowing Stroke," in Carlo Donatelli's personable and quaintly translated book *The Gondola: An Extraordinary Naval Architecture:* Donatelli's dynamometer readings and measurements of oxygen consumption seem to suggest, remarkably, that you expend the same amount of energy rowing a loaded gondola at a speed of two miles an hour as you would walking empty-handed on flat ground at the same speed. (Which explains how gondoliers can work fifteen-hour days during the busy season.) I read also Goethe's description of his father's toy gondola, which first made him want to visit Venice and record his adventures there, thus luring south a poetical crowd of Romantic and Victorian followers. And I learned that plastic model gondolas, probably identical to the one my father gave us, had a vogue in Germany in the fifties, where they went on top of television sets and were called *rauchverzehren,* which means "smoke-eaters," because their lights supposedly neutralized the effects of cigarette smoke.

We went on several more gondola rides. On a very windy morning, we got on a boat manned by a square-jawed regatta champion named Franco Grossi, a seventh-generation oarsman and a practitioner of Eastern medicine, to whom colleagues went for help with the sort of ailments (e.g., tennis elbow and back pain) that afflict rowers. I told him I wanted to use the gondola the way people would have used it in the nineteenth century, simply as a means of getting somewhere. Could he take us to the Ponte dei Pugni, or Bridge of Fists, where according to the *Blue Guide* there was an English-language bookstore? Grossi said nobody did that sort of thing anymore in a gondola—went from Ponte A to Ponte B. Everyone went in loops and ended up where they started. "But I like doing crazy things," he said. He untied the ropes and we pushed back, as a passenger plane does, from his mooring near the Doge's Palace. The gondola slots are defined by many thin twiglike sticks projecting vertically from the water; they give the hotel-crowded shoreline the appearance of fronting on a reedy marsh. We bobbed along for a while, and then, as we got closer to the mouth of the Grand Canal, there was a major gust of wind that made fine crinkles on the top of all the swells. The gust, combined with some large heaves from a ferry, made us suddenly slide around sideways, facing the Church of the Salute. I heard a "Wow!" behind me and thought Grossi had fallen off. But he hadn't. "There was a little problem back there," he conceded a few minutes later. The gondola is flat-bottomed, he said, and the wind, under certain rare conditions, can get under it and flip it over.

Things were quieter once we entered the San Trovaso canal and slid past a boatyard, or *squero*, where there are often three or four gondolas turned on their sides like dozing dugongs, having their hulls sanded down and repainted. Then we turned right on All-Saint's Canal, and right again on the Canal of Lawyers, and Grossi pointed out the center of gondola history—the shop of the Brothers Tramontin. Domenico (El Grando) Tramontin perfected the modern gondola's asymmetries in the 1880s, and Grossi was of the opinion that the Brothers Tramontin continue to make the best and longest-lived gondolas. But they cost ten million lire more than anyone else's, Grossi said. His own boat is the work of "Nino" Giuponi, another *squerarolo* of legend, now retired. Giuponi was more of an experimenter than the later Tramontins; he introduced the use of plywood in some of his boats, which some disparage, although it can help the hull keep its shape in the presence of constant motorwaves.

Finally we reached the Bridge of Fists. The bookstore was gone. Its old shelves were holding lettuces and radishes, overflow from the highly successful produce barge that moors there. But it didn't matter. We bought some spinach and went home—altogether a delightful trip.

Then, in my son's sleepy company, I took a ride with a
pilot named Marco, who worked at the gondola station at the
Church of the Salute and looked like Billy Crystal. When I
asked Marco what the most difficult thing was about being a
gondolier, he thought for a moment. "The other gondoliers,"
he said. "Mostly the old gondoliers. They have small brains,
believe me." As we passed the Church of San Trovaso, where
there is an altar for boatbuilders with a gondola carved
into it, Marco got a call on his portable phone. He set up
a rendezvous while ducking under a bridge. We went by
Tramontin's boatyard, deserted now except for a small brown
dog sniffing some new sawdust. We got onto the subject of
boat maintenance. It's important, Marco said, to wash your
boat for half an hour every day. "It's what my father teach to
me, when I was young. Every day. With new water, not salt
water. New water the gondola, then you dry the gondola."

"Some gondoliers seem very good—" I began to say.

Marco misheard the word "seem" and cut in. "Believe
me, sir," Marco said with a self-deprecating laugh, "but I
have a horrible voice. Better not to sing, just enjoy the nice
weather." In his father's time, twenty or thirty years ago, a
family would hire a gondola for the whole day, he said. I
asked how much it would cost to do that now. "I think eight
hundred thousand lire."

That's a pretty steep day rate, but (I said to myself)
one total-immersion gondolar day—with a micro-cruise
budget of 450 dollars—would give a visitor new to Venice a
comprehensive oar's-eye notion of the several neighborhoods
and many churches. And each bought ride would have a
political component: it would be an act of defiance against
the water taxis and other arriviste wave-generators, a vote for
a quieter city, something more than mere tourism. Why not

skip the twelfth or fifteenth absurdly expensive meal in which three kinds of pale shellfish are mingled with a noodle of little distinction and instead buy eight dollars' worth of cheese and olives and whatnot at the local *salumeria* and eat out at twilight in the very kind of boat that kings and popes and moody poets would have ridden in?

Next door to the Tramontin brothers' *squero* is a gondola shop run by Daniele Bonaldo. A twenty-four-year-old American anthropology student named Thomas Price recently built a life-size gondola there with the help of a Watson Fellowship. Bonaldo is childless and says he's tired of building boats, so he agreed to teach the art to Price. On the tenth of May I went to a party at Bonaldo's place to celebrate "The Launching of the First American Gondola." Price's boat looked authentic— black, with a dark-red hull and a small, tasteful, delicately rendered American flag, breeze-ruffled, carved into one of the decorative elements by an itinerant artisan. Price has built sailboats and rowboats in Maine, but he was attracted to the gondola, he told me, because there are many unusual things about it. Not only is it asymmetrical and rowed in a standing position—but also its components are bent into shape by brushing them with water over a fire of marsh reeds (a blowtorch will also work and is handier in the winter), and they are assembled without paper plans, by cutting the pieces in accordance with a wooden template, the *cantier.* The prosecco that Price poured on the prow to christen the boat mixed with the sun-warmed and not-completely-cured black lacquer to produce an inspiring Saturday-morning smell. Price told me that he would like his gondola to be rowed on the canals of Venice, but it may be that a couple of entrepreneurs in Maine buy it for a novelty riverboat service there: it's Bonaldo's boat to sell.

Before I left the party I talked to Price's sister, Anne. She was living in Mestre, making a living playing North Carolina fiddle music on the steps of Venetian churches, which is forbidden without a busker's license. I asked her if she had ever ridden in a gondola. One time she was walking across a bridge, she said, and a young, handsome gondolier with long blond hair offered her a free ride. She said okay. They went down a sludgy canal by a conservatory, where she could hear pianos and clarinets, and then out onto the Grand Canal. The whole time the gondolier was saying how sorry he was that she had no one to be kissing while she was riding the gondola. I asked her if the two of them had hit it off. "We hit it off," she said, "but I maintained my distance. I see him from time to time. It's like a musical skill to be able to row a gondola. When I see gondoliers just standing all day on bridges, saying *Gondola, gondola,* waiting, it's like they're begging. It's so similar to me when I play violin on the street, waiting for somebody to stop and listen." Her gondolier's name was Eros.

Eros the Oarboy is as familiar today as he was in *Lady Chatterley's Lover,* where Giovanni the gondolier is "devoted to his ladies, as he had been devoted to cargoes of ladies in the past." At night there is, I have noticed, a considerable amount of giggly public gondolier-kissing in the city by groups of foreign women carrying bottles of wine. My wife made up a song: *Come into my gondola, I'm going to fondle ya.* Once, in the middle of the Grand Canal at ten o'clock in the evening, we passed a gondola that was sitting motionless on the water with two women and two stripe-shirted men in close converse within; one of the men greeted our rower and called out (my wife translated for me), "How do you say 'double bed' in Spanish?"

All this is as it should be. My minor complaint is just that there is no privacy available to the passengers of these boats—privacy not to go hog wild, necessarily, but simply to talk without constraint. You are compelled to take the waters in a convertible. The *felze* (wooden winter cabin) and *tendalin* (canvas summer hood) were renounced forty or fifty years ago—too time-consuming to set up, and unnecessary, it was thought, for the demands of tourism. Unless these traditional enclosures are revived, the conventional tender moment on the water will be forever inhibited by the steady oar-plying and tour-guiding going on abaft. You tentatively take the spousal hand, and then hear, from behind, "This is Goethe house. Goethe lived in this house." All potential romance has been realigned in favor of the presiding gondolier himself. Male passengers are adjuncts, balding lumps of flesh with wallets.

The one real love story I know between a gondolier and a *straniéra* is the one between Bruno Palmarin, the profusely mustached hereditary gondolier who rowed at our wedding, and Susan Nickerson, an American mosaicist. Susie grew up in Long Island, the daughter of two judges. She came to Venice in 1972 after art school to study mosaic-making. Late in December, on her birthday, she went alone to Torcello. The sacristan unlocked the church for her; she was the only person there. Then she got a boat back to Venice and went to an antique store where she knew some people. She told them it was her birthday, and they bought a bottle of spumanti to celebrate. Just then Bruno Palmarin came by—a big, polite man carrying two baby rabbits in a cage. (They were a Christmas present for his niece and nephew.) Bruno looked a little like the bust of the Emperor Constantine, Susie thought: the same large, spiritual eyes. Later she found out he was a gondolier.

When Bruno finished work for the day, he would hitch his gondola like a horse not far from Peggy Guggenheim's palazzo (Bruno's father was Peggy Guggenheim's gondolier for a time), in the little canal where Susie shared a mosaic studio with a Russian woman. He would peek in the little window that was in the door and greet her; she would scoop away the wet cement from her work-in-progress (she was using pieces of old mirror-glass a lot then) and come out with him. In time Susie learned to row herself, and they rowed a lot—to the Rialto to shop, to entertain dinner guests, to carry Susie's heavy mosaics to her show. They, together with an American man and Bruno's brother Ambrogio (who was a gondolier until elbow problems forced him to become a businessman), competed in the first Vogalonga in 1975—the Vogalonga being a noncompetitive marathon open to any kind of international oar-powered craft. "She should be home washing the dishes!" some people called from the shore (in Italian). Others called out, *"Viva la donna!"*

They got married in Venice's City Hall in 1978; their first child, Giacomo, learned the basics of rowing when he was two, by holding a broom and standing in a wooden cradle that Bruno had built for him. Giacomo is now eighteen; he is not sure whether he wants to be a trumpet player, or a gondolier, or both. Last year he won the youth-division Regata Storica and every other race he entered. I asked him if he had any rowing tips. "You have to make the boat always go forwards and not go back," he said. "The oar has to come in strong to come out sweetly and then go back fast." Bruno is not a regatta-racer himself, but Giacomo admires his father's virtuosity. "Everybody can go fast, if you train," he said, "but not everybody can go fast in the canals."

Bruno has the *ferri,* the prow and stern ornaments, of various relatives mounted on the walls and ceilings of their house. He recently spent three winters renovating an ornately filigreed *felze* made around the turn of the century, the sort of thing that Henry James or William Dean Howells would have cruised around in. ("I don't know where, on the lagoon, my gondolier took me," James wrote; "we floated aimlessly and with slow rare strokes.") Bruno has a collection of old gondola components he keeps in a low-ceilinged storage room near where he grew up, in the Dorsoduro. (His family moved to the Giudecca in 1960, after canal water began flooding into Bruno's room.) On the wall are portraits of gondolier relatives, old paintings of regatta champions, and a photograph of Susie and him leaving City Hall on their wedding day. The radio is always softly playing. "I like old things, anyway," he said as he uncovered more and more of his collection of cloth-shrouded gondoliana. He owns two gondolas—the one that he rowed for our wedding (which seemed plenty fancy to us at the time), and a budget-busting wedding sloop that he commissioned Tramontin to make for him in 1990. Its stern-piece is an elegant twist of steel curving around a fernlike decorative whorl incised with the Palmarin coat of arms and the initials "PB." ("Handmade by a friend of mine," Bruno said.) The chairs are the ones his uncle used on his wedding gondola, re-gilded; Susie made the embroidered pillows and found the putti-and-flower pattern that the wood-carver chipped into the top panels. On the prow there is a small gold man holding a bottle of wine that Bruno had cast from a statue on an old clock he owns—the figure serves, as Bruno sees it, as the hostly Bacchus, saluting all passenger-guests and wishing them a good journey in his boat. Bruno hesitates to say how much it all cost: "Thirty thousand dollars would not be enough," he says. The boat's name is *Aurelia Stephanie*, after his daughter.

I walked with Bruno one morning to pick up the sealed results of a heart test from the Ospedale Civile. He tore open the white envelope on the front steps of the building, in front of a fifteenth-century trompe l'oeil stone facade, but the results were numerical and abbreviated and impossible to interpret. Not long ago he experienced what he calls "an episode of fast heartbeating" during an argument over the phone with Giacomo. He hasn't felt any flutters while he is rowing, though. Inactivity is his enemy. "The more I work hard, the better I feel. If I fatigue, if I feel nice and tired, I feel much better." One of the difficult things about his job is the waiting—standing in the heat in front of the Doge's Palace. Passersby ask him the same questions hundreds of times a day, and have their pictures taken next to him as if he's a monument. The sunlight reflects off the walls of the palace and off the water; it is like standing in a toaster.

We stopped at the Rialto at a small clothing store; I stood outside guarding a wicker basket that Bruno had found in a pile of trash by a canal while Bruno went inside and bought two pairs of black gondolier's pants. Then he told me another story about his grandfather Ambrogio. "In the winter, there was very little to support the family, but he was a grand man," he said. Ambrogio had a big red handkerchief, in which he put three cabbages. "Then he bought three necks of turkey—only the necks. He pinned the necks of turkey outside the handkerchief, and the cabbages were inside. Passing by San Vio like that—he wanted everybody to think he had three turkeys inside."

Bruno's childhood was not prosperous, either. He is self-educated; he left school after fifth grade and got a job carrying boxes of tripe across town on his shoulder. Later he worked for an old gondolier, cleaning out his boat and doing substitute work. Eventually he inherited his father and grandfather's gondolier's license. The licenses are valuable nowadays, like cab medallions. Recently someone introduced a measure that would prohibit the transfer of a license to one's offspring. "Someone would make me not be able to give it to my son, eventually?" Bruno asks, incredulously. "No, no, ridiculous." It was voted down. On the other hand, Bruno half hopes that he is the last Palmarin gondolier—that Giacomo will choose a different profession. "Not that I don't like this job, but I think sometimes it is restricted, if you know what I mean, limited."

He thinks of owning a place in the mountains, far from boats, and raising land creatures—horses, pigs, chickens. Venice can seem paved-over and confining. English and French he learned by spending winters abroad when he was in his twenties. "It didn't mean when I went to Paris I did the grand life, or to London. But—*ah!*—I breathe more. The life here was to be a gondolier, to get *fiancé* with some nice young Venetian and then eventually get married, and then, that is life." When he met Susie it was different. "Modestly, I had some opportunities here," he said. "But she was not suffocating. A Venetian woman would be suffocating, you see. And so something grew in between us. She very often says to me, 'You should have married a Venetian woman, cooking well, and so on.' But she doesn't know how much happy she made me, anyway."

If Giacomo does decide in time to be a gondolier, he can expect to make a comfortable, if seasonal, living. Tariffs have risen steadily, and each gondolier is a member of a cooperative that pools income and pays a percentage of health insurance and pension expenses. "The gondola is alive because of money," Bruno reminded me. "I am no angel myself." But Bruno is troubled by how narrowly income-obsessed some of his colleagues are now. They are relinquishing their traditional roles as ambassadors and civic proxies. "There used to be a gondolier who was called *Zar delle Russie,* 'Russian Czar,' because he was a very pompous guy," Bruno told me. "When somebody came to Venice, he used to go to Piazza San Marco and say, 'The gondoliers welcome you, sir.' And shake the hand. It was a bit of pathos, if you like. But it was done in an elegant way. Now gondoliers, what are they? We have no identity anymore. We have no past. We have put everything in money."

Relations with City Hall are not good these days, either. When some kooks recently hijacked a ferryboat and occupied Saint Mark's with the help of a cardboard tank, a famous Italian television commentator announced that he would be spending the next day in the square. The gondoliers, through their official representatives, lodged a protest with the city, saying that the TV equipment would interfere with their business and they wanted due compensation. Bruno thinks that was a mistake. "Our image is more important than immediate money, you see. The image pays in the long term." Formerly gondoliers rowed political dignitaries and racing champions during annual celebrations like the Regata Storica or the Sensa (the day in which the mayor of Venice celebrates the city's marriage to the sea by tossing a ring into the water out by the Lido, while a man with a microphone adds booming color commentary); now the four-oared boats of honor are manned by volunteer members of the city's rowing clubs. "It is true that the city spares money by giving these services to the rowing clubs," Bruno says. "But I was one of those on the table who said, 'No, no, no, *we* must do that. Who if not the gondoliers? We should do that for free. One day a year, we should pay our people, in order to take a place there."

Much of the ill-feeling between the city and the gondoliers is a result of the rampancy of *moto ondoso*. Speed limits are posted on the Giudecca and the Grand Canal—11 kilometers per hour for vaporetti-buses, 7 for water trucks, and 5 for water taxis—but they are seldom enforced. The gondoliers want "strict repression," by which they mean traffic cops who will stop motormen—especially water-taxi drivers—from speeding and behaving recklessly. But the motormen evidently have powerful friends. At a big *moto ondoso* conference in June that I went to, under the eighteenth-century painted ceiling of the Venice Atheneum, a group of tough-looking water-taxi drivers with gold jewelry stood along the wall, arms crossed, and jeered audibly throughout a slide presentation of decaying stonework and leaping dual-engine boats. "They are brutes," says Bruno. "They are savages. They should be thrown out the window."

In principle, gondoliers have nothing against engines. Bruno's gondola cooperative (the Ducale) owns ten big excursion launches, each carrying from thirty to fifty passengers; it also maintains the only reduced-wave water taxi in the city, the Eco, which has a lower-horsepower engine and a hull that does a better job of healing its transient water wound. In 1988, Bruno put his gondola in dry dock and drove a water taxi for a year. He returned to the oar, though, because, he said, "I wasn't sweating enough." Sweating rowers created the Venetian Republic, one recalls; the gondola is a direct link back to the glory days, when fifty-oared, ocean-roaming triremes earned or stole for the city its Renaissance fortune. The gondola's prow, not the Evinrude's screw, is Venice's omnipresent postcard symbol for good reason, and it would be sad if unregulated motor traffic succeeded in sweeping the chaotic waters in front of St. Mark's as free of black boats as the Giudecca Canal is now.

Bruno's idea these days is for the creation of an elite corps of rowing police. Each would patrol a section of the city, standing up, using a smaller type of boat called a *s'ciopon*. Such floating mounties used to exist; because their boats were smaller and nimbler than the existing police motorboats, they could keep an eye on the narrow canals, too, which are now sometimes completely blocked by scofflaws. Oar-cops would be able to feel for themselves the destabilizing effect of waves in a way that existing Polizia and Caribinieri can't; they would know better what gondoliers contend with every day. "But if I talk like that with someone, they think I come from Mars," Bruno told me.

Shouldn't it be possible to institute an *ora-remi*—an oar hour, or two, in the middle of the afternoon (when business slows down anyway) during which only human-powered vehicles would be allowed on all the canals of Venice? Several big four- or six-oared barges, like the baroque *burchielli* that once plied the river Brenta to and from Padua, could then peaceably proceed, stuffed with happy map-flapping tourists, from San Marco up the Grand Canal, in place of the ubiquitously groaning No. 1 vaporetto. Imagine daylit water that had calmed down enough to reflect, as it once did, the Redentore or the porphyritic palazzi disappearing around the curve of the Grand Canal. Imagine the water-taxi men chewing at their toothpicks from the sidelines. Imagine the history-sheltering silence. Gondolas would pour from their moorings to celebrate, wedding bells would swing in their leaning towers, women would kiss their husbands or their gondoliers, and everyone would weep and spend lots of money.

*(1998)*

# The Charms of Wikipedia

Wikipedia is just an incredible thing. It's fact-encirclingly huge, and it's idiosyncratic, careful, messy, funny, shocking, and full of simmering controversies—and it's free, and it's fast. In a few seconds you can look up, for instance, "Diogenes of Sinope," or "turnip," or "Crazy Eddie," or "Bagoas," or "quadratic formula," or "Bristol Beaufighter," or "squeegee," or "Sanford B. Dole," and you'll have knowledge you didn't have before. It's like some vast aerial city with people walking briskly to and fro on catwalks, carrying picnic baskets full of nutritious snacks.

More people use Wikipedia than Amazon or eBay—in fact, it's up there in the top-ten Alexa rankings with those moneyed funhouses MySpace, Facebook, and YouTube. Why? Because it has 2.2 million articles, and because it's very often the first hit in a Google search, and because it just feels good to find something there—even, or especially, when the article you find is maybe a little clumsily written. Any inelegance, or typo, or relic of vandalism reminds you that this gigantic encyclopedia isn't a commercial product. There are no banners for E*Trade or Classmates.com, no side sprinklings of AdSense.

It was constructed, in less than eight years, by strangers who disagreed about all kinds of things but who were drawn to a shared, not-for-profit purpose. They were drawn because for a work of reference Wikipedia seemed unusually humble. It asked for help, and when it did, it used a particularly affecting word: "stub." At the bottom of a short article about something, it would say, "This article about X is a stub. You can help Wikipedia by expanding it." And you'd think, That poor sad stub: I will help. Not right now, because I'm writing a book, but someday, yes, I will try to help.

And when people did help they were given a flattering name. They weren't called "Wikipedia's little helpers," they were called "editors." It was like a giant community leaf-raking project in which everyone was called a groundskeeper. Some brought very fancy professional metal rakes, or even back-mounted leaf-blowing systems, and some were just kids thrashing away with the sides of their feet or stuffing handfuls in the pockets of their sweatshirts, but all the leaves they brought to the pile were appreciated. And the pile grew and everyone jumped up and down in it having a wonderful time. And it grew some more, and it became the biggest leaf pile anyone had ever seen anywhere, a world wonder. And then self-promoted leaf-pile guards appeared, doubters and deprecators who would look askance at your proffered handful and shake their heads, saying that your leaves were too crumpled or too slimy or too common, throwing them to the side. And that was too bad. The people who guarded the leaf pile this way were called "deletionists."

But that came later. First it was just fun. One anonymous contributor wrote, of that early time:

> I adored the Wikipedia when it was first launched and I contributed to a number of articles, some extensively, and always anonymously. The Wikipedia then was a riot of contributors, each adding bits and pieces to the articles they were familiar with, with nary an admin or editor in sight.

It worked and grew because it tapped into the heretofore unmarshaled energies of the uncredentialed. The thesis procrastinators, the history buffs, the passionate fans of the alternate universes of Garth Nix, Robotech, *Half-Life*, P. G. Wodehouse, *Battlestar Galactica, Buffy the Vampire Slayer*, Charles Dickens, or Ultraman—all those people who hoped that their years of collecting comics or reading novels or staring at TV screens hadn't been a waste of time—would pour the fruits of their brains into Wikipedia, because Wikipedia added up to something. This wasn't like writing reviews on Amazon, where you were just one of a million people urging a tiny opinion and a Listmania list onto the world—this was an effort to build something that made sense apart from one's own opinion, something that helped the whole human cause roll forward.

Wikipedia was the point of convergence for the self-taught and the expensively educated. The cranks had to consort with the mainstreamers and hash it all out—and nobody knew who really knew what he or she was talking about, because everyone's identity was hidden behind a jokey username. All everyone knew was that the end product had to make legible sense and sound encyclopedic. It had to be a little flat—a little generic—fair-minded—

compressed—unpromotional—neutral. The need for the outcome of all edits to fit together as readable, unemotional sentences muted—to some extent—natural antagonisms. So there was this exhilarating sense of mission—of proving the greatness of the Internet through an unheard-of collaboration. Very smart people dropped other pursuits and spent days and weeks and sometimes years of their lives doing "stub dumps," writing ancillary software, categorizing and linking topics, making and remaking and smoothing out articles—without getting any recognition except for the occasional congratulatory barnstar on their user page and the satisfaction of secret fame. Wikipedia flourished partly because it was a shrine to altruism—a place for shy, learned people to deposit their trawls.

But it also became great because it had a head start: from the beginning the project absorbed articles from the celebrated 1911 edition of the *Encyclopedia Britannica,* which is in the public domain. And not only the 1911 *Britannica.* Also absorbed were Smith's *Dictionary of Greek and Roman Biography,* Nuttall's 1906 *Encyclopedia,* Chambers's *Cyclopedia,* Aiken's *General Biography,* Rose's *Biographical Dictionary,* Easton's *Bible Dictionary,* and many others. In August 2001, a group of articles from W. W. Rouse Ball's *Short Account of the History of Mathematics*— posted on the Net by a professor from Trinity College, Dublin—was noticed by an early Wikipedian, who wrote to his co-volunteers: "Are they fair game to grab as source material for our wikipedia? I know we are scarfing stuff from the 1911 encyclopedia, this is from 1908, so it should be under the same lack of restrictions. . . ." It was. Rouse Ball wrote that Pierre Varignon was an intimate friend of Newton, Leibniz, and the Bernoullis and, after l'Hopital, was the earliest and most powerful advocate in France of the use of differential calculus. In January 2006, Wikipedia imported this 1908 article, with an insertion and a few modernizing rewordings, and it now reads:

> Varignon was a friend of Newton, Leibniz, and the Bernoulli family. Varignon's principal contributions were to graphic statics and mechanics. Except for l'Hôpital, Varignon was the earliest and strongest French advocate of differential calculus.

But the article is now three times longer, barnacled with interesting additions, and includes a link to another article discussing Varignon's mechanical theory of gravitation.

The steady influx of top-hat-and-spatted sources elevated Wikipedia's tone. This wasn't just a school encyclopedia, a back-yard *Encarta*—this was drinks at the faculty club. You looked up Diogenes, and bang, you got something wondrously finished-sounding from the 1911 *Britannica*. That became Diogenes' point of departure. And then all kinds of changes happened to the Greek philosopher, over many months and hundreds of revisions—odd theories, prose about the habits of dogs, rewordings, corrections of corrections. Now in Wikipedia there is this summary of Diogenes' provocations:

> Diogenes is said to have eaten (and, once, masturbated) in the marketplace, urinated on some people who insulted him, defecated in the theatre, and pointed at people with his middle finger.

And yet amid the modern aggregate, some curvy prose from the 1911 *Britannica* still survives verbatim:

> Both in ancient and in modern times, his personality has appealed strongly to sculptors and to painters.

The fragments from original sources persist like those stony bits of classical buildings incorporated in a medieval wall.

But the sources and the altruism don't fully explain why Wikipedia became such a boomtown. The real reason it grew so fast was noticed by cofounder Jimmy "Jimbo" Wales in its first year of life. "The main thing about Wikipedia is that it is fun and addictive," Wales wrote. Addictive, yes. All big Internet successes—e-mail, AOL chat, Facebook, Gawker, *Second Life,* YouTube, *Daily Kos, World of Warcraft*—have a more or less addictive component—they hook you because they are solitary ways to be social: you keep checking in, peeking in, as you would to some noisy party going on downstairs in a house while you're trying to sleep.

Brion Vibber, who was for a while Wikipedia's only full-time employee, explained the attraction of the encyclopedia at a talk he gave to Google employees in 2006. For researchers it's a place to look stuff up, Vibber said, but for editors "it's almost more like an online game, in that it's a community where you hang out a bit, and do something that's a little bit of fun: you whack some trolls, you build some material, et cetera." Whacking trolls is, for some Wikipedia editors, a big part of why they keep coming back.

Say you're working away on the Wikipedia article on aging. You've got some nice scientific language in there and it's really starting to shape up:

After a period of near perfect renewal (in Humans, between 20 and 50 years of age), organismal senescence is characterized by the declining ability to respond to stress, increasing homeostatic imbalance and increased risk of disease. This irreversible series of changes inevitably ends in Death.

Not bad!

And then somebody—a user with an address of 206.82.17.190, a "vandal"—replaces the entire article with a single sentence: "Aging is what you get when you get freakin old old old." That happened on December 20, 2007. A minute later, you "revert" that anonymous editor's edit, with a few clicks; you go back in history to the article as it stood before. You've just kept the aging article safe, for the moment. But you have to stay vigilant, because somebody might swoop in again at any time, and you'll have to undo their harm with your power reverter ray. Now you're addicted. You've become a force for good just by standing guard and looking out for juvenile delinquents.

Some articles are so out of the way that they get very little vandalism. (Although I once fixed a tiny page about a plant fungus, *Colletotrichum trichellum,* that infects English ivy; somebody before me had claimed that 40 percent of the humans who got it died.) Some articles are vandalized a lot. On January 11, 2008, the entire fascinating entry on the aardvark was replaced with "one ugly animal"; in February the aardvark was briefly described as a "medium-sized inflatable banana." On December 7, 2007, somebody altered the long article on bedbugs so that it read like a horror movie:

> Bedbugs are generally active only at dawn, with a peak attack period about an hour before dawn, though given the opportunity, they may attempt to feed at your brain at other times.

A few weeks later, somebody replaced everything with:

> BED BUGS MOTHER FUCKER THEY GON GET YO MOTHAFUCKING ASS BRAAAAAAAT FOOL BRAAAAAAAAAAAAAAAAP.

A piece of antivandalism software, VoABot II, reverted that edit, with a little sigh, less than a minute after it was made.

Vandalism spiked in August 2006 after comedian Stephen Colbert—in the wake of Stacy Schiff's excellent but slightly frosty *New Yorker* article about Wikipedia—invited viewers of his show to post made-up facts about the increase in the population of African elephants, as proof of the existence of something that was not reality but "wikiality"—a cheap shot, but mildly funny. People repeatedly went after the elephant page, and it was locked for a while. But not for very long. The party moved on.

The Pop-Tarts page is often aflutter. Pop-Tarts, it says as of today (February 8, 2008), were discontinued in Australia in 2005. Maybe that's true. Before that it said that Pop-Tarts were discontinued in Korea. Before that Australia. Several days ago it said: "Pop-Tarts is german for Little Iced Pastry O' Germany." Other things I learned from earlier versions: More than two trillion Pop-Tarts are sold each year. George Washington invented them. They were developed in the early 1960s in China. Popular flavors are "frosted strawberry, frosted brown sugar cinnamon, and semen." Pop-Tarts are a "flat Cookie." No: "Pop-Tarts are a flat Pastry, KEVIN MCCORMICK is a FRIGGIN LOSER not to mention a queer inch." No: "A Pop-Tart is a flat condom." Once last fall the whole page was replaced with "NIPPLES AND BROCCOLI!!!!!"

This sounds chaotic, but even the Pop-Tarts page is under control most of the time. The "unhelpful" or "inappropriate"—sometimes stoned, racist, violent, metal-headed—changes are quickly fixed by human stompers and algorithmicized helper bots. It's a game. Wikipedians see vandalism as a problem, and it certainly can be, but a Diogenes-minded observer would submit that Wikipedia would never have been the prodigious success it has been without its demons.

This is a reference book that can suddenly go nasty on you. Who knows whether, when you look up Harvard's one-time warrior-president, James Bryant Conant, you're going to get a bland, evenhanded article about him, or whether the whole page will read (as it did for seventeen minutes on April 26, 2006): "HES A BIGSTUPID HEAD." James Conant was, after all, in some important ways, a big stupid head. He was studiously anti-Semitic, a strong believer in wonder-weapons—a man who was quite as happy figuring out new ways to kill people as he was administering a great university. Without the kooks and the insulters and the spray-can taggers, Wikipedia would just be the most useful encyclopedia ever made. Instead it's a fast-paced game of paintball.

Not only does Wikipedia need its vandals—up to a point—the vandals need an orderly Wikipedia, too. Without order, their culture-jamming lacks a context. If Wikipedia were rendered entirely chaotic and obscene, there would be no joy in, for example, replacing some of the article on Archimedes with this:

> Archimedes is dead.
> He died.
> Other people will also die.
> All hail chickens.
> The Power Rangers say "Hi"
> The End.

Even the interesting article on culture jamming has been hit a few times: "Culture jamming," it said in May 2007, "is the act of jamming tons of cultures into 1 extremely hot room."

When, last year, some computer scientists at the University of Minnesota studied millions of Wikipedia edits, they found that most of the good ones—those whose words persisted intact through many later viewings—were made by a tiny percentage of contributors. Enormous numbers of users have added the occasional enriching morsel to Wikipedia—and without this bystander's knowledge the encyclopedia would have gone nowhere—but relatively few users know how to frame their contribution in a form that lasts.

So how do you become one of Wikipedia's upper crust—one of the several thousand whose words will live on for a little while, before later verbal fumarolings erode what you wrote? It's not easy. You have to have a cool head, so that you don't get drawn into soul-destroying disputes, and you need some practical writing ability, and a quick eye, and a knack for synthesis. And you need lots of free time—time to master the odd conventions and the unfamiliar vocabulary (words like *smerge, POV warrior, forum shopping, hatnote, meat puppet, fancruft,* and *transclusion*), and time to read through guidelines and policy pages and essays and the endless records of old skirmishes—and time to have been gently but firmly, or perhaps rather sharply, reminded by other editors how you should behave. There's a long apprenticeship of trial and error.

At least, that's how it used to be. Now there's a quicker path to proficiency: John Broughton's *Wikipedia: The Missing Manual,* part of the Missing Manual series, overseen by the *New York Times*'s cheery electronics expert, David Pogue. "This Missing Manual helps you avoid beginners' blunders and gets you sounding like a pro from your first edit," the book says on the back. In his introduction, Broughton, who has himself made more than 15,000 Wikipedia edits, putting him in the elite top 1,200 of all editors—promises "the information you absolutely need to avoid running afoul of the rules." And it's true: this manual is enlightening, well organized, and full of good sense. Its arrival may mark a new, middle-aged phase in Wikipedia's history; some who read it will probably have wistful longings for the crazy do-it-yourself days when the whole project was just getting going. In October 2001, the first Wikipedian rule appeared. It was:

> Ignore all rules: If rules make you nervous and depressed, and not desirous of participating in the wiki, then ignore them entirely and go about your business.

The "ignore all rules" rule was written by cofounder Larry Sanger and signed by cofounder Jimbo Wales, along with WojPob, AyeSpy, OprgaG, Invictus, Koyaanis Qatsi,

Pinkunicorn, sjc, mike dill, Taw, GWO, and Enchanter. There were two dissenters listed, tbc and AxelBoldt.

Nowadays there are rules and policy banners at every turn—there are strongly urged warnings and required tasks and normal procedures and notability guidelines and complex criteria for various decisions—a symptom of something called instruction creep: defined in Wikipedia as something that happens "when instructions increase in number and size over time until they are unmanageable." John Broughton's book, at a mere 477 pages, cuts through the creep. He's got a whole chapter on how to make better articles ("Don't Suppress or Separate Controversy") and one on "Handling Incivility and Personal Attacks." Broughton advises that you shouldn't write a Wikipedia article about some idea or invention that you've personally come up with; that you should stay away from articles about things or people you really love or really hate; and that you shouldn't use the encyclopedia as a PR vehicle— for a new rock band, say, or an aspiring actress. Sometimes Broughton sounds like a freshman English comp teacher, a little too sure that there is one right and wrong way to do things: Strunk without White. But honestly, Wikipedia can be confusing, and you need that kind of confidence coming from a user's guide.

The first thing I did on Wikipedia (under the username Wageless) was to make some not-very-good edits to the page on bovine somatotropin. I clicked the "edit this page" tab, and immediately had an odd, almost light-headed feeling, as if I had passed through the looking glass and was being allowed to fiddle with some huge engine or delicate piece of biomedical equipment. It seemed much too easy to do damage; you ask, Why don't the words resist me more? Soon, though, you get used to it. You recall the central Wikipedian directive: "Be Bold." You start to like life on the inside.

After bovine hormones, I tinkered a little with the plot summary of the article on *Sleepless in Seattle,* while watching the movie. A little later I made some adjustments to the intro in the article on hydraulic fluid—later still someone pleasingly improved my fixes. After dessert one night my wife and I looked up recipes for cobbler, and then I worked for a while on the cobbler article, though it still wasn't right. I did a few things to the article on periodization. About this time I began standing with my computer open on the kitchen counter, staring at my growing watchlist, checking, peeking. I was, after about a week, well on my way to a first-stage Wikipedia dependency.

But the work that really drew me in was trying to save articles from deletion. This became my chosen mission. Here's how it happened: I read a short article on a post-Beat poet and small-press editor named Richard Denner, who had been a student in Berkeley in the sixties and then, after some lost years, had published many chapbooks on a hand press in the Pacific Northwest. The article was proposed for deletion by a user named PirateMink, who claimed that Denner wasn't a notable figure, whatever that means. (There are quires, reams, bales of controversy over what constitutes notability in Wikipedia: nobody will ever sort it out.) Another user, Stormbay, agreed with PirateMink: no third-party sources, ergo not notable.

Denner was in serious trouble. I tried to make the article less deletable by incorporating a quote from an interview in the *Berkeley Daily Planet*—Denner told the reporter that in the sixties he'd tried to be a street poet, "using magic markers to write on napkins at Cafe Med for espressos, on girls' arms and feet." (If an article bristles with some quotes from external sources these may, like the bushy hairs on a caterpillar, make it harder to kill.) And I voted "keep" on the deletion-discussion page, pointing out that many poets publish only chapbooks: "What harm does it do to anyone or anything to keep this entry?" An administrator named Nakon—one of about a thousand peer-nominated volunteer administrators—took a minute to survey the two "delete" votes and my "keep" vote and then killed the article. Denner was gone. Startled, I began sampling the "AfDs" (the Articles for Deletion debate pages) and the even more urgent "speedy deletes" and "PRODs" (proposed deletes) for other items that seemed unjustifiably at risk; when they were, I tried to save them. Taekwang Industry—a South Korean textile company—was one. A user named Kusunose had "prodded" it—that is, put a red-edged banner at the top of the article proposing it for deletion within five days. I removed the banner, signaling that I disagreed, and I hastily spruced up the text, noting that the company made "Acelan" brand spandex, raincoats, umbrellas, sodium cyanide, and black abaya fabric. The article didn't disappear: wow, did that feel good.

So I kept on going. I found press citations and argued for keeping the Jitterbug telephone, a large-keyed cell phone with a soft earpiece for elder callers; and Vladimir Narbut, a minor Russian Acmeist poet whose second book, *Halleluia*, was confiscated by the police; and Sara Mednick, a San Diego neuroscientist and author of *Take a Nap! Change Your Life;* and Pyro Boy, a minor celebrity who turns himself into a human firecracker onstage. I took up the cause of the Arifs, a Cyprio-Turkish crime family based in London (on LexisNexis

I found that the *Irish Daily Mirror* called them "Britain's No. 1 Crime Family"); and Card Football, a pokerlike football simulation game; and Paul Karason, a suspender-wearing guy whose face turned blue from drinking colloidal silver; and Jim Cara, a guitar restorer and modem-using music collaborationist who badly injured his head in a ski-flying competition; and writer Owen King, son of Stephen King; and Whitley Neill Gin, flavored with South African botanicals; and Whirled News Tonight, a Chicago improv troupe; and Michelle Leonard, a European songwriter, cowriter of a recent glam hit called "Love Songs (They Kill Me)."

All of these people and things had been deemed nonnotable by other editors, sometimes with unthinking harshness—the article on Michelle Leonard was said to contain "total lies." (Wrongly—as another editor, Bondegezou, more familiar with European pop charts, pointed out.) When I managed to help save something I was quietly thrilled—I walked tall, like Henry Fonda in *12 Angry Men*.

At the same time as I engaged in these tiny, fascinating (to me) "keep" tussles, hundreds of others were going on, all over Wikipedia. I signed up for the Article Rescue Squadron, having seen it mentioned in Broughton's manual: the ARS is a small group that opposes "extremist deletion." And I found out about a project called WPPDP (for "WikiProject Proposed Deletion Patrolling") in which people look over the PROD lists for articles that shouldn't be made to vanish. Since about 1,500 articles are deleted a day, this kind of work can easily become life-consuming, but some editors (for instance, a patient librarian whose username is DGG) seem to be able to do it steadily week in and week out and stay sane. I, on the other hand, was swept right out to the Isles of Shoals. I stopped hearing what my family was saying to me— for about two weeks I all but disappeared into my screen, trying to salvage brief, sometimes overly promotional, but nevertheless worthy biographies by recasting them in neutral language, and by hastily scouring newspaper databases and Google Books for references that would bulk up their notability quotient. I had become an "inclusionist."

That's not to say that I thought every article should be fought for. Someone created an article called Plamen Ognianov Kamenov. In its entirety, the article read: "Hi my name is Plamen Ognianov Kamenov. I am Bulgarian. I am smart." The article is gone—understandably. Someone else, evidently a child, made up a lovely short tale about a fictional woman named Empress Alamonda, who hated her husband's chambermaids. "She would get so jealous she would faint," said the article. "Alamonda died at 6:00 pm in her room. On august 4 1896." Alamonda is gone, too.

Still, a lot of good work—verifiable, informative, brain-leapingly strange—is being cast out of this paperless, infinitely expandable accordion folder by people who have a narrow, almost grade-schoolish notion of what sort of curiosity an online encyclopedia will be able to satisfy in the years to come.

Anybody can "pull the trigger" on an article (as Broughton phrases it)—you just insert a double-bracketed software template. It's harder to improve something that's already written, or to write something altogether new, especially now that so many of the *World Book*–sanctioned encyclopedic fruits are long plucked. There are some people on Wikipedia now who are just bullies, who take pleasure in wrecking and mocking people's work—even to the point of laughing at nonstandard "Engrish." They poke articles full of warnings and citation-needed notes and deletion prods till the topics go away.

In the fall of 2006, groups of editors went around getting rid of articles on webcomic artists—some of the most original and articulate people on the Net. They would tag an article as nonnotable and then crowd in to vote it down. One openly called it the "web-comic articles purge of 2006." A victim, Trev-Mun, author of a comic called *Ragnarok Wisdom,* wrote: "I got the impression that they enjoyed this kind of thing as a kid enjoys kicking down others' sand castles." Another artist, Howard Tayler, said: " 'Notability purges' are being executed throughout Wikipedia by empire-building, wannabe tin-pot dictators masquerading as humble editors." Rob Balder, author of a webcomic called PartiallyClips, likened the organized deleters to book burners, and he said: "Your words are polite, yeah, but your actions are obscene. Every word in every valid article you've destroyed should be converted to profanity and screamed in your face."

As the deletions and ill will spread in 2007—deletions not just of webcomics but of companies, urban places, websites, lists, people, categories, and ideas—all deemed to be trivial, "NN" (nonnotable), "stubby," undersourced, or otherwise unencyclopedic—Andrew Lih, one of the most thoughtful observers of Wikipedia's history, told a Canadian reporter: "The preference now is for excising, deleting, restricting information rather than letting it sit there and grow." In September 2007, Jimbo Wales, Wikipedia's panjandrum— himself an inclusionist who believes that if people want an article about every Pokemon character, then hey, let it happen—posted a one-sentence stub about Mzoli's, a restaurant on the outskirts of Cape Town, South Africa. It was quickly put up for deletion. Others saved it, and after a thunderstorm of vandalism (e.g., the page was replaced with "I hate Wikipedia, its a far-left propaganda instrument, some far-left gangs control it"), "Mzoli's" is now a model piece, spiky with press citations. There's even, as of January, an article about "Deletionism and inclusionism in Wikipedia"— it, too, survived an early attempt to purge it.

My advice to anyone who is curious about becoming a contributor—and who is better than I am at keeping his or her contributional compulsions under control—is to get Broughton's *Missing Manual* and start adding, creating, rescuing. I think I'm done for the time being. But I have a secret hope. A librarian, K. G. Schneider, recently proposed a Wikimorgue—a bin of broken dreams where all rejects could still be read, as long as they weren't libelous or otherwise illegal. Like other middens, it would have much to tell us over time. We could call it the Deletopedia.

(*2008*)

# Kindle 2

I ordered a Kindle 2 from Amazon. How could I not? There were banner ads for it all over the Web. Whenever I went to the Amazon website, I was urged to buy one. "Say Hello to Kindle 2," it said, in tall letters on the main page. If I looked up a particular writer on Amazon—Mary Higgins Clark, say—and then reached the page for her knuckle-gnawer of a novel *Moonlight Becomes You,* the top line on the page said, "*Moonlight Becomes You* and over 270,000 other books are available for Amazon Kindle— Amazon's new wireless reading device. Learn more." Below the picture of Clark's physical paperback ($7.99) was another teaser: "Start reading *Moonlight Becomes You* on your Kindle in under a minute. Don't have a Kindle? Get yours here." If I went to the Kindle page for the digital download of *Moonlight Becomes You* ($6.39), it wouldn't offer me a link back to the print version. I was being steered.

Everybody was saying that the new Kindle was terribly important—that it was an alpenhorn blast of post-Gutenbergian revalorization. In the *Wall Street Journal,* the cultural critic Steven Johnson wrote that he'd been alone one day in a restaurant in Austin, Texas, when he was seized by the urge to read a novel. Within minutes, thanks to Kindle's free 3G hookup with Sprint wireless—they call it Whispernet—he was well into Chapter 1 of Zadie Smith's *On Beauty* ($9.99 for the e-book, $10.20 for the paperback). Writing and publishing, he believed, would never be the same. In *Newsweek*, Jacob Weisberg, the editor in chief of the Slate Group, confided that for weeks he'd been doing all his recreational reading on the Kindle 2, and he claimed that it offered a "fundamentally better experience" than inked paper did. "Jeff Bezos"—Amazon's founder and CEO—"has built a machine that marks a cultural revolution," Weisberg said. "Printed books, the most important artifacts of human civilization, are going to join newspapers and magazines on the road to obsolescence."

Lots of ordinary people were excited about the Kindle 2, too—there were then about fifteen hundred five-star customer reviews at the Kindle Store, saying "I love my Kindle" over and over, and only a few hundred bitter one-stars. Kindle books were clean. "I've always been creeped out by library books and used books," one visitor, Christine Ring, wrote on the Amazon website. "You never know where they've been!" "It has reinvigorated my interest in reading," another reviewer said. "I'm hooked," another said. "If I dropped my kindle down a sewer, I would buy another one immediately."

And the unit was selling: in April, tech blogs had rumors that three hundred thousand Kindle 2s had shipped since the release date of February 24. Bezos wrote a letter to shareholders: "Kindle sales have exceeded our most optimistic expectations." He went on *The Daily Show* and laughed. (See the YouTube video called "Jeff Bezos Laughing Freakishly Hard on The Daily Show with Jon Stewart.")

Amazon's page showed a woman in sunglasses sitting on a beach with a Kindle over her knee. Below that were video testimonials from big-name writers like Michael Lewis and Toni Morrison, recycled from the launch of the original Kindle, in the fall of 2007. James Patterson, the force behind a stream of No. 1 *Times* best-sellers, said that he enjoyed reading outdoors, where he had, he confided, a "wonderful back yard, nice pool, and all that." Patterson was pleased to discover, while Kindling poolside, that the wind didn't make the book's pages flutter. "There's just the one page," he explained. Neil Gaiman had moved from skeptic to "absolute believer."

Well, well! I began to have the mildly euphoric feeling that you get ten minutes into an infomercial. Sure, the Kindle is expensive, but the expense is a way of buying into the total commitment. This could forever change the way I read. I've never been a fast reader. I'm fickle; I don't finish books I start; I put a book aside for five, ten years and then take it up again. Maybe, I thought, if I ordered this wireless Kindle 2 I would be pulled into a world of compulsive, demonic book consumption, like Pippin staring at the stone of Orthanc. Maybe I would gorge myself on Rebecca West, or Jack Vance, or Dawn Powell. Maybe the Kindle was the Bowflex of bookishness: something expensive that, when you commit to it, forces you to do more of whatever it is you think you should be doing more of.

True, the name of the product wasn't so great. Kindle? It was cute and sinister at the same time—worse than Edsel, or Probe, or Microsoft's Bob. But one forgives a bad name. One even comes to be fond of a bad name, if the product itself is delightful.

It came, via UPS, in a big cardboard box. Inside the box were some puffy clear bladders of plastic, a packing slip with

"$359" on it, and another cardboard box. This one said, in spare, lowercase type, "kindle." On the side of the box was a plastic strip inlaid into the cardboard, which you were meant to pull to tear the package cleanly open. On it were the words "Once upon a time." I pulled and opened.

Inside was another box, fancier than the first. Black cardboard was printed with a swarm of glossy black letters, and in the middle was, again, the word "kindle." There was another pull strip on the side, which again said, "Once upon a time." I'd entered some nesting Italo Calvino folktale world of packaging. (Calvino's Italian folktales aren't yet available at the Kindle Store, by the way.) I pulled again and opened.

Within, lying faceup in a white-lined casket, was the device itself. It was pale, about the size of a hardcover novel, but much thinner, and it had a smallish screen and a QWERTY keyboard at the bottom made of tiny round pleasure-dot keys that resisted pressing. I gazed at the keys for a moment and thought of a restaurant accordion.

The plug, which was combined with the USB connector, was extremely well designed, in the best post-Apple style. It was a very, very good plug. I turned the Kindle on and pressed the Home key. Home gives you the list of what you've got in your Kindle. There were some books that I'd already ordered waiting for me—that was nice—and there was also a letter of greeting from Jeff Bezos. "Kindle is an entirely new type of device, and we're excited to have you as an early customer!" Bezos wrote. I read the letter and some of *His Majesty's Dragon* (a dragon fantasy by Naomi Novick set during the Napoleonic Wars, given away free), *Gulliver's Travels*, and *Slow Hands*, a freebie Harlequin Blaze novel by Leslie Kelly. I changed the type size. I searched for a text string. I tussled with a sense of anticlimax.

The problem was not that the screen was in black-and-white; if it had really been black-and-white, that would have been fine. The problem was that the screen was gray. And it wasn't just gray; it was a greenish, sickly gray. A postmortem gray. The resizable typeface, Monotype Caecilia, appeared as a darker gray. Dark gray on paler greenish gray was the palette of the Amazon Kindle.

This was what they were calling e-paper? This four-by-five window onto an overcast afternoon? Where was paper white, or paper cream? Forget RGB or CMYK. Where were sharp black letters laid out like lacquered chopsticks on a clean tablecloth?

I showed it to my wife. "Too bad it doesn't have a little kickstand," she said. "You could prop it up like a dresser mirror and read while you eat." My son clicked around in the Kindle edition of a Bernard Cornwell novel about ancient Britain. "It's not that bad," he said. "The map looks pretty good. Some of the littler names aren't readable. I'd rather be reading that"—pointing to his Cornwell paperback, which was lying facedown nearby—"but I can definitely read this."

Yes, you can definitely read things on the Kindle. And I did. Bits of things at first. I read some of De Quincey's *Confessions*, some of Robert Benchley's *Love Conquers All*, and some of several versions of Kipling's *The Jungle Book*. I squeezed no new joy from these great books, though. The Gluyas Williams drawings were gone from the Benchley, and even the wasp passage in *Do Insects Think?* just wasn't the same in Kindle gray. I did an experiment. I found the Common Reader reprint edition of *Love Conquers All* and read the very same wasp passage. I laughed: ha-ha. Then I went back to the Kindle 2 and read the wasp passage again. No laugh. Of course, by then I'd read the passage three times, and it wasn't that funny anymore. But the point is that it wasn't funny the first time I came to it, when it was enscreened on the Kindle. Monotype Caecilia was grim and Calvinist; it had a way of reducing everything to arbitrary heaps of words.

Reading some of *Max,* a James Patterson novel, I experimented with the text-to-speech feature. The robo-reader had a polite, halting, Middle European intonation, like Tom Hanks in *The Terminal,* and it was sometimes confused by periods. Once it thought *miss.* was the abbreviation of a state name: "He loved the chase, the hunt, the split-second intersection of luck and skill that allowed him to exercise his perfection, his inability to Mississippi." I turned the machine off.

And yet, you know, many people loved it. To be fair to the Kindle, I had to make it through at least one whole book. Jeff Bezos calls this "long form" reading. I had some success one morning when I Kindled my way deep into *The Complete Idiot's Guide to Writing Erotic Romance,* by Alison Kent. There are, I learned, four distinct levels of intensity in the erotic-romance industry: sweet, steamy, sizzling, and scorching. This seemed like pertinent information, since romance readers are major Kindlers. "The success of the ebook is being fueled by the romance and erotic romance market," Peter Smith, of ITworld, reports. Smith cites the actress and Kindle enthusiast Felicia Day, of *Buffy the Vampire Slayer,* who has been bingeing on paranormals like *Dark Needs at Night's Edge.* "I've read like, 6 books this week and ordered about 10 more," Day blogged. "It's stuff I never would have checked out at the Barnes and Noble, because the gleaming and oily man chests would have made me blush too much."

But e-romances don't fully explain the Kindle's success—and the kind of devotion that it inspires. To find out more, I went to Freeport, Maine, to talk to Eileen Messina, the manager of the British-imports store just across from L.L. Bean. Messina, a thoughtful, intelligent woman in her thirties, has all kinds of things on her Kindle, including *Anna Karenina,* Murakami's *Kafka on the Shore,* books by Dan Simmons and Abraham Verghese, and the comic novel *Pride and Prejudice and Zombies.* She is so happy with it that she has volunteered, along with about a hundred others, to show it off to prospective purchasers, as part of Amazon's "See a Kindle in Your City" promotion. Her Kindle was in her purse; she'd crocheted a cover for it out of green yarn. In the past, she said, she'd taken books out of the library, but some of them smelled of smoke—a Kindle book is a smoke-free environment. I thanked her and bought some digestive biscuits and a teapot, and then I went next door to Sherman's Books and Stationery. I asked Josh Christie, who worked there, to recommend a truly gut-churningly suspenseful novel. I was going to do a comparison between the paperback and the Kindle 2 version. Christie suggested *The Bourne Identity* and a book by Michael Connelly, *The Lincoln Lawyer*—one of his colleagues at the shop swore by it. I bought them both.

Outside, I sat on a bench near L.L. Bean, eating an ice cream, and tried to order *The Bourne Identity* wirelessly from the Kindle Store. But no—there is no Kindle version of *The Bourne Identity.* What?

What else was missing? Back home, I spent an hour standing in front of some fiction bookcases, checking on titles. There is no Amazon Kindle version of *The Jewel in the Crown.* There's no Kindle of Jean Stafford, no Vladimir

Nabokov, no *Flaubert's Parrot,* no *Remains of the Day*, no *Perfume* by Patrick Suskind, no Bharati Mukherjee, no Margaret Drabble, no Graham Greene except a radio script, no David Leavitt, no Bobbie Ann Mason's *In Country,* no Pynchon, no Tim O'Brien, no *Swimming-Pool Library,* no Barbara Pym, no Saul Bellow, no Frederick Exley, no *World According to Garp,* no *Catch-22,* no *Breakfast at Tiffany's,* no *Portnoy's Complaint,* no *Henry and Clara,* no Lorrie Moore, no *Edwin Mullhouse,* no *Clockwork Orange.*

Of course, the title count will grow. It will grow because not-so-subtle forces will be exerted on publishers and writers. Below the descriptions of all non-Kindle books for sale on Amazon, there's a box that says, "Tell the Publisher! I'd like to read this book on Kindle." If you click it, Amazon displays a thank-you page: "We will pass your specific request on to the publisher."

But say you've actually found the book you're seeking at the Kindle Store. You buy it. Do you get what's described in the catalog copy? Yes and no. You get the words, yes, and sometimes pictures, after a fashion. Photographs, charts, diagrams, foreign characters, and tables don't fare so well on the little gray screen. Page numbers are gone, so indexes sometimes don't work. Trailing endnotes are difficult to manage. If you want to quote from a book you've bought, you have to quote by location range—e.g., the phrase "She was on the verge of the mother of all orgasms" is to be found at location range 1596–1605 in Mari Carr's erotic romance novel *Tequila Truth.*

When you buy the Kindle edition of Konrad Lorenz's *King Solomon's Ring,* rather than the paperback version, you save three dollars and fifty-eight cents, but the fetching illustrations by Lorenz of a greylag goose and its goslings walking out from the middle of a paragraph and down the right margin are separated from the text—the marginalia has been demarginalized. The Kindle Store offers *The Cheese Lover's Cookbook & Guide,* from Simon & Schuster. "The picture of the Ricotta Pancakes with Banana-Pecan Syrup may just inspire you enough to make it the first recipe you want to try," one happy Amazon reviewer writes. She's referring to the recipe in the print edition, the description of which is reused in the Kindle Store—there's no pancake picture in the Kindle version.

Yes, you can save nine dollars if you buy the Kindle edition of *The Algorithmic Beauty of Seaweeds, Sponges, and Corals,* by Jaap A. Kaandorp and Janet E. Kübler—it'll cost you $85.40 delivered wirelessly, versus $94.89 in print. *New Scientist* says that the book is "beautifully, if sometimes eccentrically, illustrated with photographs, drawings and computer simulations." The illustrations are there in the Kindle version, but they're exceedingly hard to make out, even if you zoom in on them using the five-way clicker switch, or "control nipple," as one Kindler called it. An award-winning medical textbook titled *Imaging in Oncology* (second edition) is for sale in the Kindle Store for $287.96. Tables are garbled. The color coding—yellow for malignancy, blue for healthy tissue—has been lost. Arrows pointing to shadowy tumors become invisible in the gray. Indeed, the tumors themselves disappear.

One more expensive example. The Kindle edition of *Selected Nuclear Materials and Engineering Systems,* an e-book for people who design nuclear power plants, sells for more than eight thousand dollars. Figure 2 is an elaborate chart of a reaction scheme, with many callouts and chemical equations. It's totally illegible. "You Save: $1,607.80 (20%)," the Kindle page says. "I'm not going to buy this book until the price comes down," one stern Amazoner wrote.

Here's what you buy when you buy a Kindle book. You buy the right to display a grouping of words in front of your eyes for your private use with the aid of an electronic display device approved by Amazon. The company uses an encoding format called Topaz. (*Topaz* is also the name of a novel by Leon Uris, not available at the Kindle Store.) There are other e-book software formats—Adobe Acrobat, for instance, and Microsoft Reader, and an open format called ePub—but Amazon went its own way. Nobody else's hardware can handle Topaz without Amazon's permission. That means you can't read your Kindle books on your computer, or on an e-book reader that competes with the Kindle. (You can, however, read Kindle books on the iPod Touch and the iPhone—more about that later—because Amazon has decided that it's in its interest to let you.) Maybe you've heard of the Sony Reader? The Sony Reader's page-turning controls are better designed than the Kindle's controls, and the Reader came out more than a year before the Kindle did; also, its screen is slightly less gray, and its typeface is better, and it can handle ePub and PDF documents without conversion, but forget it. You can't read a Kindle book on a Sony machine, or on the Ectaco jetBook, the BeBook, the iRex iLiad, the Cybook, the Hanlin V2, or the Foxit eSlick. Kindle books aren't transferable. You can't give them away or lend them or sell them. You can't print them. They are closed clumps of digital code that only one purchaser can own. A copy of a Kindle book dies with its possessor.

On the other hand, there's no clutter, no pile of paperbacks next to the couch. A Kindle book arrives wirelessly: it's untouchable; it exists on a higher, purer plane.

It's earth-friendly, too, supposedly. Yes, it's made of exotic materials that are shipped all over the world's oceans; yes, it requires electricity to operate and air-conditioned server farms to feed it; yes, it's fragile and it duplicates what other machines do; yes, it's difficult to recycle; yes, it will probably take a last boat ride to a Nigerian landfill in five years. But no tree farms are harvested to make a Kindle book; no ten-ton presses turn, no ink is spilled.

Instead of ink on paper, there's something called Vizplex. Vizplex is the trade name of the layered substance that makes up the Kindle's display—i.e., the six-inch-diagonal rectangle that you read from. It's a marvel of bi-stable microspheres, and it took lots of work and more than 150 million dollars to develop, but it's really still in the prototype phase. Vizplex, in slurry form, is made in Cambridge, Massachusetts, by a company called E Ink. E Ink layers it onto a film, or "frontplane laminate," at a plant in western Massachusetts, and then sends the laminate to Taiwan, where its parent company, P.V.I. (which stands for Prime View International, itself a subsidiary of a large paper company), marries it to an electronic grid, or backplane. The backplane tells the frontplane what to do.

The prospect of Vizplex first arose in the mind of a scientist, Joseph Jacobson, who now works at M.I.T.'s Media Lab and avoids interviews on the subject of e-paper. Sometime in the mid-nineties, according to a colleague, Jacobson was sitting on a beach reading. He finished his book. What next? He didn't want to walk off the beach to get another book, and he didn't want to lie on the beach and dig moist holes with his feet, thinking about the algorithmic beauty of seaweeds. What he wanted was to push a little button that would swap the words in the book he held for the words in some other book somewhere else. He wanted the book he held to be infinitely rewriteable—to be, in fact, the very last book he would ever have to own. He called it "The Last Book." To make the Last Book, he would have to invent a new kind of paper: RadioPaper.

At M.I.T., Jacobson and a group of undergraduates made lists of requirements, methods, and materials. One of their tenets was: RadioPaper must reflect, like real paper. It must not emit. It couldn't be based on some improved type of liquid-crystal screen, no matter how high its resolution, no matter how perfectly jewel-like its colors, no matter how imperceptibly quick its flicker, because liquid crystals are backlit, and backlighting, they believed, is intrinsically bad because it's hard on the eyes. RadioPaper also had to be flexible, they thought, and it had to persist until recycled in situ. It should hold its image even when it drew no current, just as paper could. How to do that? One student came up with the idea of a quilt of tiny white balls in colored dye. To make the letter A, say, microsquirts of electricity would grab some of the microballs and pull them down in their capsule, drowning them in the dye and making that capsule and neighboring capsules go dark and stay dark until some more electricity flowed through in a second or a day or a week. This was the magic of electrophoresis.

In 1997, Jacobson and his partners joined with Russ Wilcox, an entrepreneur from Harvard Business School, to form E Ink. "When we first got involved with this, people were, like, 'Oh, you're trying to kill the book,'" Wilcox said recently, by telephone. "And we're, like, 'No, we love the book.' Unfortunately, we fear for its future, because people just expect digital media these days. The economic pressures are immense."

The newspaper industry, Wilcox figured, was a 180-billion-dollar-a-year business, and book publishing was an additional 80 billion. Half of that was papermaking, ink mixing, printing, transport, inventory, and the warehousing of physical goods. "So you can save a hundred and thirty billion dollars a year if you move the information digitally," he told me. "There's a lot of hidden forces at work that are all combining to make this sort of a big tidal wave that's coming."

E Ink ran into some trouble after 2000, when there was less venture capital to go around. The company's direction changed slightly. It wouldn't make the Last Book, but it would sell other manufacturers the means to do so. The company's models were Coca-Cola—which grew great by selling the syrup and letting others do the bottling—and NutraSweet. "Imagine you're NutraSweet," Wilcox said. "The cola industry is already up and running. There's no way you're going to make your own diet cola and compete head to head. So what do you do? You sell the ingredient."

E Ink's first big, visible customer was Sony. Sony bought a lot of Vizplex display screens for its Reader, the PRS-500, which Howard Stringer, Sony's C.E.O., introduced at the Consumer Electronics Show in Las Vegas in January 2006, standing in front of a photograph of the electrophoretic version of Dan Brown's *The Da Vinci Code*. Sony set up an online bookstore, and sold its machines at Borders Books and the Sony Store, and, later, at Target, Costco, Staples, and Walmart. Sony is, of course, a deft hand at handheld design. Its Reader was very good, given the Etch-A-Sketch limitations of the Vizplex medium, but it lacked wirelessness—you had to USB-cable it to a computer in order to load a book onto it—and Sony had no gift for retail bookselling. Hundreds of thousands of Sony Readers have sold—and you can now read five hundred thousand public-domain Google Books on it in ePub format—but, oddly, people ignore it.

Along with Sony, several other companies rushed to develop Vizplex-based devices. Amazon was one of them. Since 2000, Amazon had been offering various kinds of e-books (to be read on a computer screen), without success. "Nobody's been buying e-books," Jeff Bezos told Charlie Rose in November 2007, at the time of the Kindle 1 launch. The shift to digital page-turning hadn't happened. Why was that? "It's because books are so good," according to Bezos. And they're good, he explained, because they disappear when you read them: "You go into this flow state." Bezos wanted to design a machine that helped a reader achieve that same flow—and also (although he didn't say this) sold for a premium, fended off Sony's trespass into the book business, and tied buyers to Amazon forever.

Thus Bezos's engineers—including Gregg Zehr, who had previously worked for Palm and Apple—ventured to design a piece of hardware. "This is the most important thing we've ever done," Bezos said in *Newsweek* at the time. "It's so ambitious to take something as highly evolved as the book and improve on it."

But the Kindle 1 wasn't an improvement. Page-turning was slow and was accompanied by a distracting flash of black as the microspheres dived down into their oil-filled nodules before forming new text. "The first thing to note is that the screen isn't like reading actual paper," Joseph Weisenthal wrote on paidContent.org. "It's not as bright and there is glare if the light is too direct."

The problem wasn't just the Vizplex screen. The Kindle 1's design was a retro piece of bizarrery—an unhandy, asymmetrical Fontina wedge of plastic. It had a keyboard composed of many rectangular keys that were angled like cars in a parking lot, and a long Next Page button that, as hundreds of users complained, made you turn pages by accident when you carried it around. "Honestly, the device is fugly," a commentator named KenC said on the Silicon Alley Insider: "The early 90s called and they want their device back." The comments on Engadget.com were especially pointed. "It looks like a Timex Sinclair glued to the bottom of an oversized 1st gen Palm device," Marcus wrote. "That's some ugly shit," Johan agreed. "Was this damned thing designed by a band of drunken elves?" Jerome asked. CB summed it up: "It is truly butt ugly. wow. ugly."

Undeterred, the folks at Amazon gave the Kindle 1 a hose blast of marketing late in 2007. To counter the threat, Sony boosted its advertising for the PRS-500, but it couldn't compete. Amazon sold out of Kindles before Christmas of 2007. Then came another lucky break: Oprah announced on TV that she was obsessed with the Kindle. "It's absolutely my new favorite, favorite thing in the world," she said. "It's life-changing for me."

Reading the one-star reviews for this device, which accumulated throughout 2008, must have been a painful experience for Amazon's product engineers. Yet they soldiered on, readying the revised version—smoothing the edges and fixing the most obvious physical flaws. They made page-turning faster, so that the black flash was less distracting, and they got the screen to display sixteen shades of gray, not four, a refinement that helped somewhat with photographs.

Despite its smoother design, the Kindle 2 is, some say, harder to read than the Kindle 1. "I immediately noticed that the contrast was worse on the K2 than on my K1," a reviewer named T. Ford wrote. One Kindler, Elizabeth Glass, began an online petition, asking Amazon to fix the contrast. "Like reading a wet newspaper," according to petition-signer Louise Potter.

There was another problem with the revised Kindle— fading. Some owners (not me, though) found that when they read in the sun the letters began to disappear. Readers had to press Alt-G repeatedly to bring them back. "Today is the first day when we have had bright sunshine, so I took the Kindle out in the sun and was dismayed to see that the text (particularly near the center of the screen) faded within seconds," one owner, Woody, wrote. Another owner, Mark, said, "I went through 4 kindles til I found a good one that doesn't fade in the sun. It was a hassle but Amazon has a great CS." (CS is customer service.)

Amazon remains fully committed to electrophoresis. "We think reading is an important enough activity that it deserves a purpose-built device," Bezos told stock analysts in April. Heartened by the Kindle 2's press, Amazon introduced, in mid-June, a bigger machine—the thumb-cramping, TV-dinner-size Kindle DX. The DX can auto-flip its image when you turn it sideways, like the iPod Touch (although its tetchy inertial guidance system sometimes sends the page twirling when you don't want it to), and on it you can view—but not zoom on or pan across—unconverted PDF files. Some engineer, tasked with keyboard design, has again been struck by a divine retro-futurist fire: the result is a squashed array of pill-shaped keys that combine the number row with the top QWERTY row in a peculiar tea party of un-ergonomicism. Pilot programs have arisen at several universities, including Princeton, which will test the Kindle DX's potential as a replacement for textbooks and paper printouts of courseware. The Princeton program is partly funded by the High Meadows Foundation, in the name of environmental sustainability; for Amazon, it's also a way to get into the rich coursepack market, alongside Barnes & Noble, Kinko's, and a company called XanEdu.

The real flurry over the new DX, though, has to do with the fate of newspapers. The DX offers more than twice as much Vizplex as the Kindle 2—about half the area of a piece of letter-size paper—enough, some assert, to reaccustom Web readers to paying for the digital version of, say, the *Times*, thereby rescuing daily print journalism from financial ruin. "With Kindle DX's large display, reading newspapers is more enjoyable than ever," according to Amazon's website.

It's enjoyable if you like reading Nexis printouts. The Kindle *Times* ($13.99 per month) lacks most of the print edition's superb photography—and its subheads and callouts and teasers, its spinnakered typographical elegance and variety, its browsableness, its website links, its listed names of contributing reporters, and almost all captioned pie charts, diagrams, weather maps, crossword puzzles, summary sports scores, financial data, and, of course, ads, for jewels, for swimsuits, for vacationlands, and for recently bailed-out investment firms. A century and a half of evolved beauty and informational expressiveness is all but entirely rinsed away in this digital reductio.

Sometimes whole articles and op-ed contributions aren't there. Three pieces from the July 8, 2009, print edition of the *Times*—Adam Nagourney on Sarah Palin's resignation, Alessandra Stanley on Michael Jackson's funeral, and David Johnston on the civil rights of detainees—were missing from the Kindle edition, or at least I haven't managed to find them (they're available free on the *Times* website); the July 9 Kindle issue lacked the print edition's reporting on interracial college roommates and the infectivity rates of abortion pills. I checked again on July 20 and 21: Verlyn Klinkenborg's appreciation of Walter Cronkite was absent, as was a long piece on Mongolian shamanism.

The Kindle DX ($489) doesn't save newspapers; it diminishes and undercuts them—it kills their joy. It turns them into earnest but dispensable blogs.

Amazon, with its Listmania Lists and its sometimes inspired recommendations and its innumerable fascinating reviews, is very good at selling things. It isn't so good, to date anyway, at making things. But, fortunately, if you want to read electronic books there's another way to go. Here's what you do. Buy an iPod Touch (it costs seventy dollars less than the Kindle 2, even after the Kindle's price was recently cut), or buy an iPhone, and load the free "Kindle for iPod" application onto it. Then, when you wake up at 3 a.m. and you need big, sad, well-placed words to tumble slowly into the basin of your mind, and you don't want to disturb the person who's in bed with you, you can reach under the pillow and find Apple's smooth machine and click it on. It's completely silent. Hold it a few inches from your face, with the words enlarged and the screen's brightness slider bar slid to its lowest setting, and read for ten or fifteen minutes. Each time you need to turn the page, just move your thumb over it, as if you were getting ready to deal a card; when you do, the page will slide out of the way, and a new one will appear. After a while, your thoughts will drift off to the unused siding where the old tall weeds are, and the string of curving words will toot a mournful toot and pull ahead. You will roll to a stop. A moment later, you'll wake and discover that you're still holding the machine but it has turned itself off. Slide it back under the pillow. Sleep.

I've done this with Joseph Mitchell's *The Bottom of the Harbor* ($13.80 Kindle, $17.25 paperback) and with Wilkie Collins's *The Moonstone*. The iPod screen's resolution, at 163 pixels per inch, is fairly high. (It could be much higher, though. High pixel density, not a reflective surface, is, I've come to believe, what people need when they read electronic prose.) There are other ways to read books on the iPod, too. My favorite is the Eucalyptus application, by a Scottish software developer named James Montgomerie: for $9.99, you get more than twenty thousand public-domain books whose pages turn with a voluptuous grace. There's also the Iceberg Reader, by ScrollMotion, with fixed page numbers, and a very popular app called Stanza. In Stanza, you can choose the colors of the words and of the page, and you can adjust the brightness with a vertical thumb swipe as you read. Stanza takes you to Harlequin Imprints, the Fictionwise Book Store, O'Reilly Ebooks, Feedbooks, and a number of other catalogs. A million people have downloaded Stanza. (In fact, Stanza is so good that Amazon has just bought Lexcycle, which makes the software; meanwhile, Fictionwise has been bought by a worried Barnes & Noble.)

Forty million iPod Touches and iPhones are in circulation, and most people aren't reading books on them. But some are. The nice thing about this machine is (a) it's beautiful, and (b) it's not imitating anything. It's not trying to be ink on paper. It serves a night-reading need, which the lightless Kindle doesn't. And the wasp passage in *Do Insects Think?* is funny again on the iPod.

The paperback edition of *The Lincoln Lawyer* ($7.99 at Sherman's in Freeport) has a bright-green cover with a blurry photograph of a car on the front. It says "Michael Connelly" in huge metallic purple letters, and it has a purple band on the spine: "#1 *New York Times* Bestseller." On the back, it says, "A plot that moves like a shot of Red Bull." It's shiny and new and the type is right, and it has the potent pheromonal funk of pulp and glue. When you read the book, its gutter gapes before your eyes, and you feel you're in it. In print, *The Lincoln Lawyer* swept me up. At night, I switched over to the e-book version on the iPod ($7.99 from the Kindle Store), so that I could carry on in the dark. I began swiping the tiny iPod pages faster and faster.

Then, out of a sense of duty, I forced myself to read the book on the physical Kindle 2. It was like going from a Mini Cooper to a white 1982 Impala with blown shocks. But never mind: at that point, I was locked into the plot and it didn't matter. Poof, the Kindle disappeared, just as Jeff Bezos had promised it would. I began walking up and down the driveway, reading in the sun. Three distant lawn mowers were going. Someone wearing a salmon-colored shirt was spraying a hose across the street. But I was in the courtroom, listening to the murderer testify. I felt the primitive clawing pressure of wanting to know how things turned out.

I began pressing the Next Page clicker more and more eagerly, so eagerly that my habit of page-turning, learned from years of reading—which is to reach for the page corner a little early, to prepare for the movement—kicked in unconsciously. I clicked Next Page as I reached the beginning of the last line, and the page flashed to black and changed before I'd read it all. I was trying to hurry the Kindle. You mustn't hurry the Kindle. But, hell, I didn't care. The progress bar at the bottom said I was 91 percent done. I was at location 7547. I was flying along. Gray is a good color, I thought. Finally, I was on the last bit. It was called "A Postcard from Cuba." I breathed an immense ragged sigh. I read the acknowledgments and the about-the-author paragraph—Michael Connelly lives in Florida. Good man. The little progress indicator said 99 percent. I clicked the Next Page button. It showed the cover of the book again. I clicked Next Page again, but there was no next page. My first Kindle-delivered novel was at its end.

*(2009)*

# *Papermakers*

There are two paper mills in the town of Jay, in Maine, on the Androscoggin River. One mill, now owned by Verso Paper Corp., makes the paper for *Martha Stewart Living, National Geographic, Cosmopolitan,* and other magazines. It's a big plant, built by International Paper in the sixties. The other mill is older and made of brick and stone. It's called the Otis Mill, and it was built by Hugh Chisholm, the founder of International Paper, in 1896. Back then it was a prodigy—THE LARGEST PAPER MILL PLANT IN THE WORLD, according to a headline in the *Lewiston Weekly Journal,* which was exaggerating, but only a little.

The Otis Mill has produced all sorts of paper over the years—paper for postcards, ornate playing cards, wallpaper, copier paper, inkjet paper, and the shiny, peel-off paper backing for sticky labels. Now, though, the Otis Mill doesn't make anything. The paper industry is in a slump. The new owner, Wausau Paper, shut down one of Otis's two paper machines in August 2008. The number of employees dropped from about 250 to 96. Then, this spring, Wausau's CEO, Thomas J. Howatt, closed the plant altogether. The closure was a difficult decision, he said in a press release, but it was necessary in order to "preserve liquidity and match capacity with demand during a period of severe economic difficulty." The final reel of paper came off the mill at 6:50 a.m. on June 1, 2009. It was parchment paper, the kind bakers use to bake cookies.

I drove up to Jay on a fine day in mid-October, thinking as I drove about forests with logging trails, and about 400,000-square-foot Internet data centers going up around the country with cooling towers and 28,000-gallon backup tanks of diesel fuel, and about mountaintop coal removal, and about relative carbon footprints. I'd been talking on the phone to Don Carli, a research fellow at the Institute for Sustainable Communication. Carli said that the risk to Maine's forests—and to forests in Washington and Wisconsin and elsewhere—was not from logging, but from what happens if the logging stops. A thinned or even a completely felled woodland grows back, but when a landowner loses his income from cutting down trees, he has to find another way to make money. Low-density development, with all of its irrevocabilities—paved roads, parking lots, power lines, propane depots, sewage plants, and mini-malls—is one way of getting a return. "Hamburgers and condos kill more trees than printed objects ever will," Carli told me. "If the marketplace for timber, harvested sustainably from Maine's forests, collapses because of the propagation of a myth—which some might say is a fraud—that says that using the newspaper is killing trees, then what happens is the landholder can no longer generate the revenue to pay a master logger for sustainable timber harvesting, and can't pay the taxes. Then a developer offers to buy the land at a steep premium over what it was worth as a forest, and the developer clear cuts the land and turns it into a low-density development. Then it really is deforested."

I drove through Auburn and Turner, north on Route 4, past many FOR-LEASE signs, past the Softie Delight (closed), past the White Fawn Trading Post, which once sold deerskin gloves (closed), past the Antique Snowmobile Museum (open) and the apple-processing factory (closed) and Moose Creek log cabin homes (open). The road curves as you come into Jay, and you drive along the railroad track toward the Otis Mill. The tower is made of brick and, oddly, looks a little like the Campanile in Venice. It still says, at the top: INTERNATIONAL PAPER CO. / 1906.

At a little variety and pizza shop I bought a Coke and three newspapers. The headline on one of the papers, the *Franklin Journal,* was WAUSAU MILL SOLD, CLOSING. The Lewiston *Sun Journal* had a big front-page article: OTIS MILL SOLD. A couple from Jay, owners of Howie's Welding & Fabrication, had bought the mill from Wausau, with financing from a consortium of local towns. They were just figuring out what to do with it, according to the *Sun Journal.* They wanted to save the building and get some people back to work. As for the machinery, "We'll be doing a lot of liquidating."

I drove through Otis's plant gate and into one of the parking spaces near the railroad tracks. When I got out, a man was standing near a shiny red pickup truck. I told him I was writing about the paper industry for a newspaper in San Francisco and he said I should talk to Larry, because Larry had been there over thirty years. He himself had only been there for ten, he said. He asked me inside.

We walked into a low white room with blue trim. Fabric banners announcing yearly corporate safety awards hung from the ceiling. So did the American flag. There were several corkboards for union announcements, but the announcements had all been taken down and the colored pushpins neatly clustered in the cork. There was a bench strewn with flyers for employment retraining and adult-education flyers—also brochures from church groups, job-loss support groups, and workshops on starting a new business. Something from the United Way said: "YOU CAN SURVIVE UNEMPLOYMENT!"

Larry, a man in his sixties, gestured me upstairs to the darkened, unkempt office suite. Larry's own office was still well organized, though. It was officially his last day as an employee of Wausau—October 15, 2009. He'd worked at the plant for thirty-three years, first in maintenance and then in engineering. Schematics and electrical diagrams of the mill that he knew better than almost anyone else were neatly ranked in a file caddy, and pictures of his grandchildren were angled on the bookcase behind him. "When I first started here," he said, "they were making copier-type paper. Then those markets grew so big that we couldn't compete with bigger mills. We started getting into specialty grades, like release base paper—the paper that you throw away behind a self-sticking stamp or a bumper sticker. We did a lot of that. We did some inkjet early in the inkjet era. Again we got competed out of that. Our niche was specialty grades, small orders."

Larry didn't smile much, except when he talked about taking care of his grandchildren. Everyone knew everyone in the plant, he said, and the closing of the second paper machine came as a shock to the town. "It's not good news, for sure," Larry said. "The expectation was that we had a few years left to run the one machine."

Could the plant be brought back online by another owner, I asked, if paper markets picked up? No, said Larry: Wausau had sold the plant to the proprieters of Howie's Welding & Fabrication under the condition that its machines never again be used to make paper in North or South America. "It was sold with a non-compete clause," he explained. Wausau had not only closed the plant down, it had effectively ended any possibility of its resurrection as a paper mill.

As he was shaking my hand, Larry told me I should get in touch with Sherry Judd, who was in charge of Maine's Paper & Heritage Museum.

I got in the car, sighed, and drove on down the road, trying to figure out where to go next. Passing the Otis Federal Credit Union, I saw an electric sign, which said: "Benefit Spaghetti Supper for PAPER & HERITAGE MUSEUM Saturday October 17th 4:30 to 7PM St. Rose Parish Hall Jay." I stopped and took a picture of the sign. Then I drove a few miles upriver to the big Verso Paper mill—"Andro," as the locals call it—where they make the paper for *Cosmo* and *Martha Stewart Living.* More than nine hundred employees work there. I parked near a vintage green Jaguar in the parking lot.

I stood for a while, looking at the sun as it sank behind the two digester towers, with their manelike plumes of steam. Not smoke—steam. The plant was enormous and boxy and clean and, I thought, elegant in its own way. It was heavy industry, but it carried its weight well. There was no sulphurous paper-mill stench. I felt a surge of pride that the paper for many magazines—filled with photographs of food and jungles and expensive New York City interiors and classy brassieres—was being made right here, in Jay, Maine. The biggest building said VERSO in big letters on the side.

We may not make steel anymore, in our hollowed-out

husk of a country, I thought, and we may not make shoes or socks or shirts or china or TVs or telephones or much of anything else except pills and pilotless drones—but we do make very heavy, twenty-four-foot rolls of clean-smelling, smooth-surfaced paper.

I took some pictures of trucks filled with cut logs queued up in one of the feeder roads. Then I went to the security desk and announced myself and drove home. A few days later I got a call from Sondra Dowdell, one of Verso's corporate spokespersons. She explained how efficient the Verso plant was—that it used river power, tree bark, and "black liquor," the lignin-rich waste product of papermaking, as sources of energy. She forwarded me Verso's sustainability report, "A Climate of Change." A chart diagrammed the sources of Verso's energy: more than 50 percent came from recycled biomass—i.e., bark and black liquor—another 1.2 percent came from hydroelectric power. Dowdell had visited one of Verso's customers, Quad/Graphics, in Wisconsin, which prints many magazine titles. "It is amazing," she said, "the talent of the graphic artists and the technical savvy of the people who can lay lovely ink on paper. It is just beautiful to watch."

That Saturday, my wife and I drove back to Jay to go to the spaghetti fund-raiser. We got there early, so that we could have a tour of Maine's Paper & Heritage Museum, which is in a mansion on Church Street in Livermore Falls, where mill managers and their families once lived. The front walk is dug up now, because they're installing a new community walkway and wheelchair ramp.

Walter Ellingwood and Norman Paradis, whose father and grandfather worked at the Otis Mill, and whose son now works at Andro, gave us the museum tour. Walter showed us the burst tester, and the opacity and absorption tester, and a piece of wood that helped you compute the speed of the paper machine—and the two of them pointed out the old steam whistle from the Otis Mill. Walter said that one night long ago he got lost in the swamp in Chesterville and they blew the steam whistle for him so that he could find his way home. Norm showed us a diagram of Andro, with light-up buttons, and he pointed out the medal that his father had gotten for working for International Paper for forty years. It had four diamonds, one for each decade. "He thought that was really really something from International Paper company. It didn't take much to make these people say, 'Jeez, look how nice that is.'" Norm himself also worked for forty years for International Paper, first as a kid in school, and eventually as a supervisor at Andro, with four hundred people under him. "These are some of my buckles that I won," he said, showing us some metal pieces in a glass case. His grandfather, who came from Quebec, had worked in the Otis Mill barefoot, he said, because the chemicals ruined any shoes you wore.

We paused in front of an aerial photograph of the Otis Mill in winter. Norm pointed out the town's skiing hill, just on the other side of the river. The old mill's hydro plant had always powered the ski lifts; now, Norm said, he didn't know what would happen. Then he and Walter had to hurry on over to work at the spaghetti event. We went there, too, to the Rose Church Parish Hall.

There were two other public fund-raisers happening in town that night, but even so, a good crowd came out to have the seven-dollar dinner. Mostly they were retired mill workers, but there were some who had just lost their jobs. Norm greeted everyone—he knew everyone. We sat next to two women who had, long ago, cleaned the offices at the mill. "You can't be delicate eating spaghetti," said one of the women—she was about seventy—when I wiped my mouth. There were two sculptures of saints on the walls, each nearly life-size.

Sherry Judd, the founder of the museum, a smiley woman with short curly hair who wore a western-style blue shirt, was serving spaghetti. Sherry worked at both Otis and Andro, and also at a paper mill in California, and her father was a mason at Otis Mill. She started raising money for the museum several years ago, she said. "I had a vision that someday there was not going to be papermaking in these towns," she told me. "Somebody needs to tell the children about what their ancestors did, how hard they worked to develop this community and the communities around it." For two years she raised money for the museum by towing around a caboose replica filled with papermaking artifacts and giving talks on the need to preserve the past. She had a video made, "Along the Androscoggin," about the history of papermaking in the area, with good clips from mill workers, including Norm Paradis and his son. She wants people to walk into the museum and hear the sound of the papermaking machinery, and see how it worked. "I have a lot of ideas up here," she said, tapping her head, "but we need a curator. And a grant writer."

We bought some tickets for the quilt raffle and a brick to go into the museum's new front walkway, and then we drove home talking about Sherry, Norm, Walter, and the skiing hill next to the river.

Don Carli, of the Institute for Sustainable Communication, told me that this year eighteen paper mills have closed in the United States, and more than thirty-four papermaking machines have been permanently put out of commission. Meanwhile, the power demand from the Internet is growing hugely. "If you do a simple extrapolation of the consumption of energy by data centers, we have a crisis," Carli said. In 2006, the Energy Information Administration estimated that data centers consumed about 60 billion kilowatt hours of electricity—just the centers themselves, not the wireless or fiber-optic networks that connect them or the end-user computers that they serve—while paper mills consumed 75 billion kilowatt hours of electricity, of which more than half was green power from renewable sources. "And that was in 2006," Carli said, "when print wasn't kicked to the curb and declared all but dead and buried. It was still fighting the good fight." Not only is there now a roughly comparable carbon footprint between server farms and paper mills, but the rate of growth in server and data center energy consumption is "metastasizing," he said. "It doubled between 2000 and 2005, and it's due to double again at current rates by 2010." That's one reason why gigantic data centers are now going up far away from cities, Carli added. "You can't go to ConEd and get another ten megawatts of power. You can buy the computers, you can buy the servers. You just can't get juice for them, because the grid is tapped out."

"That's kind of amazing," I said.

"So when we start thinking about transforming more and more of our communication to digital media," Carli said, "we really do have to be asking, Where will the electrons come from?"

I nodded and looked out at the trees.

*(2009)*

# Google's Earth

I'm fond of Google, I have to say. I like Larry Page, who seems, at least in the YouTube videos I've watched, shy and smart, with salt-and-pepper bangs; and Sergey Brin, who seems less shy and jokier and also smart. Ken Auletta, the author of an absorbing, shaggy, name-droppy book called *Googled: The End of the World As We Know It,* doesn't seem to like either of them much—he says that Page has a "Kermit the Frog" voice, which isn't nice, while Brin comes off as a swaggering, efficiency-obsessed overachiever who, at Stanford, aced tests, picked locks, "borrowed" computer equipment from the loading dock, and once renumbered all the rooms in the computer science building. "Google's leaders are not cold businessmen; they are cold engineers," Auletta writes—but "cold" seems oddly wrong. Auletta's own chilliness may be traceable in part to Brin's and Page's reluctance to be interviewed. "After months of my kicking at the door, they opened it," he writes in the acknowledgments. "Google's founders and many of its executives share a zeal to digitize books," he observes, "but don't have much interest in reading them."

They'll probably give more than a glance at *Googled.* I

read the book in three huge gulps and learned a lot—about Google's "cold war" with Facebook, about Google's tussles with Viacom, about Google's role in the "Yahoo-Microsoft melee," and about Google's gradual estrangement from its former ally Apple. Auletta is given to martial similes and parallels, from Prince Metternich in nineteenth-century Europe to Afghanistan now: "Privacy questions will continue to hover like a Predator drone," he writes, "capable of firing a missile that can destroy the trust companies require to serve as trustees for personal data." And he includes some revealing human moments: Larry Page, on the day of Google's hugely successful stock offering, pulls out his cell phone and says, "I'm going to call my mom!"

But what Auletta mainly does is talk shop with CEOs, and that is the great strength of the book. Auletta seems to have interviewed every media chief in North America, and most of them are unhappy, one way or another, with what Google has become. Google is voracious, they say, it has gargantuan ambitions, it's too rich, it's too smug, it makes big money off of O.P.C.—other people's content. One unnamed "prominent media executive" leaned toward Auletta at the 2007 Google Zeitgeist Conference and whispered a rhetorical question in his ear: What real value, he wanted to know, was Google producing for society?

Wait. What real value? Come now, my prominent executive friend. Have you not glanced at Street View in Google Maps? Have you not relied on the humble aid of the search-box calculator, or checked out Google's movie showtimes, or marveled at the quick-and-dirtiness of Google Translate? Have you not made interesting recherché nineteenth-century discoveries in Google Books? Or played with the amazing expando-charts in Google Finance? Have you not designed a strange tall house in Google SketchUp, and did you not make a sudden cry of awed delight the first time you saw the planet begin to turn and loom closer in Google Earth? Are you not signed up for automatic Google News alerts on several topics? I would be very surprised if you are not signed up for a Google alert or two. Surely no other software company has built a cluster of products that are anywhere near as cleverly engineered, as quick-loading, and as fun to fiddle with as Google has, all for free. Have you not *searched*?

Because, let me tell you, I remember the old days, the antegoogluvian era. It was okay—it wasn't horrible by any means. There were cordless telephones, and people wore comfortable sweaters. There was AltaVista, and Ask Jeeves, and HotBot, and Excite, and Infoseek, and Northern Light—with its deep results and its elegant floating schooner logo—and if you wanted to drag through several oceans at once, there was MetaCrawler. But the haul was haphazard, and it came in slow. You chewed your peanut-butter cracker, waiting for the screen to fill.

Then Google arrived in 1998, sponged clean, impossibly fast. Google was like a sunlit white Formica countertop with a single vine-ripened tomato on it. No ads in sight—Google was anti-ad back then. It was weirdly smart, too; you almost never had a false hit. You didn't have to know anything about the two graduate students who had aligned and tuned their secret algorithms—the inseparable Page and Brin—to sense that they were brilliant young software dudes, with all the sneakered sure-footedness of innocence: the "I'm Feeling Lucky" button in that broad blank expanse of screen space made that clear. Google would make us all lucky; that was the promise. And, in fact, it did.

So why are the prominent media executives unhappy? Because Google is making lots of ad money, and there's only so much ad money to go around. Last year almost all of Google's revenue came from the one truly annoying thing that the company is responsible for: tiny, cheesy, three-line text advertisements. These AdWords or AdSense ads load fast, and they're supposedly "polite," in that they don't flicker or have pop-ups, and they're almost everywhere now—on high-traffic destinations like the *Washington Post* or MySpace or Discovery.com, and on hundreds of thousands of little websites and blogs as well. "It's all of our revenue," Larry Page said in a meeting that Auletta attended in 2007.

The headlines say things like "Laser Hair Removal," "Christian Singles," "Turn Traffic Into Money," "Have You Been Injured?" "Belly Fat Diet Recipe," "If U Can Blog U Can Earn," "Are You Writing a Book?" and so on. Countless M.F.A., or Made for AdSense, websites have appeared; they use articles stolen or "scraped" or mashed together from sites like Wikipedia, and their edges are framed with Google's text ads. The ads work on a cost-per-click scheme: the advertiser pays Google only if you actually click on the ad. If you do, he's billed a quarter, or a dollar, or (for some sought-after keywords like "personal injury" or "mesothelioma lawyers") ten dollars or more.

But think—when was the last time you clicked on a three-line text ad? Almost never? Me neither. And yet, in 2008, Google had $21.8 billion in revenue, about 95 percent of which flowed from AdWords/AdSense. (A trickle came from banner and video ads sold by Google's new subsidiary DoubleClick, and from other products and services.) These unartful, hard-sell irritants—which have none of the beauty or the humor of TV, magazine, radio, or newspaper advertising—are the foundation of Google's financial empire, if you can believe it. It's an empire built on tiny grains of keyword-searchable sand.

The advertising revenue keeps Google's stock high, and that allows the company to do whatever it feels like doing. In 2006, when Google's stock was worth $132 billion, the company absorbed YouTube for $1.65 billion, almost with a shrug. "They can buy anything they want or lose money on anything they choose to," Irwin Gotlieb, the chief of GroupM, one of Google's biggest competitors in the media market, told Auletta. If Microsoft is courting DoubleClick, Google can swoop in and buy DoubleClick for $3.1 billion. If the business of cloud computing seems to hold great promise, Google can build twenty or fifty or seventy massive data centers in undisclosed locations around the world, each drawing enough power to light a small city. Earlier this month, Google announced it would pay $750 million in stock for a company called AdMob, to sell banner ads on cell phones. "Once you get to a certain size, you have to figure out new ways of growing," Ivan Seidenberg, the chief executive of Verizon, said to Auletta. "And then you start leaking on everyone else's industry." That's why Auletta's CEOs are resentful.

True, the miracles keep coming: Google Voice, which can e-mail you a transcript of your voice mail messages; and Chrome, a quick, clever Web browser; and Android, the new operating system for mobile devices. One of the latest is an agreement to print books on an ATM-style on-demand printer, the Espresso Book Machine. But perhaps there are too many miracles emanating from one campus now; perhaps brand fatigue is setting in. Google's famous slogan, "Don't be evil," now sounds a little bell-tollingly dystopian. When they were at Stanford, Page and Brin criticized search engines that had become too "advertising oriented." "These guys were opposed to advertising," Auletta quotes Ram Shriram, one of Google's first investors, as saying. "They had a purist view of the world." They aren't opposed now. Now they must be forever finding forage for a hungry, $180 billion ad-maddened beast. Auletta describes an unusual job-interview test that Sergey Brin once gave to a prospective in-house lawyer: "I need you to draw me a contract," Brin said to her. "I need the contract to be for me to sell my soul to the Devil." That was in 2002, the year Google began work internally on what would become AdSense.

Now Page and Brin fly around in a customized Boeing 767 and talk sincerely about green computing, even as the free streamings of everyone's home video clips on YouTube burn through mountaintops of coal. They haven't figured out a way to "monetize"—that is, make a profit from—their money maelstrom YouTube, although I notice that Coffee-mate and Samsung banners appear nowadays in Philip DeFranco's popular video monologues. "The benefit of free is that you get 100 percent of the market," Eric Schmidt, Google's chief executive, explained to Auletta. "Free is the right answer." For a while, perhaps—but maybe free is unsustainable. For newspapers, Auletta writes, "free may be a death certificate." Maybe in the end, even on the Internet, you get what you pay for.

*(2009)*

# Steve Jobs

The other day, I ordered a new machine from Apple, and just before bed I went to the Apple website to check when it was going to ship. There, looking at me, instead of the normal welcome page announcing the latest mojo miracle of euphoric minimalism, was a man with round John Lennon glasses and an intense gaze and a close-cropped beard, photographed in black-and-white. It was Steve Jobs from some years ago, before he got sick. He looked like he wanted to tell me something, but I didn't know what it was. To the left of the photograph, on this simple white screen—not an ounce of color on it anywhere—I saw his birth date: 1955. Then there was a hyphen, and then: 2011.

I was stricken. Everyone who cares about music and art and movies and heroic comebacks and rich rewards and being able to carry several kinds of infinity around in your shirt pocket is taken aback by this sudden huge vacuuming-out of a titanic presence from our lives. We've lost our techno-impresario and digital dream granter. Vladimir Nabokov once wrote, in a letter, that when he'd finished a novel he felt like a house after the movers had carried out the grand piano.

That's what it feels like to lose this world-historical personage. The grand piano is gone.

The next morning, I picked up my latecomer's MacBook Pro—I'd bought it only this year, after more than two decades of struggling with and cursing at software from outside Apple's fruitful orchard—and opened the aluminum top. I went to the website again, and there he was, still Steve, still looking at us. His fingers were in a sort of delicate pinch at his chin, in a pose that photographers like, because they want to see your hands. And the pose made sense, since one of the really noble things that Apple has done is to apply the ancient prehensile precision of pinching, sliding, or tapping fingers to screens and touch pads. Other companies had touch screens. Only Apple made them not seem ridiculous.

I saw Jobs just once, last year, at the first iPad unveiling, in San Francisco. A mass of tech journalists surged into the auditorium while, over the P.A. system, Bob Dylan sang "How does it feel?" The live-bloggers flipped open their laptops. Joshua Topolsky, who was then the head of Engadget, told me that this was bigger than the iPhone. "In a way, I would almost hate to be Apple right now," he said.

Jobs was talking to Al Gore in the front row—Gore appeared to be, amazingly, chewing gum. Then the show began, and Steve went onstage, looking thin but fit, like some kind of aging vegan long-distance runner. He told us that so many millions of iPods had been sold and so many million people had visited the retail stores, with their blue-shirted Geniuses waiting to help you. He said it was kind of incredible, and it was—I found myself applauding joyfully and unjournalistically. And then came the announcement: "And we call it—the iPad."

Immediately afterward, the carping began. Meh, the iPad wasn't magical at all, it was just a big iPhone, the journalists said. One expert called it "D.O.A."—disappointing on arrival. But it was a smash; people immediately began figuring out new ways to use this brilliant, slip-sliding rectangle of private joy.

When he was young, Jobs looked remarkably like James Taylor. When he was older and sick, his blue jeans hung off his body. Even so, I thought that he, like a true marathoner, was going to make it—make it to the iPhone 5, to the iPad 3. Instead, he died, too weak at the end, according to the *Times*, to walk up the stairs of his house.

But Jobs lived to see the Beatles on iTunes, to see Tim Cook, Apple's new CEO, not muff the latest iPhone announcement, and then he left us on our own. He died absolutely the king of the world of talking to people who aren't in the same room with you and of book reading when you don't have a real book and of movie editing and of e-mail and of music distribution—the king of the world of making good things flow better. You have to love him.

*(2011)*

# War

# Why I'm a Pacifist

Six months after the Japanese attack on Pearl Harbor, Abraham Kaufman, the executive secretary of the War Resisters League, stood up in the auditorium of the Union Methodist Church in Manhattan and said something that was difficult to say. Kaufman, a man of thirty-three, who had put himself through City College at night and had worked Sundays selling magazines and candy in a subway station, insisted that we needed peace now—and that to get peace now, we needed to negotiate with Hitler. "This tremendous war can be ended by just one small spark of truth and sanity," he said.

To those who argued that you couldn't negotiate with Hitler, Kaufman replied that the Allies were already negotiating with Hitler, and with Japan, too—over prisoners of war, for example, and the sending of food to Greece. It was important to confer *right away*, Kaufman believed, before either side had lost. Our aim should be what Woodrow Wilson had hoped for at the end of the First World War: a peace without victory. "We ask for peace now," Kaufman said, "while there is still a world to discuss aims, not when it is too late."

What explained Kaufman's urgency? It was simple: he didn't want any more people to suffer and die. Civilian massacres and military horrors were reported daily, and Kaufman feared that the war would prove to be, as he'd written to the *New York Times* two years earlier, "so disastrous as to make the 1917 adventure seem quite mild." He understood exactly what was at stake. In his view, a negotiated peace with Hitler was, paradoxically, the best chance the Allies had of protecting the world from Hitler's last-ditch, exterminative frenzy.

Kaufman was one of a surprisingly vocal group of World War II pacifists—absolute pacifists, who were opposed to any war service. They weren't, all of them, against personal or familial self-defense, or against law enforcement. But they did hold that war was, in the words of the British pacifist and parliamentarian Arthur Ponsonby, "a monster born of hypocrisy, fed on falsehood, fattened on humbug, kept alive by superstition, directed to the death and torture of millions, succeeding in no high purpose, degrading to humanity, endangering civilization and bringing forth in its travail a hideous brood of strife, conflict and war, more war." Along with Kaufman and Ponsonby—and thousands of conscientious objectors who spent time in jail, in rural work camps, in hospitals, or in controlled starvation studies—the ranks of wartime pacifists included Vera Brittain, Rabbi Abraham Cronbach, Dorothy Day, and Jessie Wallace Hughan.

I admire these people. They believed in acts of mercy rather than in fist-shaking vows of retribution. They kept their minds on who was actually in trouble. They suffered, some in small ways, some in large, for what they did and said. They were, I think, beautiful examples of what it means to be human. I don't expect you to agree, necessarily, that they were right in their principled opposition to that enormous war—the war that Hitler began—but I do think you will want to take their position seriously, and see for yourself whether there was some wisdom in it.

Praising pacifists—using the *P*-word in any positive way, but especially in connection with the Second World War— embarrasses some people, and it makes some people angry. I found this out in 2008, when I published a book about the beginnings of the war. *Human Smoke* was a mosaic of contradictory fragments and moments in time, composed largely of quotations; it made no direct arguments on behalf of any single interpretation of World War II. But in an afterword, I dedicated the book to the memory of Clarence Pickett—a Quaker relief worker—and other British and American pacifists, because I was moved by what they'd tried to do. "They tried to save Jewish refugees," I wrote, "feed Europe, reconcile the United States and Japan, and stop the war from happening. They failed, but they were right."

They were *what*? In a review in the *Nation,* Katha Pollitt said she pored over my book obsessively, for hours at a time—and she hated it. "By the time I finished," she wrote, "I felt something I had never felt before: fury at pacifists." Pollitt's displeasure hurt, as bad reviews from thoughtful readers generally do. But I still think the pacifists of World War II were right. In fact, the more I learn about the war, the more I understand that the pacifists were the only ones, during a time of catastrophic violence, who repeatedly put forward proposals that had any chance of saving a threatened people. They weren't naïve, they weren't unrealistic—they were psychologically acute realists.

Who was in trouble in Europe? Jews were, of course.

Hitler had, from the very beginning of his political career, fantasized publicly about killing Jews. They must go, he said, they must be wiped out—he said so in the 1920s, he said so in the 1930s, he said so throughout the war (when they were in fact being wiped out), and in his bunker in 1945, with a cyanide pill and a pistol in front of him, his hands shaking from Parkinson's, he closed his last will and testament with a final paranoid expostulation, condemning "the universal poisoner of all peoples, international Jewry."

Throughout Hitler's tenure, then, the question for the rest of the world was how to respond to a man who was (a) violent; (b) highly irrational; (c) vehemently racist; (d) professedly suicidal; and (e) in charge of an expanding empire. One possibility was to build weapons and raise armies, make demands, and threaten sanctions, embargoes, and other punishments. If Hitler failed to comply, we could say, "This has gone too far," and declare war.

Pacifists thought this was precisely the wrong response. "The Government took the one course which I foresaw at the time would strengthen Hitler: they declared war on Germany," Arthur Ponsonby said in the House of Lords in 1940. The novelist Vera Brittain, who published a biweekly *Letter to Peace Lovers* in London, agreed. "Nazism thrives, as we see repeatedly, on every policy which provokes resistance, such as bombing, blockade, and threats of 'retribution,'" she wrote in her 1942 masterpiece, *Humiliation with Honour*.

The Jews needed immigration visas, not Flying Fortresses. And who was doing their best to get them visas, as well as food, money, and hiding places? Pacifists were. Quaker pacifist Bertha Bracey helped arrange the *Kindertransport*, which saved the lives of some ten thousand Jewish children; pacifists Runham Brown and Grace Beaton of War Resisters International organized the release of Jews and other political prisoners from Dachau and Buchenwald; pacifists André Trocmé and Burns Chalmers hid Jewish children among families in Southern France; and pacifist Eva Hermann spent two years in prison for her actions as a *judenhelfer* ("Jew helper"). "I am fully conscious of the fact that my late husband and I did nothing special," Hermann said when she later received an award from Yad Vashem. "We simply tried to remain human in the midst of inhumanity."

"We've got to fight Hitlerism" sounds good, because Hitler was so self-evidently horrible. But what fighting Hitlerism meant in practice was, above all, the five-year-long Churchillian experiment of undermining German "morale" by dropping magnesium firebombs and two-thousand-pound blockbusters on various city centers. The firebombing killed and displaced a great many innocent people—including Jews in hiding—and obliterated entire neighborhoods. It was supposed to cause an anti-Nazi revolution, but it didn't. "The 'experiment' has demonstrated, so far, that mass bombing does not induce revolt or break morale," Vera Brittain wrote in 1944:

> The victims are stunned, exhausted, apathetic, absorbed in the immediate tasks of finding food and shelter. But when they recover, who can doubt that there will be, among the majority at any rate, the desire for revenge and a hardening process, even if, for a time it may be subdued by fear.

If you drop things on people's heads, they get angry, and they unite behind their leader. This was, after all, just what had happened during the Blitz in London.

"Even so," you may say, "I don't like the word *pacifist*. If somebody came after me or someone I loved, I'd grab a baseball bat, or a gun, and I'd fight him off." Of course you would. I would, too. In fact, that's exactly what I said in college to my girlfriend—who's now my wife—when she announced that she was a pacifist. I also said, What about Hitler? She made two observations: that her father had served in World War II and had come back a pacifist, and that sending off a lot of eighteen-year-old boys to kill and wound other eighteen-year-old boys wasn't the way to oppose Hitler. I said, Well, what other way was there? Nonviolent resistance, she replied. I wasn't persuaded. Still, her willingness to defend her position made a permanent notch, an opening, in my ethical sense.

Next came my brief, insufferable Young Republican phase. For a year, just out of college, I worked on Wall Street, at a company called L. F. Rothschild, Unterberg, Towbin. (They're gone now.) I became a confused but cocky neoconservative. I subscribed to *Commentary*, enthralled by its brilliant pugnacity. I read F. A. Hayek, Irving Kristol, Jeane Kirkpatrick, Karl Popper, Robert Nozick, and Edmund Burke.

I wasn't interested in wars, because wars are sad and wasteful and miserable-making, and battleships and gold epaulettes are ridiculous. But I was excited by the notion of free markets, by the information-conveying subtlety of daily price adjustments, and I thought, Heck, if *Commentary* is right about F. A. Hayek, maybe they're right about fighting communism, too. Surely we had to have hardened missile silos and Star Wars satellites and battalions of Abrams tanks.

And the winning of World War II was unquestionably a plume in our cap, was it not? We'd stepped into the fray; we'd turned the tide of battle. At that point I put aside political thought altogether. It was beyond me. Its prose was bad. I concentrated on writing about what struck me as funny and true.

Then came the Gulf War. I'd just finished writing an upbeat novel about phone sex. My wife and I watched Operation Desert Storm on TV, while it was actually happening. Peter Arnett and Bernard Shaw were up on the roof of the Hotel Al-Rasheed in Baghdad. We saw the tracer fire sprout up over that enormous complicated green city with its ancient name, and we saw the slow toppling of the communication tower, which looked like Seattle's Space Needle, and then, within hours (or so I remember it), we were shown grainy black-and-white clips of precision-guided bombs as they descended toward things that looked like blank, cast-concrete bunkers. Soundless explosions followed. Wolf Blitzer seemed unfazed by it all.

I thought: people are probably dying down there. They can't not be. There was something awful in being able to witness feats of violent urban destruction as they unfolded—to know that big things that had been unbroken were now broken, and that human beings were mutilated and moaning who had been whole—and to comprehend that I was, simply by virtue of being a compliant part of my country's tax base, paying for all this unjustifiable, night-visioned havoc.

Afterward we learned that those early "surgical" strikes had gone astray, some of them, and had killed and wounded large numbers of civilians. We also learned that there were many thousands of bombing runs, or "sorties"—such a clean-sounding word—and that only about 10 percent of the flights had employed "smart" weaponry. Most of the bombing of Iraq in those years, it turned out, was just as blind and dumb as the carpet bombings of World War II. There was, however, a new type of incendiary weapon in use: depleted uranium shells, fired from Gatling guns and helicopter gunships, which became unstoppably heavy burning spears that vaporized metal on contact, leaving behind a wind-borne dust that some said caused birth defects and cancers. Then came the medical blockade, years of it, and punitive bombings. What President Bush began, President Clinton continued. I thought, No, I'm sorry, this makes no sense. I don't care what *Commentary* says: this is not right.

Later still, I saw a documentary on PBS called *America and the Holocaust: Deceit and Indifference,* about the State Department's despicable blockage of visas for Jewish refugees, which permanently broke my trust in Franklin Roosevelt. Then Bill Clinton's Air Force bombed Belgrade. They used the BLU-114/B "soft-bomb," which flung a fettuccine of short-circuiting filaments over power stations in order to bring on massive blackouts, and they also dropped a lot of conventional explosives from high altitudes, killing hundreds of people. And then, in 2002, we bombed Afghanistan, using 15,000-pound "daisy cutters," and killed more people; and then we bombed Iraq again and destroyed more power plants and killed more people—wedding parties, invalids sleeping in their beds. And as we debated the merits of each of these attacks, we inevitably referred back to our touchstone, our exemplar: the Second World War.

War is messy, we say. It's not pretty, but let's be real—it has to be fought sometimes. Cut to the image of a handsome unshaven G.I., somewhere in Italy or France, with a battered helmet and a cigarette hanging from his mouth. World War

II, the most lethally violent eruption in history, is pacifism's great smoking counterexample. We "had to" intervene in Korea, Vietnam, and wherever else, because *look at World War II*. In 2007, in an article for *Commentary* called "The Case for Bombing Iran," Norman Podhoretz drew a parallel between negotiating with Iran's President Mahmoud Ahmadinejad and negotiating with Hitler: we must bomb Iran now, he suggested, because *look at World War II*.

True, the Allies killed millions of civilians and absurdly young conscripts, and they desolated much of Europe and Japan—that was genuinely sad. But what about the Holocaust? We had to push back somehow against that horror.

Yes, we did. But the way you push is everything.


The Holocaust was, among many other things, the biggest hostage crisis of all time. Hostage-taking was Hitler's preferred method from the beginning. In 1923, he led a group of ultranationalists into a beer hall in Munich and, waving a gun, held government officials prisoner. In 1938, after Kristallnacht, he imprisoned thousands of Jews, releasing them only after the Jewish community paid a huge ransom. In occupied France, Holland, Norway, and Yugoslavia, Jews were held hostage and often executed in reprisal for local partisan activity.

By 1941, as Congress was debating the Lend-Lease Act, which would provide military aid to Britain and other Allies, the enormity of the risk became clear, if it wasn't already, to anyone who could read a newspaper. On February 28, 1941, the *New York Times* carried a troubling dispatch from Vienna: "Many Jews here believe that Jews throughout Europe will be more or less hostages against the United States' entry into the war. Some fear that even an appreciable amount of help for Britain from the United States may precipitate whatever plan the Reichsfuehrer had in mind when, in recent speeches, he spoke of the elimination of Jews from Europe 'under certain circumstances.'"

In response to this threat, the *American Hebrew*, a venerable weekly, ran a defiant front-page editorial. "Reduced to intelligibility this message, which obviously derives from official sources, warns that unless America backs down, the Jews in Germany will be butchered," the paper said. So be it. The editorial went on:

> We shall continue, nay, we shall increase our efforts to bring
> about the downfall of the cutthroat regime that is tyrannizing
> the world, and we are not blind to the price we may have to
> pay for our determination. But no sacrifice can be too great,
> no price too dear, if we can help rid the world of the little
> Austrian messiah and his tribe, and all they stand for.

Other Jews, a minority, disagreed. ("In wars it is the minorities that are generally right," Ponsonby once said.) In 1941, Rabbi Cronbach, of Hebrew Union College in Cincinnati, began talking to Rabbi Isidor B. Hoffman, a friendly, bald, hard-to-ruffle student counselor at Columbia University, and Rabbi Arthur Lelyveld of Omaha, Nebraska, about forming a Jewish Peace Fellowship. The fellowship would help support Jewish conscientious objectors who were then in alternative service camps or prisons, and it would, according to the first issue of its newsletter, *Tidings*, "strengthen the devotion to pacifism of self-respecting, loyal Jews."

"Crony" Cronbach became the honorary chairman of the Jewish Peace Fellowship. He was a fine-boned man, always in a suit and tie, and he had a horror of vengeance as an instrument of national policy. He'd seen what happened in the Great War. "People of gentleness, refinement, and idealism became, in the war atmosphere, hyenas raging to assault and kill not merely the foreign foe but equally their own dissenting countrymen," he recalled in his 1937 book *The Quest for Peace.* By supporting the earlier conflict, he suggested, America's Jews had "only helped prepare the way for the Nazi horror which has engulfed us."

The American middle class, still dimly recalling the trenches, the mud, the rats, the typhus, and the general obscene futility of World War I, was perhaps slightly closer to Cronbach's pacifism than to Roosevelt's interventionism— until December 7, 1941. Once Pearl Harbor's Battleship Row burned and sank, the country cried for the incineration of Tokyo. Abraham Kaufman gave his version of what happened in a letter to a historian in 1974: "Roosevelt," Kaufman said, "was willing to use the natural Jewish opposition to Hitler to get US public opinion in favor of his war measures (was unsuccessful as far as the country at large)—and finally managed to force us in with the worst kind of skull-duggery of which history is yet to be written. Shalom, Abe."

With the country demanding vengeance, the false-flag "peace" groups, such as America First, disbanded immediately; the absolute pacifists stuck to their principles. "Our Country Passes from Undeclared to Declared War; We Continue Our Pacifist Stand," wrote Dorothy Day, in her *Catholic Worker.* She quoted Jesus Christ: "Love your enemies, do good to those who hate you and pray for those who persecute and calumniate you." A Catholic newspaper, in response, charged that Day was sentimental and soft. Day, whose life was spent in poverty, caring for homeless people, wrote back: "Let those who talk of softness, of sentimentality, come to live with us in cold, unheated houses in the slums." She said: "Let them live with rats, with vermin, bedbugs, roaches, lice. (I could describe the several kinds of body lice.)" She said: "Let their noses be mortified by the smells of sewage, decay, and rotten flesh. Yes, and the smell of the sweat, blood, and tears spoken of so blithely by Mr. Churchill, and so widely and bravely quoted by comfortable people."

At the War Resisters League headquarters on Stone Street in Manhattan, the executive committee members, including Kaufman, Jessie Hughan, John Haynes Holmes, Sidney E. Goldstein, Isidor Hoffman, Frieda Lazarus, A. J. Muste, and Edward P. Gottlieb (a schoolteacher who had changed his middle name to "Pacifist"), published a post-Pearl Harbor flyer, "Our Position in Wartime." "We respect the point of view of those of our fellow citizens to whom war presents itself as a patriotic duty," the flyer said; nonetheless, the league could not abandon its principles. "The methods chosen determine the ends attained," they wrote. They promised to assist in relief work, to help conscientious objectors, to work for economic justice—and also to call for an early negotiated peace. "The war must end some time and it is proper that we should urge an early rather than a late ending on a basis of benefit and deliverance for all the peoples of the earth." The flyer got a good response, and won them some new enrollees; only a few angry letters came in, one written on toilet paper. The FBI visited the offices and began making a series of what Kaufman called "exhaustive inquiries."

Meanwhile, Hitler's anti-Semitism had reached a final
stage of Götterdämerungian psychosis. As boxcars of war-
wounded, frostbitten German soldiers returned from the
Russian front, and as it became obvious to everyone that the
United States was entering the war, Hitler, his arm tremor
now evident to his associates, made an unprecedented
number of vitriolic threats to European Jewry in close
succession—some in speeches, and some in private meetings.
(The Jew, Hitler now claimed, was a *Weltbrandstifter,* a
world arsonist.) A number of Holocaust historians—among
them Saul Friedländer, Peter Longerich, Christian Gerlach,
and Roderick Stackelberg—have used this concentration of
"exterminatory statements" (the phrase is Friedländer's) to
date, in the absence of any written order, Hitler's decision to
radically accelerate the Final Solution.

The shift, Friedländer writes, came in late 1941,
occasioned by the event that transformed a pan-European
war into a world war: "the entry of the United States into
the conflict." Roderick Stackelberg summarizes: "Although
the 'Final Solution,' the decision to kill all the Jews under
German control, was planned well in advance, its full
implementation may have been delayed until the US entered
the war. Now the Jews under German control had lost their
potential value as hostages." On December 12, 1941, Hitler
confirmed his intentions in a talk before Goebbels and other
party leaders. Goebbels, in his diary, summarized Hitler's
remarks: "The world war is here. The annihilation of the Jews
must be the necessary consequence."

Chelmno, the first killing factory, had already commenced
operation on December 8, 1941: Jews from the ghetto in
a town called Kolo were suffocated with exhaust gasses in
sealed trucks. Beginning in March 1942, the Lublin ghetto

in Poland was liquidated: Jews by the thousands were taken to a second extermination camp, Belzec, and gassed there. More Jews, including orphaned children and old people who had until then been excluded from the camps, were taken from Vienna at the beginning of June. Leonhard Friedrich, a German Quaker arrested in May for helping Jews, later wrote: "In the six months after the United States entered the war, the Gestapo felt under no restraints."

It was an open secret in the United States. On June 2, 1942, a story ran in many American newspapers about Hitler's plan. It was written by Joseph Grigg, a United Press journalist who had been interned by the Germans for five months, then freed with other Americans as a result of negotiations. "There apparently was an effort to create a 'Jew-free' Reich by April 1, as a birthday gift for Hitler," Grigg reported, "but due to transportation and other difficulties the schedule could not be maintained." The massacres in Russia, Poland, and the Baltic states were, Grigg said, "the most terrible racial persecution in modern history."

Meanwhile, that June, the United States was "fighting Hitler" by doing—what? By battling the Japanese navy, by building big bombers, and by having war parades. On June 13, 1942, with the Allied land assault on Europe still two years away, Mayor Fiorello La Guardia threw an enormous war parade in Manhattan. It went on for a full day. There were tanks, planes, and picturesque international costumes, but there were also floats meant to stir emotions of enmity and fear. A float called "Death Rides" moved slowly by: it was a giant animated skeleton beating two red swastika-bearing drums. There was a huge mustachioed figure in a Prussian helmet and body armor, riding a Disney-style dinosaur that strode heedlessly through corpses—the float was called "Hitler, the Axis War Monster." There was a float called "Tokyo: We Are Coming!" in which American airplanes set fire to the city, frightening off a swarm of large yellow rats. The *New York Herald Tribune's* reporter wrote that the only thing missing from the parade was subtlety. This is what the United States was doing during the early phase of the Holocaust: beating big red toy death drums on Fifth Avenue.

During this same mid-war period, the Royal Air Force's attacks on German civilian life crossed a new threshold of intensity. The militarily insignificant city of Lübeck, on the Baltic Sea, crowded with wood-timbered architectural treasures, was the target of the first truly successful mass firebombing, on the night of March 28, 1942, which burned much of the old city and destroyed a famous, centuries-old painting cycle called *Totentanz* ("The Dance of Death"). "Blast and bomb, attack and attack until there is nothing left," said the Sunday *Express*. "Even if 'Lübecking' does not crack the morale of Germany, it is certainly going to raise our spirits," said the *Daily Mail*. "We have no hesitation on any humanitarian grounds in writing over the whole map of Germany, as we have done at Lübeck and Rostock, 'This was once a city.'" Vera Brittain, reading through a pile of these newspaper clippings, exclaimed: "We are Gadarene swine, inhabited by devils of our own making, rushing down a steep place into the sea."

Operation Millennium was the RAF's next large-scale fire raid, at the end of May. Nearly a thousand bombers flowed toward the city of Cologne, where they dropped about 1,600 tons of bombs—more firebombs than high explosives—in half an hour, destroying tens of thousands of houses and apartments and more than twenty churches. The area around the city's main cathedral was a roasted ruin. "You have no idea of the thrill and encouragement which the Royal Air Force bombing has given to all of us here," wrote Roosevelt's personal aide, Harry Hopkins, to Churchill. He added: "I imagine the Germans know all too well what they have to look forward to."

No doubt the Germans did know—in any case, they promptly blamed the Jews for the bombings. On the radio, Goebbels said that Germans were now fighting for their very skins. Then again came the overt threat: "In this war the Jews are playing their most criminal game and they will have to pay for it with the extermination of their race throughout Europe and, maybe, even beyond." American newspapers gave wide coverage to Goebbels's speech. GOEBBELS SAYS JEWS WILL DIE FOR R.A.F. RAIDS, said the *New York Herald Tribune*. NAZIS BLAME JEWS FOR BIG BOMBINGS, said the *New York Times*. JEWS FACE MASS EXTERMINATION BY ENRAGED NAZIS, said the headline in the *Altoona Mirror*. GOEBBELS THREATENS TO WIPE OUT JEWS, said the *Pittsburgh Press*.

The Jewish press took the threat seriously, too. "The Jews were to be used, Hitler often promised, as hostages to assure the good behavior of the democracies," said *Opinion: A Jewish Journal of Life and Letters*. "The terrific RAF poundings of Cologne, Essen, Emden, Rostock and other German cities are being answered by the nazis with threats of reprisals—against the Jews." And Rabbi Louis I. Newman, of Temple Rodeph Sholom, devoted part of his sermon that Saturday to Goebbels's speech. "The dastardly threat of Goebbels that the Nazis will exterminate the Jews if the

WHY I'M A PACIFIST

R.A.F. continues its bombardment of German cities should be clear evidence that the Jews of Germany and occupied countries have been and are merely hostages in the hands of brigands and gangsters," Newman said, as reported in the *New York Times*. "Jews have been martyrs before in the annals of mankind, and if the slaying of Jews is necessary to redeem humanity from the blight of nazism those who are the victims will prove again the stuff of which the prophet and the martyr race is fashioned."

In the Warsaw ghetto, that same June of 1942, Emanuel Ringelblum read the reports and remembered an old story about a profligate nobleman. Shlomo, the nobleman's moneylender, auctioned the man's land in payment for debts. The nobleman, enraged, bought a dog, named him Shlomo, and beat him daily. The same thing, wrote Ringelblum, was happening to the Germans: "They are being defeated, their cities are being destroyed, so they take their revenge on the Jews." Ringelblum and his friends, although of several minds about the need for retribution, agreed on one thing: "Only a miracle can save us: a sudden end to the war, otherwise we are lost."

*A sudden end to the war, otherwise we are lost.* This, then, was the context for Abraham Kaufman's June 16, 1942, talk at the Union Methodist Church. First worry about the saving of lives, his logic went—everything else is secondary. In July, the SS began the liquidation of the Warsaw ghetto, loading six thousand people onto freight cars every day. The head of the Jewish Council, Adam Czerniaków, committed suicide rather than comply; the Germans were holding his wife hostage. Knowing what we know now, wouldn't we all have stood and said what Kaufman said?

Confirmation of the Final Solution didn't get out widely
in the Western press until November 1942, when Rabbi
Stephen Wise, after inexplicable delays, called a press
conference to reveal the substance of an urgent telegram he
had received from Switzerland in August. The Associated
Press reported: "Dr. Stephen S. Wise, chairman of the World
Jewish Congress, said tonight that he had learned through
sources confirmed by the State Department that about half
the estimated 4,000,000 Jews in Nazi-occupied Europe have
been slain in an 'extermination campaign.'"

Once Wise broke his silence, there was a surge of press
coverage. President Roosevelt promised retribution and,
as Churchill had done not long before, quoted Longfellow:
"The mills of God grind slowly, yet they grind exceeding
small." Yiddish papers carried black bars of mourning. And
in December, Anthony Eden, Churchill's foreign minister,
read an Allied condemnation in Parliament. "The German
authorities," Eden declared, "not content with denying to
persons of Jewish race in all the territories over which their
barbarous rule has been extended the most elementary
human rights, are now carrying into effect Hitler's oft
repeated intention to exterminate the Jewish people in
Europe." Like Roosevelt, Eden promised that the culprits
would "not escape retribution." After Eden was finished,
there was a moment of silence: a minute or two of grief
for the Jews of Europe. "The whole crowded House—an
unprecedented thing to do and not provided for by any
Standing Order—rose to its feet and stood in silent homage
to those who were about to die," Sydney Silverman, MP,

recollected after the war. "We could not do much to help them. No one desired that our war activity should be moderated in any sort of way or that our war effort should be in any way weakened in order to bring succor to those threatened people."

The atrocity was so gargantuan, wrote the *Nation* a week later, that it would have to await the perspective of history to be understood. Again came the question—what to do? "Peace with Hitler for the sake of saving hostages is out of the question," the *Nation*'s editors asserted. "Such a surrender would mean disaster for the world, for the Jews above all. Yet the harder we fight, the nearer the doom of the Nazis approaches, the fiercer will grow their homicidal mania. Let it be admitted in all solemnity that there is no escape from this ghastly dilemma." The only thing to do was fight on.

No, there was a better way, thought Jessie Wallace Hughan, founder of the War Resisters League. Hughan, a soft-faced, wide-smiling woman in her late sixties, was a poet and high-school teacher (she had been Abraham Kaufman's English teacher at Textile High School). On November 27, 1942, she sent a letter to two fellow pacifist leaders, asking them to help her mount a campaign.

It seems that the only way to save thousands and perhaps millions of European Jews from destruction would be for our government to broadcast the promise of a speedy and favorable armistice on condition that the European minorities are not molested any further. I know how improbable it is that our U.S. government would accept this but if it is the only possibility, ought not our pacifist groups to take some action?

Hughan gave talks on the necessity of rescue, she wrote letters to the State Department and the White House, and she and Abraham Kaufman, with the help of volunteers, distributed thousands of pro-armistice flyers. We must look beyond slogans like "unconditional surrender," Hughan wrote. "The European Jews, helpless victims of the Nazism we are fighting, are being ruthlessly massacred as the war goes on. Victory will not save them, for imminent defeat may be the signal for their extermination: only an armistice can rescue them, by including in its terms the immediate release of all Jews to allied guardianship." A peace without delay, conditional upon the release of Jews and other political prisoners, might bring the end of Hitler's reign, she suggested: "There are many anti-Nazis in the Reich, and hope is a stronger revolutionary force than despair." She wrote a blunt letter on the subject to the *New York Times*: "We must act now, because dead men cannot be liberated." The *Times* didn't print it.

Other pacifists publicly took up this cause. In a peace letter, Vera Brittain said that Jewish rescue required "the termination or the interruption of the war, and not its increasingly bitter continuation." Dorothy Day wrote a front-page article in the *Catholic Worker* in May 1943, headlined PEACE NOW WITHOUT VICTORY WILL SAVE JEWS:

> If we persist in our present war of unconditional surrender; if we promise only executions, retributions, punishments, dismemberments, indemnities and no friendly participation with the rest of the world in a post-war world, we shall be depriving not only the German people of all hope, but we shall be signing the death sentence of the remnant of Jews still alive. If, on the contrary, we demand the release of all

Jews from the ghettos of occupied Europe and work for a peace without victory, offering some hope, as Wilson did in his fourteen points, then there is a chance of saving the Jews.

In the following issue Day laid out a detailed plan: loosen immigration quotas, reopen Palestine, issue Nansen passports to stateless Jews, establish safe havens and sanctuaries in neutral countries, and feed those who are trapped where they are: "In view of the fact that mass starvation is the design of the Nazi regime, the United Nations should take appropriate steps without delay to organize a system for the feeding of the victims of Nazi oppression who are unable to leave the jurisdiction and control of the action." The Jewish Peace Fellowship called for an armistice to prevent Jewish extermination and "make an end to the world-wide slaughter."

Even lapsed or near pacifists—including Eleanor Rathbone in the House of Commons, and the publisher Victor Gollancz—urgently echoed this sentiment: If we failed to make some kind of direct offer to Hitler for the safe passage of Jews, we shared a responsibility for their fate. Gollancz printed a quarter of a million copies of an extraordinary pamphlet called "Let My People Go," in which he questioned the Churchill government's promise of postwar retribution. "This 'policy,' it must be plainly said, will not save a single Jewish life," he wrote.

Will the death, after the war, of a Latvian or Lithuanian criminal, or of a Nazi youth who for ten years has been specially and deliberately trained to lose his humanity—will the death of these reduce by one jot or tittle the agony of a Jewish child who perhaps at this very moment at which I write, on Christmas day, three hours after the sweet childish carol, 'O come, all ye faithful,' was broadcast before the seven o'clock news, is going to her death in a sealed coach, her lungs poisoned with the unslaked lime with which the floor is strewn, and with the dead standing upright about her, because there is no room for them to fall?

What mattered, Gollancz held, was, and he put it in italics, *the saving of life now.* The German government had to be approached immediately and asked to allow Jews to emigrate. The Allies had nothing to lose with such a proposal. "If refused, that would strip Hitler of the excuse that he cannot afford to fill useless mouths," Gollancz wrote. "If accepted, it would not frustrate the economic blockade, because Hitler's alternative is not feeding but extermination."

Nobody in authority in Britain and the United States paid heed to these promptings. Anthony Eden, who'd been tasked by Churchill with handling queries about refugees, dealt coldly with one of many importunate delegations, saying that any effort to obtain the release of the Jews from Hitler was "fantastically impossible." On a trip to the United States, Eden candidly told Cordell Hull, the secretary of state, that the real difficulty with asking Hitler for the Jews was that "Hitler might well take us up on any such offer, and there simply are not enough ships and means of transportation in the world to handle them." Churchill agreed. "Even were we to obtain permission to withdraw all Jews," he wrote in reply to one pleading letter, "transport alone presents a problem which will be difficult of solution."

Not enough shipping and transport? Two years earlier,

the British had evacuated nearly 340,000 men from the beaches of Dunkirk in just nine days. The U.S. Army Air Forces had many thousands of new planes. During even a brief armistice, the Allies could have airlifted and transported refugees in very large numbers out of the German sphere.

In the American press, calls for a negotiated peace were all but inaudible. The only significant publicity that any U.S. peace advocacy group got after 1942 was negative— witheringly negative, in one instance, and rightly so. It came in connection with the formation of something called the Peace Now Movement, which set up an office on Manhattan's East Fortieth Street in July 1943. Abraham Kaufman, while admiring the antiwar writings of the new group's chairman, George Hartmann, remained wary of this group, and not just because its name appropriated his own group's most stirring and useful phrase. What disturbed him was that the Peace Now Movement was willing, as the War Resisters League was not, to accept support from pro-fascists or anti-Semites, or even from "the devil himself," according to Hartmann, in order to bring the war to an end.

Kaufman also had doubts about the past of one of the group's organizers, John Collett, who'd been institutionalized for a mental disorder, and whose Norwegian visa imparted a fascist taint. In any case, Collett, out on a speaking tour, self-destructed: he was arrested in Cincinnati for peeping into a sorority shower and fined a hundred dollars.

After Collett resigned, another Peace Now staffer, Bessie Simon, carried on her friendly overtures to prominent isolationists and Nazi apologists, including Charles Lindbergh. Simon also hired a pretty blonde secretary, who turned out to be a plant working under an assumed name ("Virginia Long"), and whose stolen haul of damning correspondence soon found its way to the *New York Post*. PEACE NOW ENLISTS BUNDISTS! was one front-page headline in a week-long exposé. *Life* called the Peace Now Movement "not only dangerous but subversive"; the House Un-American Activities Committee condemned one of the group's mailings, which encouraged churchmen to ask their congregations to follow Christ and lay down their arms. It was, the Dies Committee determined, "a plan for mass treason which was truly colossal in its conception."

As Kaufman had foreseen, the scandal of Hartmann's Peace Now Movement eclipsed much of the work he and his colleagues had done. Now, if you were willing to say publicly that the killing should stop, you weren't just a harmless simpleton, you were a fascist fellow-traveler. According to David Lawrence, a widely syndicated conservative columnist and editor of *U.S. News,* peace talk diminished Allied soldiers' fighting zeal. "It is a weapon which is worth more to the enemy than any other," he wrote. "That's why it is vital to squelch any 'peace now' activities at their very inception."

And yet Kaufman, Hughan, and the other pacifists— the real ones—regrouped and carried on. In March 1944, with thousands of Jews still living who were not destined to survive, the War Resisters League published an updated demand that the Allies call a peace conference, stipulating Jewish deliverance. "The fortunes of war have turned, and with them the responsibility for war," Jessie Hughan wrote. "The guilt is upon our heads until we offer our enemies an honorable alternative to bitter-end slaughter. Are we fighting for mere victory or, as enlightened adults, for humanity and civilization?"

We were fighting, it seems, for mere victory. It was inconceivable that we could stop, even though an end to the fighting was the solvent that would have dissolved quicker than anything the thick glue of fear that held Hitler and Germany together. By 1944, Hitler's health was failing. He was evil, but he wasn't immortal. Whether or not the German opposition, in the sudden stillness of a conditional armistice, would have been able to remove him from power, he would be dead and gone eventually. And some of his millions of victims would have lived.

Peace and quiet was what the world needed so desperately then. Time to think, and mourn. Time to sleep without fear. Time to crawl out of the wreckage of wherever you were and look around, and remember what being human was all about. Instead, what did we do? Bomb, burn, blast, and starve, waiting for the unconditional surrender that didn't come until the Red Army was in Berlin. We came up with a new kind of "sticky flaming goo," as the *New York Times* called what would later be known as napalm. Allied airplanes burned the Rouen cathedral, so that the stones crumbled to pieces when touched, destroyed Monte Cassino, and killed two hundred schoolchildren during a single raid in Milan. A conservative MP, Reginald Purbrick, who had wanted the Royal Air Force to drop a big bomb into the crater of Mount Vesuvius ("to make a practical test as to whether the disturbances created thereby will give rise to severe earthquakes and eruptions"), began asking the prime minister whether the Royal Air Force might bomb Dresden and other cities in eastern Germany. Churchill eventually obliged him. Remorse works well, but it works only in peacetime.

When Vera Brittain argued against the Allied program of urban obliteration in her 1944 pamphlet *Massacre by Bombing*, the Writers' War Board, a government-funded American propaganda agency, pulled out all the stops in attacking her. MacKinlay Kantor (who later cowrote Curtis LeMay's memoir, the one that talked about bombing Vietnam "back into the Stone Age") published a letter in the *Times* dismissing Britain's "anguished ramblings." The Japanese and Germans well understood the "language of bombs," Kantor said. "May we continue to speak it until all necessity for such cruel oratory has passed."

Some historians, still believing that bombing has a magical power to communicate, conclude from this dismal stretch of history that the Allied air forces should have bombed the railroad tracks that led to the death camps, or bombed the camps themselves. But bombing would have done absolutely nothing except kill more Jews (and Jews were already dying when Allied fighter planes routinely strafed boxcars in transit). A cease-fire—"a pause in the fury of hostilities," as Vera Brittain called it in one of her newsletters—was the one chance the Allies had to save Jewish lives, and the pacifists proposed it repeatedly, using every means available to them.

They were ignored. The Holocaust continued, and the firebombing continued: two parallel, incommensurable, war-born leviathans of pointless malice that fed each other and could each have been stopped long before they were. The mills of God ground the cities of Europe to powder—very slowly—and then the top Nazis chewed their cyanide pills or were executed at Nuremberg. Sixty million people died all over the world so that Hitler, Himmler, and Goering could commit suicide? How utterly ridiculous and tragic.

Pacifism at its best, said Arthur Ponsonby, is "intensely practical." Its primary object is the saving of life. To that overriding end, pacifists opposed the counterproductive barbarity of the Allied bombing campaign, and they offered positive proposals to save the Jews. Create safe havens, call an armistice, negotiate a peace that would guarantee the passage of refugees. We should have tried. If the armistice plan failed, then it failed. We could always have resumed the battle. Not trying leaves us culpable.

At a Jewish Peace Fellowship meeting in Cincinnati some years after the war, Rabbi Cronbach was asked how any pacifist could justify opposition to World War II. "War was the sustenance of Hitler," Cronbach answered. "When the Allies began killing Germans, Hitler threatened that, for every German slain, ten Jews would be slain, and that threat was carried out. We in America are not without some responsibility for that Jewish catastrophe."

If we don't take seriously pacifists like Cronbach, Hughan, Kaufman, Day, and Brittain—these people who thought as earnestly about wars and their consequences as did politicians or generals or think-tankers—we'll be forever suspended in a kind of immobilizing sticky goo of euphemism and self-deception. We'll talk about intervention and preemption and no-fly zones, and we'll steer drones around distant countries on murder sorties. We'll arm the world with weaponry, and every so often we'll feel justified in taxiing out a few of our stealth airplanes from their air-conditioned hangars and dropping some expensive bombs. Iran? Pakistan? North Korea? What if we "crater the airports," as Senator Kerry suggested, to slow down Gaddafi? As I write, the United States has begun a new war against

Libya, dropping more things on people's heads in the name of humanitarian intervention.

When are we going to grasp the essential truth? War never works. It never has worked. It makes everything worse. Wars must be, as Jessie Hughan wrote in 1944, renounced, rejected, declared against, over and over, "as an ineffective and inhuman means to any end, however just." That, I would suggest, is the lesson that the pacifists of the Second World War have to teach us.

*(2011)*

# We Don't Know the
# Language We Don't Know

One Saturday last month I went to Lafayette Park in Washington, D.C., across the street from the White House, in order to protest several wars. The squirrels were out doing seasonal things. A tree was balancing big buds on the finger-ends of its curving branches; the brown bud coverings, which looked like gecko skins, were drawing back to reveal inner loaves of meaty magnolial pinkness. A policeman in sunglasses, with a blue and white helmet, sat on a Clydesdale horse, while two tourists, a father and his daughter, gazed into the horse's eyes. The pale, squinty, early-spring perfection of the day made me smile.

The demonstration wasn't officially supposed to start until noon, but already off in the distance a few hundred people had gathered near a platform festooned with a row of black-and-white Veterans for Peace flags. It was March 19, the eighth anniversary of the shock-and-aweing of Iraq, and there was an air of expectancy: arrests were going to happen that day. I sat down on a bench and watched volunteers setting up loudspeakers. Birds were getting in as much chirping as they could before the human noise began. A woman with an armful of red and black signs passed by. Her signs said:

STOP THESE WARS
EXPOSE THE LIES
FREE BRADLEY MANNING

Jay Marx, head of Proposition One, a nuclear disarmament group, took the microphone. He was wearing a knit hat. "Testing, one, two, three," Marx said into the microphone. "Testing our patience. Testing, four, five, six, seven, eight years of war. Eight years of lies! And we're live! This park is live! The Vets for Peace are live in Lafayette Park!" (Cheering.)

Code Pink, a women's antiwar group, was in charge of the pre-noon proceedings. Jodie Evans, Code Pink's founder, sang "When we make peace instead of war," to the tune of "Oh when the saints go marching in." She had on a black hat and a pink vest. She introduced a retired army colonel, Ann Wright, who had resigned her job at the State Department in 2003 because she couldn't countenance the invasion of Iraq. "I'll tell you, when Code Pink's in the house, you know it!" said Wright, to hollers of approval. She pointed across the street. "And the White House knows it!" Wright told us that she had just gotten back from Afghanistan, where the Obama administration was building a $500 million embassy complex. "It's going to be the largest embassy in the world—larger than Baghdad," she said. "As a retired colonel, as a former member of the US State Department, and as a citizen, I say that it is our obligation to raise hell! To raise cain! To get these endless wars stopped, and take care of America!" (Big cheering.)

I hurried off to buy some double-A batteries for my audio recorder, and when I got back a group called Songrise was performing a heartbreaking a capella version of John Lennon's "Imagine." The crowd was bigger now, about eight hundred people. More police had gathered, too.

Caroline Casey, another patroness of Code Pink, came on the stage to explain, in a strong contralto voice, what it meant to be advocating peace at the time of vernal equinox and lunar perigee. The culture of cataclysmic dominance was going down, Casey told us, and the culture of reverent ingenuity was rising up out of the cracks. She invited us to spiral the best of ourselves forth into what she called "the memosphere." She also offered a quote from Hafiz, a Persian poet: "The small man builds prisons for everyone he meets, but the wise woman ducks under the moon and tosses keys to the beautiful and rowdy prisoners." She tossed a figurative key to young WikiLeaker Bradley Manning, in solitary confinement in Quantico, as an agent of democracy, and she tossed a second key to President Obama, to help him see the wrong of Manning's imprisonment. Obama was himself, she said, "a prisoner of empire."

A group of Code Pinkers arranged themselves in a row and opened seventeen pink umbrellas that spelled BRING OUR WAR $$ HOME. The crowd was up to about fifteen hundred people by now. A small but committed group of pro-defense protesters—eight of them by my count—were standing out in the street holding flags. Some of their signs seemed to date from another era: CHE IS DEAD GET OVER IT! (held by a woman in sunglasses), and JANE FONDA TRAITOR (held by a man in a black biker jacket). One woman, wearing a gigantic red hat with a red bow, had a sign that said:

I Stand 4
CODE RED, White & BLUE
NOT Pink & YELLER

I went back nearer the platform to hear some of the Vets for
Peace speakers. Mike Ferner, who worked in a navy hospital
during the Vietnam War and was the author of *Inside the
Red Zone: A Veteran for Peace Reports from Iraq,* was the
master of ceremonies—he was an immediately likable guy
with a thick asymmetry of graying hair. He introduced
Debra Sweet, director of World Can't Wait, another antiwar,
anti-occupation group that had its beginnings during the
Bush era. "We have to take a stand against these immoral,
illegitimate wars, and this torture being done in our name,"
she said. "I'll see you in front of the White House!" (Huge
cheer.)

Caneisha Mills, who had successfully sued the city of
Washington for setting up military-style police checkpoints
in poor neighborhoods, said: "The president of the United
States, Barack Obama, said that he was going to make a
change in the United States. The change that we've seen
has only been for the worse." Obama and the government
were claiming, falsely, that there was no money for education
and health care, Mills argued—and now he was calling for
military intervention in Libya, even after Libya announced
a cease-fire. "We can see that he only cares about wars of
occupation and massive slaughter," Mills said.

Zach Choate, injured in Iraq, read a Dear Mr. Obama
letter, which he then rolled up and put in a pill bottle that had
held one of the medications that he's had to take since the
war. "You said you would bring my brothers and sisters home,
and they're still there," he read. "5,938 of my buddies have

died. I'm here today to act peacefully in civil disobedience for my disapproval of these wars."

I walked around the crowd and took some pictures of a six-foot-long scale model of a Reaper drone. It was painted gray, with wide wings and underwing missiles tipped with red and orange paint, and it was balanced on a pole above our heads. What would daily life be like, it prompted us to ask, if we lived in a country where real drones were flying around high overhead, able to murder by remote control? It would be deeply radicalizing and terrorism-sustaining—obviously.

A woman held a white cloth with lettering on it: "How Many Lives Will You End? How Many Billions Will You Spend? Before You End This Madness?" Meanwhile someone—I missed his name—began talking about the heavy "F.O.G.," or Forces of Greed, which surrounded us. "President Obama—with his very lovely smile and lovely family, and beautiful rhetoric—sometimes fools people. Now we know that he's part of the F.O.G. The F.O.G. needs to be lifted."

A woman shook my hand and said, "You are so familiar— have we been arrested together?" I said no, I'd never been arrested.

Ralph Nader was up eventually. He began with some words of sympathy for the victims of the disaster in Japan. Then he said, "General Petraeus said there are fifty al-Qaeda, they estimate, in Afghanistan. Why are we blowing that country apart? Why are we sending our injured and sick home day after day?" Iraq, too—we'd blown that country apart. He quoted a coinage from a recent book called *Erasing Iraq:* "sociocide."

Someone near me with yellow dyed hair abruptly turned his back on Nader and said "I'm still pissed off at that son-of-a-bitch about Florida." Everyone else was clapping, though. How was it, Nader asked, that twenty-five or thirty thousand Taliban fighters, with no air force, no navy, no tanks—armed only with Kalishnikovs and suicide belts and rocket-propelled grenades—were able to resist the most powerful military force in history? "Because," said Nader, "they have a cause that says 'Expel the invader.' Expelling the invader will be forever the cause of anybody in the world who is invaded."

A duct-taped bucket came around for donations to Vets for Peace, and I stuffed in some money. Then Brian Becker of the ANSWER Coalition, a socialist group that sponsored some of the biggest peace demonstrations before the Iraq War, tore into the Libyan intervention, which had begun with the launch of a hundred cruise missiles that morning. "We have to learn the lessons that are so crystal clear, as Obama and the Pentagon and France and Britain prepare in the next few hours to start dropping bombs on the people of Libya in the name of democracy," Becker said. "Let's know this: Libya is the largest oil producer in Africa, and there's no possible way that if the U.S. goes into Libya it's ever going to come out." Libya must be the masters of their own destiny, he continued. "We ourselves reject the idea, fed to us once again, that U.S. imperialism, with all of its guns and bombs and missiles, is going to help an oppressed people. The only help we can give to the people of Libya and Egypt and Tunisia and Yemen is to make our own revolution right here!" (Whooping and cheering.)

Watermelon Slim, a craggy country blues singer and Vietnam vet in a camouflage T-shirt, told President Obama to listen up. "Mr. Obama, these wars were George Bush's wars," he said. "They are now your wars. I hate to say that, but it's a fact." Vietnam vets, Slim said, were now standing at the

White House to make known their opposition, just as they'd done back in 1971: "Mr. Obama, you and Mr. Nixon got that in common. We're paying attention to you. We say, bring our brothers and sisters home, right now!"

Somebody gave me a flyer for the next protest, on April 9 in New York City. Somebody else handed me another flyer, "How Is the War Economy Working for You?" It was published by Veterans for Peace's Smedley D. Butler Brigade. On it was a quote from Marine Corps General Smedley Butler (1881–1940): "I spent 33 years in the Marines being a high-class muscle man for big business, for Wall Street and the bankers," Butler wrote. "The general public shoulders the horrible bill in lives, shattered minds, and back-breaking taxes for generations."

Then Daniel Ellsberg, former Marine Corps company commander and distributor of Vietnam War secrets, was on. He wore a blue blazer and a blue shirt and a sober tie. He was only a few weeks away from his eightieth birthday. He looked great. "Can one person make a difference?" Ellsberg asked. "I would say that without Bradley Manning having released the cables through WikiLeaks that inspired the uprising in Tunisia—along with the self-sacrifice of a Tunisian named Muhammad Bouazizi, who burned himself to death in protest against the oppression there—without either of those individuals, Ben Ali, our dictator there, whom we were supporting, would still be there. And Mubarak would still be in Egypt. So one person can make a difference."

Ellsberg asked us if we knew the names of the two languages of Afghanistan. Almost nobody in the audience knew. "The two languages are Dari—which is eastern Farsi, or Persian—and Pashto," he said. "In Vietnam, none of us spoke the language, but we knew the language that we didn't speak—that it was Vietnamese. We're fighting in a country now where we don't know the language we don't know."

Kings, Ellsberg said, once locked their critics away in dungeons till they were forgotten; the French, he reminded us, referred to these dungeons as *oubliettes*. Kings also once declared wars without parliamentary approval. Bradley Manning was now in an oubliette at Quantico for revealing America's war crimes; and the Libyan intervention was, like Korea, an illegal war, waged without congressional approval. President Obama believed that he was in a throne room in the oval office, said Ellsberg, with a crown on his head. It was up to us to knock that crown off. (Wild cheers, including Indian war-cry ululations.)

Ellsberg said: "One of the groups in Tahrir Square, that had been fighting Mubarak for some time, called itself Kafaya, 'enough.' We need an 'enough' movement: enough to empire, enough to imperial wars, enough to oubliettes." And he ended with: "This is a good day to get arrested at the White House, and tomorrow at Quantico." (Mad applause.)

Mike Ferner took the mic. "If you're planning on getting arrested, if you have any questions, Matt Daloisio is back here behind the stage. Come on up and see Matt." Once arrested, you had to pay a hundred dollars to be freed, or else you had to appear later in court, Ferner advised. He introduced Chris Hedges, columnist for Truthdig, who said, "If you want to stop terrorism, you must first stop committing acts of terror." Ferner then gave us guidance on the march. "This is going to be a silent march," he said. "We need to keep in mind what we're here for, which is to observe the eighth anniversary of the invasion of Iraq. We're here for a solemn purpose. So let's be that way, purposeful and thoughtful in our march." He thanked us for coming and then he said, "I'd like to add one personal note to this, which has really been rubbing me raw for some time now." The people in Afghanistan and Iraq were bearing the brunt of the military aggression, Ferner said, while our cities, our veterans, and our public institutions were all collateral damage. "Our infrastructure and our public institutions may not be being bombed, but they're being allowed to slowly rot. And that has got to stop."

The last speaker was Ryan Endicott, an Iraq marine veteran. He was full of powerful indignation, and he spoke at the top of his lungs. "When we joined the military, we rose our right hand, and we swore to defend the people of this country against all enemies foreign and domestic," he said. "And the biggest enemies to the people of this country do not live in the sands of Iraq. They do not live in the caves of Afghanistan." He gestured toward the White House. "They live hundreds of yards away!" (Roar of agreement.)

Endicott said: "We know the realities of these brutal occupations, and we know that these people are not our enemies. The fact is that these wars have cost the American people more than just our lives and our limbs." The wars had cost trillions of dollars, he cried—trillions that could have gone toward free education and health care, that could have prevented millions from losing their homes, and that could have helped thousands of homeless veterans get off the streets. "And that's why we're here today in the streets! The streets that we built! With our sweat, and our tears, and our blood!"

Revolutionary change was possible, Endicott believed: Harvey Milk, Martin Luther King, the people of Tunisia, the people of Egypt, had all made revolutionary change. "We're going to shut down our workplaces. We're going to shut down our factories and our schools. And we're going to tell this government not one more dollar! Not one more bullet! Not one more bomb! Not one more day of U.S. imperialism!" (Cacophony of applause.)

People began arranging their banners and signs and assembling to march. "While everybody is waiting, will you please remove your hats?" said Watermelon Slim. "Except those of us who have chemical gear on." Then he came to attention. "Present—arms!" He played taps on his harmonica, with a slow mournful vibrato. "We must mourn, we must also show our anger," he said. "We must also bear this war evenly. Let's go let them bear some of it, too. Come on."

Then we marchers set out, led by a World War II vet from the 90th Infantry Division, Third Army. We walked silently around several blocks to the west of the White House (evidently the police didn't want us to actually circle the White House), and then half an hour later, we massed where we'd begun, in front of the black, sharp-tipped White House fence.

There were many policemen now: motorcycle cops, park police, horseback police, K-9 police, and sinister-looking SWAT teams in black hats and black uniforms tucked into high black boots. It was a strangely varied festival of police "protection." They were hauling out segments of a metal crowd-control fence. They locked together the segments, fencing off a large area of public sidewalk and street. (The street, Pennsylvania Avenue, is normally open to public foot traffic and closed to cars.) And then they announced that if you stood on the wrong side of the temporary fence you were going to get arrested. The police created, in other words, a potential criminal infraction where there should have been no infraction. For standing on a public sidewalk, in a place where people had strolled undisturbed moments before, you could now be arrested for "disobeying an official order." I decided that this was ridiculous and that I wanted to be arrested. But after consulting my wallet, I realized that because I'd given forty dollars to Veterans for Peace, I didn't have enough cash to bail myself out. Next time, I thought.

More than a thousand of us stood against the new barricade, shouting, along with the hoarse-voiced bullhornist, "This is what democracy looks like!" And "Money for jobs and education, not for wars and occupation!" And "Stop these wars! Free Bradley Manning!" And "From Wisconsin to Iraq, stand up, fight back!" And "They say more war, we say no more!" I suddenly felt the rising power of an outraged crowd. It has a different kind of persuasiveness than any verbal argument does. I watched a blind man in a wheelchair, missing several fingers, chanting "U.S. out of the Middle East, no justice no peace."

A hundred and thirteen protesters were eventually arrested in front of President Obama's White House that afternoon. (Obama, meanwhile, was down in South America trying to sell F-18 warplanes to Brazil.) The arrests took hours. Someone called out, "You're arresting the wrong people! Arrest Bush I, arrest Bush II, arrest Obama!" One of the women, when she was out of sight in the arrest tent, began a series of blood-curdling screams of protest. "Let us see what's happening," someone called. As a paddy wagon drove off, someone called out, "The Jell-O's no good in the slammer, don't eat it."

In the end the SWAT team had to summon two city Metro buses, in addition to the wagons, to carry off the detainees. Both buses carried ads for breakfast at McDonald's: PUTS THE A.M. BACK IN AMAZING. The police so parked the paddy wagons and the buses that the crowd couldn't witness the arrests. As a man with a ponytail was pushed into the back of a paddy wagon, a woman in our crowd read from the Constitution, the part about how Congress cannot abridge the right of the people "peaceably to assemble and to petition the government for a redress of grievances." I applauded her. There was no question that the police were denying the public the right of peaceable assembly.

There were cheers when Daniel Ellsberg, forty years after his arraignment for leaking the Pentagon Papers, was led toward the arrest tent. He turned toward the White House, obliging a policeman who wanted to take his picture. His wrists were zip-corded behind his back. He flashed us a double peace sign from his cuffed hands.

When the arrests were all done, one of the cops collected some FREE BRADLEY MANNING signs and put them in a garbage bag in the trunk of his cruiser.

*(2011)*

# Painkiller Deathstreak

I'd never held a video-game controller until last fall. Which is a pretty sad admission, as if I'd said in 1966 that I'd never watched *Bonanza* or heard a song by the Rolling Stones. My sixteen-year-old son and his friends—his male friends, that is, all of them polite, funny, good-hearted kids—play video games just about every day. They don't watch much TV; they don't have time. Most of the games they play are on the Xbox 360 console—not the Wii or the PlayStation 3—and most involve killing and dying. The big one for the first half of last year was *Nazi Zombies,* a mini-game included with the best-selling *Call of Duty: World at War.* In it, you and your friends, linked by audio headsets, hide out in a ruined building, and yellow-eyeballed zombies in Nazi uniforms lurch toward you, mumbling and waving their arms and trying to eat your head. You have to shoot them or stab them or set them on fire, and they never stop coming. If they swarm you, you call out, "Dude, they're on me!" and a friend struggles over to save you. If you're near death, you call out, "Dude, revive me!" and a friend jabs you with a revivifying hypodermic. There's a lot of wild laughing.

I still haven't played *Nazi Zombies.* But since last fall

I've been buying some of the biggest new game releases and trying them out. I say "trying" because the first thing I learned is that video games—especially the vivid, violent ones—are ridiculously hard to play. They're humbling. They break you down. They kill you over and over. Eventually, you learn how to crouch and crawl through grass and hide behind boxes. You fight your way to a special doorway and you move up to the next level. Suddenly, you feel smart and euphoric. You reload, with a reassuring metallic click, and keep on going.

To begin, you must master the controller. On the Xbox 360 controller, which looks like a catamaran, there are seventeen possible points of contact. There's the left trigger and the right trigger, the left bumper and the right bumper, two mushroom-shaped joysticks, a circular four-way pad, two small white buttons, each with triangles molded into them, and a silver dome in the middle that glows green when you press it. Then, there are the very important colored buttons: the blue X, the green A, the red B, and the yellow Y. On the slightly smaller Sony PlayStation 3's controller, the buttons are similar, except that in place of the colored letters you've got the green triangle, the pink square, the red O, and the blue X. (The PlayStation 3's blue X button is in a different place than the Xbox 360's blue X button—madness.) In order to run, crouch, aim, fire, pause, leap, speak, stab, grab, kick, dismember, unlock, crawl, climb, parry, roll, or resuscitate a fallen comrade, you must press or nudge or woggle these various buttons, singly or in combination, performing tiny feats of exactitude that are different for each game. It's a little like playing "Blue Rondo à la Turk" on the clarinet, then switching to the tenor sax, then the oboe, then back to the clarinet.

The second thing I learned about video games is that they are long. So, so long. Playing one game is not like watching one ninety-minute movie; it's like watching one whole season of a TV show—and watching it in a state of staring, jaw-clenched concentration. If you're good, it might take you fifteen hours to play through a typical game. If you're not good, like me, and you do a fair amount of bumping into walls and jumping in place when you're under attack, it will take more than twice that.

On the other hand, the games can be beautiful. The "maps" or "levels"—that is, the three-dimensional physical spaces in which your character moves and acts—are sometimes wonders of explorable specificity. You'll see an edge-shined, light-bloomed, magic-hour gilded glow on a row of half-wrecked buildings and you'll want to stop for a few minutes just to take it in. But be careful—that's when you can get shot by a sniper. Stay frosty.

The first game I bought was *Halo 3: ODST*, developed by Bungie and published by Microsoft Game Studios last September. It's not one of the really beautiful games, but it's instructive. *Halo* was Microsoft's first hit on the Xbox, in 2001, and this is the latest offering in the long-running series. It's set in 2552, during a space war. ODST stands for Orbital Drop Shock Troopers—people who say things like "You know the music, time to dance," and then drop down through the atmosphere into battle. I plummeted into the city of New Mombasa, Africa, which looked like a dim, cast-concrete parking garage but with grand staircases. An alliance of bad creatures called the Covenant had killed billions of people, and this drop might be an opportunity to save humankind.

Mostly I glided up and down ramps and stairs, shooting at enemies, listening to chilly electronica. I played the

game in "easy" mode, as opposed to "normal," "heroic," or
"legendary"—the menu option reads "Laugh as helpless
victims flee in terror from their inevitable slaughter"—but
it didn't seem all that easy to me. Short-statured, stocky
aliens called Grunts popped up frequently, and with hostile
intent—they had munchkin voices and cackled nastily and
they said things like "Die, heretic!" I had to kill many of
these. Other alien enemies, called Brutes, said, "I will split
your bones." They sounded as if they had ripped up their
vocal cords by popping steroids. I used several different
weapons to kill them, including the needler, which shot
explosive needles, and I plundered dead alien bodies for
more guns and ammunition. The Grunts and the Brutes
jeered and tried to end my life. I got lost and hit cul-de-sacs
and said bad words and hopped up and down near a burning
car. Sometimes I died.

Whenever you're injured, the screen begins to go red and
you hear yourself gasping. Red arrows point in the direction
of your attackers. As you near your end, your gasps come
quicker and they become odd little yips and yelps of pain.
Finally, you die, and the camera lifts. For the first time in
New Mombasa—this being a first-person shooter—you see
yourself from the outside: a rookie in a helmet falling to the
pavement. Another life consumed in this endless war. But
immediately you "respawn"—that is, you reappear, ready to
try again, at a point a little earlier in the game.

The good thing about *Halo 3: ODST* is . . . I don't
know. If I was fonder of 1970s cast-concrete architecture,
I'm sure I would have enjoyed the experience more. The
game seemed to me to be both desolate and repetitive, with
incomprehensible biblical and race-war undermeanings. I
flipped through the game guide, published by an imprint of

Random House, and read a list of some of the medals you can earn. Killtacular is what you get if you kill five enemies in quick succession in firefight mode; Killtrocity if you add a sixth; Killimanjaro if you reach seven. "Dash about with the Gravity Hammer," I read, "killing large groups of enemies for lengthy kill chains and hammer sprees before swapping to the Magnum and running to the next group of foes, plugging Grunts and Jackals in the head to keep the kill chain going." Forget it.

*Uncharted 2: Among Thieves,* a production of the Naughty Dog studio, in Santa Monica, was the next game I tried, and it's good. It was a Sony exclusive, meaning that I needed a PlayStation 3 to play it, and I didn't have a PlayStation 3. Just coincidentally, in October my son's Xbox developed the famous red ring of death, a total hardware failure signaled by a warning light around the On/Off button. This seemed a sign from the gods of war to get a PS3, which I did.

*Uncharted 2* is about a blue-jeans-wearing male model, Nate, who wakes up with fresh blood on his hands and climbs around on a cold train wreck that is hanging off a cliff. It's literally a cliff-hanger, you see. Nate (whom we can see, because this is a third-person game) is remarkably good at climbing on things, and his hands never stick to frozen metal, because he's an action hero. He grunts realistically when he hurls himself up and over the edge of something—the voice actor who plays Nate, Nolan North, is an inspired grunter, and there must be a hundred different expressions of strain on this soundtrack.

Then the screen goes white, and we're in a flashback. We learn that Nate, who can sight-translate medieval-Latin prose, is in search of Marco Polo's lost treasure and that he must break into a museum in Istanbul, dart-gunning or punching or choking its numerous flashlight-wielding security guards. His goal is to find an ancient, precious green lamp that holds a clue. He finds it and, being an American action hero, immediately breaks it like a piggy bank on the floor. The clue within leads him to the jungles of Borneo, where he shoots some Russian-accented mercenaries—people are always shooting Russians in video games—and then it's time to hurry off to sunny Nepal, where there are prayer flags, more mercenaries, and incredible vistas. The acting is often good and includes some funny ad-libs—not just by Nolan North but also by Richard McGonagle, who plays a crusty cigar-puffer. Two women appear in the game—one a tanned Aussie with black unruly bangs and sparkly eyes, who wears a red crop-top shirt that we see a lot of, and the other an old flame of Nate's, an American journalist with Jennifer Aniston hair pulled back—both of them joshing and likable.

It's a visual glory hallelujah of a game. Zebra shadows on leaves and rocks never looked better, nor did sunlit onion domes, nor bombed-out laundromats with puddles in them—and the shirts of the guards glimmering in the plum-purple half-light of the Istanbul Palace Museum are a sight to behold. I wish so many foreigners didn't have to be shot, so many historical sites damaged without comment, but evidently they do or the game wouldn't exist, and it's diverting to clamber around on stone Buddhas, solving (or repeatedly failing to solve) spatial puzzles. When you die, the image desaturates to black-and-white and there's a tactful moment of funereal bagpipery.

The best time I had with *Uncharted 2* (which went on to win several game-of-the-year awards) was while eating a submarine sandwich and watching the making-of videos that came with the game disk, fantasizing about what it would be like to work for Naughty Dog as a late-afternoon-lighting designer or a stony-ledge-placement specialist. These people know how to have fun. They've even included an optional zero-gravity mode, in which mercenaries, when shot, flip up rag-dollingly in the air and drift there. After one battle, there were two riot shields and six bulletproof-vested dead people peacefully hanging like barrage balloons in the air in front of a temple.

After *Uncharted 2* came the biggest release of the year—*Call of Duty: Modern Warfare 2*, developed by Infinity Ward and published by Activision on November 10. My son and his friends went to a local GameStop at midnight to get their reserved copies; they played it all night and then fell asleep in school assembly. *Modern Warfare 2* sold fast—it reportedly made more money in its first twenty-four hours than *Titanic* or *Avatar* did. Millions of people play it every day. In less than a year, it has become the second-best-selling video game of all time, after *Wii Play*.

Here's what it's about. It's about killing, and it's about dying. Also, it's about collecting firearms. And it's modern warfare, which means it's set in places like Afghanistan. As in *Halo*, you are a gun that moves—in fact, you are many guns, because with a touch of your Y button you can switch from one gun to another. But this game has a much crisper, brighter look than the murky *Halo*, and the graphics engine is better, and the telescopic rifle scopes, their lenses pale blue and curvingly reflective, are a delight to peer through. "Yesterday's enemies are today's recruits," says the narrator, General Shepherd, who is full of little bits of wisdom like that, until he slides over to the dark side.

The first thing you have to do is learn how to aim and

shoot, and to do that you run through a training course in Afghanistan with pop-up wooden targets. Some targets depict enemies—they have angry frowns and wear turbans and look like Khomeini—and some depict civilians: boys in blue-striped polo shirts, little girls in dresses, and a plump man in a button-down shirt. The training course keeps track of how many civilians you've killed and how many frowning Khomeinis, while a corporal shouts at you to hurry up: "Go, go, go!"

You do so well as Private Allen, shooting Arabs in Kabul, that you are enlisted to help out the CIA, which is up to nothing good in Russia. Then, as part of something called Task Force 141, you begin dying in earnest. I don't know how many times I was killed as I tried to work toward the northeast section of a runway in order to plant a bomb. (This was at a military base in Kazakhstan.) I wandered tensely through cold Quonset huts. Each time, a jeep would park, and there was a sudden surge of Russian voices and men would aim at me and shoot me. I was shooting them, too. My name during this phase of the game was Roach. "Roach, search the northeast part of the runway for the fueling station!" my commander, Soap MacTavish, said repeatedly, in his Scottish burr. When I got someone in the head, MacTavish would say, "Nicely done," or "Good kill." When I shot badly, he would say, "That was sloppy." I always felt better when MacTavish was telling me what to do.

When you're hit in *Modern Warfare 2*, the bullets make a zing and then a flump. Your field of view jolts and gets alarmingly blood-dropletted around the edges. You begin to gasp. The sound goes hollow, as if you're listening through a long tube, the controller vibrates, and you know that you have only a moment of life left. As your head hits the ground, the screen's image turns suddenly diagonal and fuzzes out. There's a swooshing in your ears, followed by a brief whistling-teakettle sound. The last thing you hear is MacTavish shouting, once again, from far away, "Roach, search the northeast corner of the runway!"

Then, at the blood-blurred moment of death, you are rewarded with a literary quotation. These come from Einstein, Voltaire, Zora Neale Hurston, Edward R. Murrow, Churchill, Machiavelli, Dick Cheney—all sorts of apropos people—and they are confusingly contradictory. Some quotes are cynical, some pacifist, some earnestly pro-war. Cheney says, "It is easy to take liberty for granted when you have never had it taken from you." Gandhi says, "An eye for an eye only ends up making the whole world blind." These neat word packets, displayed just as you've been shot or blown up by a grenade, mock the notion that there is any body of aphoristic wisdom that can be applied to a fatal firefight. You're lying in the snow, dead. Words of wisdom mean nothing now.

But of course you're not really dead. Almost immediately, you respawn. You're given another chance. You're given many, many chances, because *Modern Warfare 2* is just about the dyingest game out there. It isn't, in my reading, a glorification of modern warfare. You play for three hours and you think, This? This chaotic chattering absurdity and panic and wasted ardor is what we mean by "troop surge"? It is an unjingoistic, perhaps completely cynical amusement. The CIA, covertly making everything worse, gets mixed up in an airport atrocity in Russia, which prompts Russia to attack a residential neighborhood in northeastern Virginia, not far from the Pentagon and CIA headquarters (both in flames), with paratroopers and helicopter gunships. "Ramirez," a sergeant shouts, voice-acted by Keith David, "take your team and secure the Burger Town!" Also: "Be advised multiple enemy mobiles have been sighted near the taco joint, over!"

I'd been playing alone, but the "single-player campaign," with its improbable story, is not what *Modern Warfare 2* is really about. Most people want to go online and shoot at other real people, not at software soldiers controlled by artificial intelligence. "Single player is like taking a Spanish class," my son explained. "Multiplayer is like going to Spain." In multiplayer, you choose a locale—for instance, the submarine base—and a style of competition. There's Team Deathmatch, Capture the Flag, Domination, and others. And then you run around shooting and setting claymore mines where other players won't see them when they walk into a room. If you kill three people without dying, you can get a U.A.V.—a Predator drone. A kill streak of nine gives you a Stealth Bomber air strike. If you kill twenty-five people in a row, you can get a tactical nuclear weapon, and the game is over. You get frequent bonuses and awards—new weapons, new ammunition, new scopes, new camouflage, new proficiencies. "It's like they've got you on a drip feed of sugar," my son said. "The only way you get the next little drip is by playing a little more."

In multiplayer you kill and die so often that a single statistic becomes extremely important to you: your kill-to-death ratio. As you get better—reviewing your deaths on "killcam" instant replay to see who got you—your kill-to-death ratio goes to one and then to more than one. One of my son's friends, a good student, has a kill-to-death ratio of 1.65. In 219 hours of game-playing, he has killed 32,884 times and died 19,956 times. My son, who believes that wars serve no purpose, has played for 96 hours, and he has a kill-to-death of 1.17; it was 1.4 when he was playing every day. Mine is 0.08.

In order to give me a taste of multiplayer madness, as I practiced my shooting and my sprinting skills, my son set us up by ourselves in a location called Rust—a place in Afghanistan where there is an old oil installation. Sitting side by side and watching our characters on the split screen, we spawned out in Rust, and he began running circles around me. I could hear his feet going *pad pad pad pad* in the sand, and then the sound changed and became hollow as he ran onto a pipe. I would look around, trying to find him—and then I'd see that he was a few feet away, pointing his gun at my head. His character was an American soldier, I noticed. My character, which I saw when I looked at his split-screen image, was some bad jihadist with Arabic writing on my head scarf.

We were very considerate of each other in the beginning. My son could have shot me many times, but he didn't. "Go ahead!" I said. "No, Dad," he said, "I'm not going to shoot you." He followed me around, waiting for me to take some shots. We carried on this peculiar chivalry for fifteen minutes, sometimes using riot shields, whose glass cracks realistically under repeated fire. Finally I wounded him, and he stabbed me, and we relaxed and began shooting and sniping and running and laughing, just as he did with his friends via inter-couchal headsets. We switched to another map, Afghan, which has as its centerpiece a C-130 transport plane that has crashed somewhere in the mountains of Afghanistan. There were thick-budded poppies growing in the sun, with PVC irrigation pipes over them. Again I heard my son's sprinting footsteps—he had a multiplayer perk that allowed him to run forever without tiring. He knew a way to get up on the fuselage—I could hear him running down the metallic skin—and onto the tail, and from there up onto a high cliff. I'd spray bullets in a semicircle, and then there would be a single quick sniper shot and I'd be dead. Then he'd apologize. "Sorry, Dad, I didn't mean to kill, only to maim." I died often enough that I received a temporary health boost called a "painkiller deathstreak." By the end, I'd improved—so he said—and I'd machine-gunned him a few times. We went off to dinner full of weird camaraderie.

Altogether, it took me an astounding twenty-four hours to get through the single-player version of *Modern Warfare 2*—three times longer than the average player takes. But I made a lot of notes, and that stretched the time out some. What fascinated me most were those moments in the midst of a fierce firefight when you were given a chance to find some "intel"—on the second floor of a house on the Russian border, say, where Makarov, the paleo-Soviet terrorist, was rumored to be hiding out. During these tranced lulls, I found, you could wander at your leisure from room to room while your squadron-mates stood around waiting for you to act. As they waited, they cracked their necks from side to side and scratched themselves, as idle men seem always to do under the guidance of artificial intelligence.

I found many interesting things while exploring this house, not wanting, particularly, to get back into the action and be killed again. Some Russians lay in pools of blood in the upstairs hall. In the master bedroom were books on a bookshelf, including *The Jungle Book*, a law treatise, and what appeared to be a biography of the Dutch painter Gerard van Honthorst. I'd seen these same books back in northern Virginia, during a break in the frantic action there, before the bloodbath at Burger Town. In the bathroom there were sections of illegible newspaper and a Teddy bear fixed to the wall with a knife through its nose. I went into a smaller bedroom.

In it were seven or eight sleeping bags, unrolled, empty, and a lot of rollaway suitcases. Also a pinup of a clothed woman wielding a machine gun. There was something touching about this tableau of sleeping bags, since I knew that the soldiers who had slept there were now dead. If I got down on my stomach, I could crawl right through the sleeping bags, which was an interesting experience—seeing the underside of the texture. I could even crawl through a dead body, and I did once—for everything in a video game is just a contortedly triangulated, infinitely thin quilt of surface. What, I wondered, was in the suitcases?

The only way I knew how to look inside a random object was to shoot it. So I shot at a suitcase. A dingy striped shirt flew out. I shot at another suitcase: another dingy shirt. These rang a bell: I'd seen them hanging from a clothesline in the Brazilian favela, the setting for an earlier battle. In the master bedroom, I shot at some cardboard boxes. Bags of potato chips and beef jerky popped out, and little cherry pies. Down in the kitchen, I noticed an old crate of potatoes—also bags of flour and basmati rice. These staples, too, I'd seen in the favela.

I began to think a lot about the hardworking set dressers for this game, who cleverly reused the same props in different ways in different countries. What moral were they offering— that people were basically the same everywhere? That most of life was getting up in the morning, putting on your clothes, and eating basmati rice? That war, even for the soldier, was the aberration? Or were they just being thrifty, or playful?

*Modern Warfare 2*, at that moment, felt truer, realer than almost all war movies—although it owes much to them, of course, especially *Black Hawk Down*. In fact, when I watched *The Hurt Locker* I sensed the rifle-scopic influence of the entire *Call of Duty* series—as in the long, still standoff in the desert with the tiny figure at the window. Cinematographers and movie directors think more like snipers now because of the Xbox. I went downstairs in the Russian house to resume the battle. When I was shot and died, I was offered a quotation from Confucius: "Before you embark on a journey of revenge, dig two graves."

Next on my master list, appearing on November 17, was the ultra-stealthy, silver-hooded *Assassin's Creed II,* set in Renaissance Florence and Venice. (This list, by the way, I'd made with my son's help. He reads the video-game websites and listens every week to the charmingly garrulous "Giant Bombcast," which is like "Car Talk" but with four vastly knowledgeable gamers.) In *Assassin's Creed II,* you are Ezio, a man with many missions. You deliver letters and hurry around cities with a loping stride, climbing up the facades of palazzos and churches when the mood moves you. You leap from rooftop to rooftop, and sometimes you leap in the wrong direction and fall, and if you fall too far you die, whereupon the screen goes red and then white, crisscrossed with many schematic lines, and it says "desynchronized"—because in the game's frame story you're not really in Renaissance Italy; you're really a twenty-first-century man (again voice-acted by Nolan North) reclining in a comfortable virtual-reality machine with an orange cushion.

Sometimes you have to assassinate someone—that's your creed, after all—which you can do with hidden wrist knives or poison blades or swords or even an early gun, and sometimes you just have to beat someone up. One of your first tasks, in fact, is to find a lout who is cheating on your sister. You call him a lurid pig, and when you beat him up you make money. You can hire thieves, you can loot dead bodies, you can steal florins from pedestrians (although they will fuss if you do), and you can buy Renaissance paintings from a small art stand. You can even hire a group of murmurously flirty courtesans who wear low-cut pastel gowns and coo provocatively, and if you suddenly decide to parkour around on the roof once again they will wait for you down below.

The game, made by Ubisoft Montreal, has moments of loveliness, as when you reach a lookout high up over Venice and allow your gaze to sweep across the sfumatoed city. The colors are brown stone, weathered brick, the occasional red flapping banner, and pale Mediterranean blue. The wind sounds just the way wind should sound. Not much that's noble or witty or soul-stirring happens in these lovingly re-created cities. If you hang in there for many hours, you get to fly Leonardo da Vinci's bat-winged glider by night. But mostly it's death, death, death—and fistfights, and the accumulation of wealth by acts of thuggery. You leap down on the Borgia Pope in the middle of Mass and punch him out. You're forever pressing the pink square to stab. (Or, on the Xbox, the blue X.) "There's a lot of face and neck stabbing, if you like to stab dudes in the face and neck," Ryan Davis explained on the Giant Bombcast. "There's one really good move where you will stab a dude five or six times super quickly, shank style, like, uh uh uh uh uh, just jabbing—and that's oddly satisfying." The most fun I had was jumping off a building into a pile of hay. My son showed me how to rock-climb to the top of the Tower of San Marco, keeping a lookout for the slightly darker brick where the handholds were. That was a pleasure.

To avoid competing with *Modern Warfare 2*, many game publishers took cover and postponed their launches, so after *Assassin's Creed II* there wasn't much going on till late in

January. Out of curiosity, I played the demo for *Bayonetta,*
a Japanese game in which a woman dressed in her own hair
kickboxes her way through battles with fearsome creatures.
She wears hip eyeglasses and looks like Tina Fey. When
she goes wild with a kick combination, her hair suddenly
swooshes out and forms itself into a swirling lethal force that
helps her defeat her enemy. I also fought zombies with a
fry pan and a crowbar in *Left 4 Dead 2.* A zombie called the
Spitter doused me with corrosive stomach acid that emerged
in a flume from her enormous toothy mouth. That was the
only game that gave me a bad dream: in it, I crouched in a
jet engine with my family, hiding out from evil people on the
runway, wishing I had a fry pan.

Meanwhile, my son and his friends were laboriously
working their way up the multiplayer ladder of *Modern
Warfare 2.* The goal is to reach the top rank, level 70, in
which you unlock an AK-47. At that point, you start again at
level 1, but with a fancy star icon next to your name to signal
that you've gone "Prestige." My son quit playing the game at
that point—many of his friends have continued.

Then came BioWare's gigantic opus, *Mass Effect 2,*
released on January 26, 2010. Commander Shepard (no
relation to *Modern Warfare*'s General Shepherd) is in control
of a gracefully elongated spaceship, the *Normandy,* which
has bunk beds, fish tanks, and a wisecracking mess officer
who also cleans the bathrooms. "This ain't no luxury liner,"
he says. "I catch what falls through the cracks, heh-heh."
Young ensigns flirt outrageously with Shepard as they give
him messages, and Miranda, a brunette with "extensive
genetic modification" (i.e., breast implants), accompanies you
sometimes on your travels. You visit a strip club where a blue
alien dances for you and a bartender tries to poison you. You

avert a plague by using some big fans to spread an antidote around.

*Mass Effect 2* is the most novelistic of the games I played. It's an elaborately cataloged scatterment of worlds in which you slingshot yourself around using mass-effect generators that make you go at light speed. You meet many colorful humanoids, with whom you converse by choosing bits of dialogue with your control stick. It sounds awkward, but it works. After one battle, Shepard encounters a young Krogan standing in a corner. The Krogan, a hulking monster with a huge reptilian neck, was born in a tank the week before. "You are different," the Krogan says. "You don't smell like this world. Seven night cycles and I have felt only the need to kill. But you—something makes me speak."

"How can you speak if you're only a week old?" Commander Shepard asks, providing you prompt this query with your control stick.

"There was a scratching sound in my head, and it became the voice," the Krogan replies. "It taught things I would need—walking, talking, hitting, shooting." Walking, talking, hitting, shooting—that just about sums it up. Video games aim to find and nurture the tank-born Krogan in all of us.

I played for a while, visiting planets and shooting incendiary bullets at waves of venomous antagonists. Then I stopped. It's two DVD disks. It's really enormous. In order to do all the missions and side missions of *Mass Effect 2,* you can easily spend fifty hours or more, especially if you like trying all the dialogue options, as I do. I craved more sunshine pouring in through the helmet visors, more leaf shadow, more wind, more air—maybe some little Krogans riding on bicycles. Finally, I gave up. I was dying too much, and when you die the music goes bom-bom-bom-bom-bom-bom-bom, while terrible red and black retinal veins grow in from the edges of the screen.

By then it was the end of February, and time to play the most self-consciously artistic game on the list: *Heavy Rain,* by Quantic Dream, a studio in Paris that got development funding from Sony. Sony kindly sent me an early copy, in a faux-battered shoebox. When I lifted the lid, an audio clip of a woman's voice asked, "Are you prepared to suffer to save your son?" David Cage, Quantic Dream's founder, calls the game an interactive drama. In one interview, in the *Independent,* Cage said that he feels close to Orson Welles, advancing an art form. And in fact he's right.

For the first half hour, the game is a stunner. "It's flipping genius, Dad!" my son called out as he began playing. The faces have complicated eyes and eyelids, and you, a sad-faced father with a strong resemblance to David Duchovny, do pleasant things with your kids and your wife. Then comes grief: one of your sons dies in front of your eyes. Whereupon you enter the gloomy *Heavy Rain* universe, switching among several characters, one of whom may possibly be a serial murderer who likes paper folding. You are a woman with amazingly good posture and an impassive face who high-steps around her apartment in her underwear. You are a private detective with a big stomach and a big heart. You are an FBI agent with virtual-reality sunglasses. It's always raining, and the music is lush, and everyone's face is sad and empty, until you can't stand the pop of droplets anymore and you're slogging around in the runoff at the side of the street, wondering whether the clouds will ever part. No, they never will.

Is it a good game? It has realistic eyeblinks and moments of ecstatic mundanity, as when you use the controller to put a frozen pizza in a microwave for your TV-watching son (who is soon to be kidnapped) and then dump it onto a plate. It's forward-looking, too, in the way it uses the control buttons: at moments of high tension, you have to hold down several at once, like Lon Chaney playing a Bach arpeggio, till you've accomplished a difficult action—fought off an attacker, say, or chopped off one of your own fingers. But the plot and the conversational tropes will be familiar—too familiar—to crime-drama watchers. It's an homage to *NYPD Blue* episodes and the movie *Seven:* cops who squabble in Brooklyn accents, some serial killing, some split personality, some amnesia, more lush music—nothing that has any reality in any conceivable life lived anywhere on planet Earth. The endings vary based on what you do—the script is more than two thousand pages long—but my son and I both arrived independently at similar endings, in which the character that we liked the most turned out to be the Origami Killer. Which made us unhappy and made no sense dramatically. In my version of the story, my second son died, too. I suffered, to be sure, but I didn't manage to save him.

*Heavy Rain* feels like a clinical depression served up in a shoebox. Possibly that's what David Cage intended it to be—and more than a million copies have sold, so it's a successful depression.

The next game on my list was another eagerly sought-after PlayStation 3 showpiece: *God of War III*, a single-player game set on and under Mt. Olympus. I got about eight hours into it, during which time I cut off the Chimera's tail, ripped off Helios's head, and stabbed somebody in the eye with his own horn. I hooked into the flesh of middle-aged naked birdwomen who flew around as Harpies. I injured a horse and saw its intestines pour out. I cut off Hades's chest muscle and watched it jump around on the floor like a toad; I had to destroy the muscle before the huge Hell god could grab it and slap it back into place. I took hold of the Cyclops's eye like a beach ball and pulled on it till the optic nerve dangled.

Why did I do this? Because I was the muscleman Kratos, a Spartan-born hero who wears a lot of eye makeup and wanders the mythosphere with a spoiled scowl on his face. Kratos is on a rampage, bent on revenge, because one of the gods tricked him into killing his family. He has a flaming bow and arrow, some claws he won from Hades, a long blue sword, and two big blades, and every time he whirls around—and he whirls a lot, because that's how he fights—he's slashing at something. If he slashes well, the words "Brutal Kill!" come on-screen. Once, he runs into a toga-wearing civilian on a window ledge of Olympus. "Curse the gods and their war," the civilian says, quite sensibly, weeping. "My home—everything I own—destroyed!" Kratos knocks the civilian's head against the wall and tosses him down the mountain.

This game isn't satire. It's a slasher movie over which you have control. It uses the Greek stories to trick you, or your parents (few families abide by the rating system), into tolerating a level of participatory gore that would be otherwise impossible in a mass-market entertainment. You think it must be okay to make your hero, Kratos, slowly tear off someone's head by whanging away on the O button because the someone is a Greek god and everyone knows that Greek myths are dark, brutal, and Oedipal. It's all in the name of classical culture, isn't it? No—it's a trick.

Even so, *God of War III* has visual astonishments in almost every scene. You walk around on Gaia's gigantic rocky body. You see her giant stony breast. You climb into her chest cavity and see her stony heart beating. You cut her wrist so that she falls away. The game, to a surprising degree, is about hacking away at half-naked women, or naked half-women. Whenever you see female breasts, you have a pretty good idea that the breasted person is going to die horribly, and soon. *God of War III* is a confused confection, and the brilliant, smiley, jokey designers who made it should hang their claws in shame for so misdirecting their obvious talents.

The last big game I played was a Western called *Red Dead Redemption*, made by Rockstar, the people who created *Grand Theft Auto*. I bought it on its release day, May 19, 2010. You are John Marston, a polite whoreson cowboy with virtuous instincts who has done bad things in the past. John is handy with a lasso and he has dirty hair, as does everyone in the game. He collects medicinal herbs like feverfew, he keeps cows from panicking in a storm and running off a cliff, he shoots and skins skunks, wolves, bears, raccoons, vultures, and coyotes—"Ugh, what were you eating?" he mutters to the dead coyote as blood splatters on the screen—and he travels the dry borderlands of Texas and Mexico helping or hurting innocent people: your choice. When he loots a bounty hunter's corpse, he says, "This ain't nice, I know." A kind woman named Bonnie tries to draw him out, but he's not chatty. "You are being deliberately obscure as a substitute for having a personality," Bonnie says, as she and John canter around her ranch on horseback.

You kill and you die in *Red Dead Redemption*, of course—with "dead eye" aiming, you can queue up several shots in slow motion, while on horseback—and when you die the word "dead" appears on the screen in fat red cracked letters. But after an exhausting day of shooting and skinning and looting and dying comes the real greatness of this game: you stand outside, off the trail, near Hanging Rock, utterly alone, in the cool, insect-chirping enormity of the scrublands, feeling remorse for your many crimes, with a gigantic predawn moon silvering the cacti and a bounty of several hundred dollars on your head. A map says there's treasure to be found nearby, and that will happen in time, but the best treasure of all is early sunrise. *Red Dead Redemption* has some of the finest dawns and dusks in all of moving pictures. Albert Bierstadt couldn't make morning light look this good. When you do eventually wander back into town, a prostitute pipes up, "I can't stand to see a man walking around town with such a dry pecker. Can I help?"

So those were the games I tried. They showed me many sights I'm glad I've seen, and some I wish I hadn't seen. I liked *Uncharted 2* best, but *Red Dead Redemption* had the prettiest clouds and hootiest owls, and the taciturn *Modern Warfare 2* had the deepest moral snowdrifts. My son has been trying out *Crackdown 2*, where you leap around a city shooting mutant freaks and collecting energy from green orbs. But he's playing less now; he's waiting for September's release of *Halo: Reach*, which will let players construct intricately ramped battle structures that hang out over rocky coastlines. I think it's time for me to take a break. No war, no gods, no bounties, no kill chains, no vengeance. No convoys in Afghanistan. Just end it. Maybe I'll try a game like *Flower*, for the PlayStation 3, which is a sort of motocross game for wind and petals. Or even go outside, with my pants legs tucked into my socks so that the midsummer ticks don't crawl up my legs. I miss grass.

*(2010)*

# Last Essay

# Mowing

Sometimes everything seems simple. This morning, a Saturday in July, I reached down to the books beside my bed and pulled up a Dover collection of old Robert Benchley columns. I looked at the copyright page and I saw the dates—1930, 1931. The dates meant something to me. I knew people who had lived through those dates. I knew who Robert Benchley was, and I knew what Dover Books was. I came downstairs and tried to pour a cup of coffee. The coffeepot was empty, but as soon as I determined that it was empty I knew that my wife had very kindly transferred the coffee into the red thermos so that it would stay hot. And indeed there it was, in the red thermos. My wife was out walking the dog. It was nine-thirty. It had been nine-thirty on many Saturday mornings before this. All the sounds I heard were familiar: the tires swooshing intermittently by, and the birds—the nearby rapid chirpers and the distant screechers—and the single cricket just getting revved up for the day. I understood the kitchen tablecloth perfectly—a white cotton tablecloth with faded blue and yellow stripes. It had dried outside on the drying rack that we stuck into a flagpole socket in the yard.

I felt I understood the *New York Times* on the tablecloth as well, why it was there, and when I walked out through the dining room into the front hall and paused in front of a bookcase there, I looked at all the titles. Every title in the bookcase meant something to me. Most of the books I had packed and unpacked several times. I already had a place in my head that held each book. Each was one I wanted in my life in this unobtrusive way, on the shelf in the front hall where nobody would pay much attention to it. The door was open and the cool air from outside pushed gently through the screen and reached me. I was barefoot. Never had I known quite this particularity of peace.

So I thought again, Sometimes everything seems simple. Today I'm going to mow part of the lawn. I enjoy mowing the lawn—I know this lawn well, and I sing mildly obscene songs while I mow and think about the way grass looks. My son will mow part of the lawn. I will pay him for the part he mows. I understand how money works, green dollar bills—they're in my wallet. My daughter will sunbathe on the mown lawn near the asparagus plant, reading a book. What book is she reading? Nabokov's *Pnin.* How comprehensible is that! I have read Nabokov's *Pnin,* more than once. My wife wrote a paper on *Pnin* in college for a Russian literature class. She and I have talked about *Pnin* many times. Everything around me is anchored somehow or other in a familiar past.

Pnin is a scholar, "ideally bald." He is a figure of fun. What's the point of scholarship? Why do I sometimes, indeed often, want to be surrounded by lots of things I don't understand? Why do I want to travel to some historical society and ask to see a dead man's papers and work slowly through them, learning hundreds of new names? Is it because I want to be responsible for a piece of life that nobody else is responsible for? Is it because I want some heretofore unchronicled episode in deep time to become almost as familiar to me as the surroundings in my own life, so that I can walk around the bonsai arrangement that I have resurrected out of letters and guest lists and memos, and be as unsurprised by any part of it as I am unsurprised by my own red thermos bottle and bookcase? I don't really know why I'm drawn to do scholarship of this old-fashioned sort. I know I like finding things out—I like rationed chaos. I feel sorry for newspaper reporters who have only a day or two to research a story. Each story deserves five years. Not ten—ten years and the story goes stale. But five.

Finding things out: there is an infinitude of things you don't know, but it's not a very interesting infinitude, because it has no grain. Only some of the unknown things, a much smaller subset, are things that you are aware of not knowing, and then within that subset is a smaller set still— the unknowns that pull at you. Curiosity is a way of ordering and indeed paring down the wildness of the world. Of all the unmown fields, all the subjects I don't know anything about, this one right here is the one I would like to pursue. Why? Because nobody else is, and because it happens to be here and it draws me. I will contribute most efficiently to the whole if I pursue this topic, knowing that it is obscure enough that nobody would be foolish enough to duplicate my efforts. I will mow my own lawn, part of it, anyway.

Sometimes, though, I have a very different sort of ambition. I want to write a short book called *The Way the World Works*. I want it to be a book for children and adults, that explains everything about history, beauty, wickedness, invention, the meaning of life. The whole unseemly, bulging ball of wax. One of those books that Dover Books reissues, retaining the original typography, like *On Growth and Form*. I get this ambition most powerfully when I have the feeling I have right now, that everything is simple. I know it isn't really simple, and I know I'll never write the book, but still, I sense that I'm on the verge of understanding the rules, the laws, the sleights of hand, that govern every human action. I know why people are angry, why they laugh, why they sue other people, why they wear certain kinds of hats, why they get fat, why they say the things they do—or I almost know it. Another half an hour of frowningly careful thought and I will have it figured out. Why am I the lucky one who almost knows all this? It's because I did some patient research into a few forgotten areas. I filled out the call slips and summoned the acid-free boxes stuffed with archival folders. I half mastered several isolated turf-squares of history, and I know a little about my own lived world as well, and with these several stake-points to steady me, I can pitch my moral tent.

The feeling will pass; in fact it's already passing. But that's all right. One's head is finite. You pour more and more things into it—surnames, chronologies, affiliations—and it packs them away in its tunnels, and eventually you find that you have a book about something that you publish. Then you can forget most of the details—eject them, clean those warrens out, make room for more. And once in a while, as on a perfect morning such as this, you'll have the rapturous illusion that everything you know adds up.

*(2004)*

# ACKNOWLEDGMENTS

The essays in this book first appeared in the following publications, sometimes under different titles.

## Periodicals

*The American Scholar:* "String," "Narrow Ruled," "No Step," "I Said to Myself," and "Mowing."

*Areté:* "The Nod."

*Columbia Journalism Review:* "Defoe, Truthteller."

*Duke University Libraries:* "If Libraries Don't Do It, Who Will?"

*Granta:* "La Mer."

*Harper's Magazine:* "Why I'm a Pacifist."

*Literaturen:* "Sunday at the Dump" (in German translation).

*Married Woman:* "How I Met My Wife."

*McSweeney's, "San Francisco Panorama"* issue: "Papermakers."

*The New Yorker:* "Coins," "Truckin' for the Future," "Grab Me a Gondola," "Kindle 2," "Steve Jobs," and "Painkiller Deathstreak."

*The New York Review of Books:* "The Charms of Wikipedia."

*The New York Times:* "The *Times* in 1951."

*The New York Times Book Review:* "From A to Zyxt," "Sex and the City (Circa 1840)," and "Google's Earth."

*NYRblog:* "We Don't Know the Language We Don't Know."

*Papers of the Bibliographical Society of America:* "Reading the Paper."

*Port:* "David Remnick."

*The Washington Post Magazine:* "One Summer."


*Books*

"Inky Burden," preface to *A Book of Books,* by Abelardo Morell.

"Take a Look at This Airship!" introduction to *The World on Sunday,* by Nicholson Baker and Margaret Brentano.

"Thorin Son of Thráin," in *The Most Wonderful Books: Writers on Discovering the Pleasures of Reading*, edited by Michael Dorris and Emilie Buchwald.

"What Happened on April 29, 1994," in *240 Ecrivains Racontent une Journée du Monde: l'Album Anniversaire: 1964–1994*, edited by *Le Nouvel Observateur* (in French translation).

"Why I Like the Telephone," in *Once upon a Telephone: An Illustrated Social History*, by Ellen Stock Stern and Emily Gwathmey.

"Writing Wearing Earplugs," in *How I Write: The Secret Lives Of Authors*, edited by Dan Crowe with Philip Oltermann.

# ABOUT THE AUTHOR

Nicholson Baker was born in 1957 and grew up in Rochester, New York. He studied at the Eastman School of Music and Haverford College. He has published nine novels, the latest of which is *House of Holes,* and four previous works of nonfiction. His work has appeared in *Best American Short Stories* and *Best American Essays*. A nonfiction work, *Double Fold,* won a National Book Critics Circle Award. He lives with his family in Maine.